Illustrator:
Jose L. Tapia
Keith Vasconcelles
Agi Palinay

Editor:
Ruth Nauss Stingley, M.A.

Editorial Project Manager:
Ina Massler Levin, M.A.

Editor-in-Chief:
Sharon Coan, M.S. Ed.

Art Director:
Elayne Roberts

Cover Artist:
Blanca LaBounty

Product Manager:
Phil Garcia

Imaging:
Hillary Merriman

Publishers:
Rachelle Cracchiolo, M.S. Ed.
Mary Dupuy Smith, M.S. Ed.

Everyday Activities for PRESCHOOL

Author:
Grace Jasmine

Teacher Created Materials, Inc.
P.O. Box 1040
Huntington Beach, CA 92647
©*1995 Teacher Created Materials, Inc.*
Made in U.S.A.

ISBN-1-55734-484-1

Table of Contents

Neat and Tidy—Funny Faces—Costume Party—Skip, Hop, Stop! ABC Game Around-the-World Dance Party—Kitchen Marching Band—When I Feel...I Look Like This—How Do I Feel Today? Like Me—Laundry Line—Kids' Olympics—I Can Help—Family/Multicultural Puppets—Family Scrapbook—Family Words

My Favorite Breakfast—Our Very Own Restaurant—Doll Dinner Party—Our Own Movie Theater—Race Course—Yummy Mud Buckets—Sharing Cube—Finders Keepers—Even Steven!—Birthday-Party Fun: We Make It!—We Wrap It!—We Give It!—We Have Friends/Name Game—Painting My Friend's Picture—Come-Back Cards—Shoe Hunt Game—Alphabet Matching —Rhyming Words

Mathematics and Order

Look Who's on TV—Finger-Counting Pals—Kid Counting—Sound Patterns—Pattern Jewelry—Rainbow Pattern Art—Washing the Socks—Big and Small—Vegetable-Tasting Party—Out of My Window—A Day at the Beach—Cut Out Shapes Blindfold Game—Tea Party—How Tall Am I?—Hand Measuring—Can You Set the Table?—Play-Money Banks—Teddy Bear Addition and Subtraction

Science and Curiosity

Mud Pie Bakery—Nature Sort—Garden Explorers—My Voice Recording—Sound-Effect Fun—Guess This Sound—Pet Masks—Classroom Pets—Lollipop Dragon—What Will the Weather Be?—The Sky/Cotton Clouds—How Should We Dress?—Planting Seeds/Indoor Garden—I Live in the Garden—Fun with Watercolors—Water Painters —Pretend Seasons

Appendix

Rhyming Words—Uppercase Alphabet—Lowercase Alphabet—Numbers—Number Sets

Introduction

Making It Work

Teachers are special people, juggling a variety of populations—parents, administrators, the community, volunteers, and all the taxpayers. And, oh yes—children! With your responsibilities and busy schedule, you don't need another problem. That is why *Everyday Activities for Preschool* has been written. You will find it is a quick and easy way to add center-based, self-directed and/or directed activities to your curriculum, every day—without a great deal of planning or preparation. It also conforms with current National Association for the Education of Young Children (NAEYC) educational trends and philosophies. The activities in this book are designed to access your already existing centers, adding activities that begin the process of prelearning in self-esteem and socialization, socialization and language arts, mathematics, and science and curiosity.

Easy Steps

A variety of components has been pulled together here to make organizing and implementing your program for preschool-age children easy and enjoyable.

❖ First, each activity will easily adapt to either a directed or self-directed philosophy. Therefore, you may tailor the activities to fit your already existing teaching style or philosophy and have the best of both worlds. Most teachers find that a combination of both directed and self-directed activities encourage their children to learn in the most beneficial and comprehensive way possible.

❖ Second, easy-to-follow steps are included to make your existing learning centers also work as centers relevant to each theme or subject area. As a result, the activities can be incorporated into your existing setup and children can be learning new and important skills every day. Most of the manipulatives used in this book are household or common items.

Introduction *(cont.)*

Easy Steps *(cont.)*

❖ Third, each activity includes the appropriate National Association of Education of Young Children (NAEYC) justification in a section called "NAEYC Appropriate Practices." This way you can be sure that your lesson plan is cutting-edge and based on sound educational philosophy. So, without a lot of worry, you will be able to explain the purpose behind your curriculum choices to anyone who is interested, without having to spend hours creating accurate justification.

A Natural Progression

Everyday Activities for Preschool follows a format that corresponds to the natural learning pattern of the very young child. Research has determined that the young child begins as egocentric and self-involved and gradually develops and begins to de-center. This book begins by focusing on activities related to self-esteem, allowing the child to start with solitary and parallel play activities that fit the learning needs of a young child in this area. The second section is socialization and language. These two learning areas go hand in hand; there cannot be one without the other. In order to understand themselves, others, or any concept of learning, children must have the ability to think. And while children may think in pictures, they need words to describe these pictures to themselves and to the rest of the world.

Therefore, a child beginning to acquire language begins to communicate and, eventually, to become socialized. (It is a process that really lasts all of our lives.) Once children have mastered the fundamentals of socialization and language, they have a context that allows them to learn the other wonderful things the world offers them—numbers and mathematics, science and curiosity.

This natural learning progression is the format of *Everyday Activities for Preschool*. It will help your children learn no matter where they are. We understand and celebrate our children's differences, their differing abilities and uniqueness. *Everyday Activities for Preschool* is designed to enable you to empower the children you teach by giving them an enriched preschool experience.

Foundations for Learning

Early Childhood Experts Know

Early childhood experts know that what happens in the early childhood classroom sets the stage for all later learning. That is why it is so crucial that we prepare children to learn on the primary level with a firm and relevant foundation. While preschool children should not be made to parrot facts and figures and recite by rote, there is a certain amount of relevant information we can give them in both self-directed and directed activities that will create a firm foundation for the rest of their educational experience.

Everyday Activities for Preschool speaks to the needs of young children. While later on children will be introduced to social studies, reading and language arts, and math and science, young children need to first be introduced to socialization and self-esteem skills to best learn a context for the world around them. Children will then learn to enjoy books and see them as pleasurable and entertaining and to see letters and numbers as part of the enjoyment of figuring out the world. Finally, the curiosity and natural interest that all children have in the world around them will begin to form the basis for learning about the sciences.

A Solid Foundation

Everyday Activities for Preschool has been set up to provide a solid foundation of learning that will translate into superior learning skills in any subject area. The activities do not attempt to rush children into facts, figures, and memorization, but rather to provide the context for later learning and the beginning of thinking skills. Each activity is totally in keeping with the philosophy of NAEYC and may be used in the particular type of classroom you feel works best for your children. The philosophy is one of exposure to experience. The activities in no way suggest that mastery should be expected in the early childhood years.

Early Childhood Trends

A variety of teaching trends exists in early childhood education. *Everyday Activities for Preschool* gives you the guidelines you need to tailor each activity to address the philosophies and teaching styles that you feel are most relevant to your students.

Everyday Activities for Everyone

The activities in this book are designed to make being a child in a preschool more enjoyable and more positive. With deep concern for the treatment and education of all children, these activities have been designed to enhance your already existing personal philosophy of caring and commitment to the children you teach and to all children.

The Learning Crown

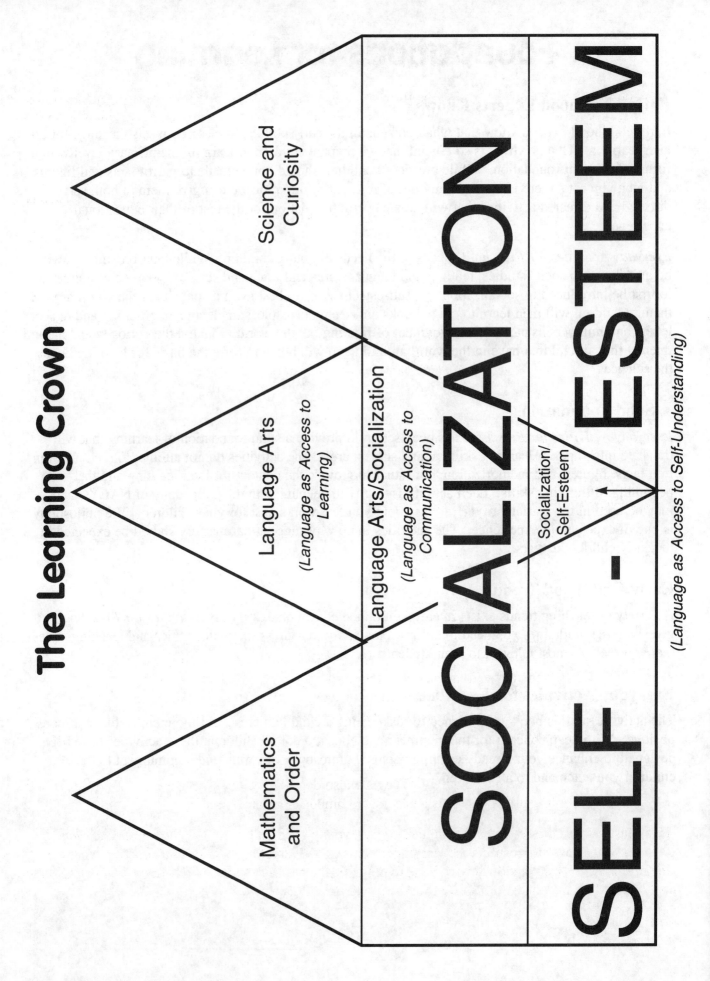

Science and Curiosity

Language Arts
(Language as Access to Learning)

Language Arts/Socialization
(Language as Access to Communication)

Mathematics and Order

Socialization/Self-Esteem

SOCIALIZATION - ESTEEM

SELF

(Language as Access to Self-Understanding)

The Learning Crown *(cont.)*

To understand better the idea behind the format of *Everyday Activities for Preschool*, take a look at the learning "crown" on the previous page. This simple diagram provides a visual demonstration of how all of the areas of learning feed into one another and are dependent on one another.

Look at the sections of the graphic in this way:

◆ Notice the diamond shape in the center of the crown. This area represents language. Language is a common thread in all of the sections of this book, and it is illustrated here to suggest the following:

— Language is necessary in the process of thinking about and understanding oneself; therefore, it is an important part of a child's ability to form a healthy sense of self (self-esteem).

— Language is necessary in the process of communication; therefore, it is a crucial component of socialization. When children begin to talk and listen and to understand words, they have the basis upon which to become socialized (socialization).

— Language is necessary to learning. Words are used to convey meaning, and the more fluent a child is in his own language, the better able he will be to think, to read, to understand mathematical concepts, and to explore science (language arts, mathematics, and science).

After looking at the language diamond, notice how it fits into the rest of the diagram.

◆ The base of the crown is self-esteem. The language diamond rests in self-esteem. A healthy self-esteem is boosted by good language skills and is essential to learning socialization.

◆ Socialization is the next step: This first building block that rests on self-esteem gives children information about how to live in the world and how to get along with others. The diamond pattern in the middle of the crown emphasizes that socialization cannot exist without language, and language is the crucial ingredient in socialization. These two areas, perhaps more than any of the others, work hand in hand to help facilitate the healthy development of the very young child.

◆ Mathematics and order, and science and curiosity form the remainder of the crown diagram. They are also dependent upon language, because language is a necessary component of any learning.

This illustration serves as an easy reminder of how young children learn. The format of *Everyday Activities for Preschool* respects the learning process of the very young child by facilitating what we already know to be true and what we have found to be the best way to introduce the very young child to the world of learning in a nurturing, stress-free, and natural way.

The Sections
Section One: Self-Esteem and Socialization

A Great Start

Before children can begin to learn, they must have a context of the surrounding world as a starting point. The first section of *Everyday Activities for Preschool* focuses on the learning foundation that will set the stage for social studies. This area is called self-esteem and socialization. Children must know who they are in relation to the world. They must have an understanding of their immediate and everyday surroundings, their families, friends, and neighborhoods, and of how they fit in with other people around them. All of these realizations work together to form a child's self-concept. Each of the activities in this section stresses a child's ability to understand where he or she is in the world and to feel good about that place.

The Self-Esteem Connection

As early childhood educators, we realize the importance of a child's socialization and development. From Piaget forward, we have attempted to recognize a child's needs for self-awareness, concept, and esteem. Before children can begin to learn, they must have a sense of themselves; the more valuable and worthwhile they feel, the better they will be able to learn, not only as young children but also as older children and adults.

To help create the solid base of self-esteem and socialization needed for learning, the first section of the activities in *Everyday Activities for Preschool* is devoted to helping you, the teacher, facilitate classroom activities. These activities, both directed and self-directed, will foster and increase students' sense of self-worth. All of the activities follow this basic format:

- ❖ teaching attainable skill mastery
- ❖ teaching autonomy and personal competence
- ❖ encouraging personal creativity
- ❖ encouraging a positive sense of self, including body image and awareness

Until recently, the current trend in self-esteem centered on praise regardless of achievement. Lately, however, there has been a shift back to achievement-oriented self-esteem encouragement. The four basic areas of mastery covered in *Everyday Activities for Preschool* provide students early on with a real and lifelong formula for achieving and maintaining a sense of their own value and worth. Each activity will enhance a child's self-awareness, mastery, sense of self, and self-concept. It is important to remember as we teach to the "whole child" that each individual starts at a different place. That is, each student you teach may be at a different level of mastery. Try to direct your children in such a manner that the skills they attempt will be at a level attainable for them where they are today, not where a peer is or where a curriculum predicts a student of two, three, four, five, or six years of age should be in development. If we teach to the whole child, and the whole individual child, each child benefits by an increased sense of mastery at every level. As a result everybody wins!

The Sections *(cont.)*

Learning About Me

In the first activity section of *Everyday Activities for Preschool*, children will take part in activities both directed and self-directed that will help them to master their awareness of themselves, their families, their communities and neighborhoods, and each step of the world as they know it. The emphasis of this book is on the diversities in our classroom, with activities centering on themes that show the differences and similarities of peoples, and that celebrate the many forms our lives, families, and cultures take. Students are validated in the beginning about who they are, whoever they happen to be. To create self-esteem in children, or adults for that matter, you must attempt to create an environment of empowerment, acceptance, and support. In such a classroom, every child benefits, and every child gets the opportunity to form the best possible personal foundation upon which to build an education.

The first section of activities addresses the following areas (Hendrick):

❖ fostering competency
❖ fostering creativity
❖ fostering positive body awareness

This self-esteem and socialization section gives children a clear understanding of where they fit in their own worlds.

Section Two: Language Arts and Socialization

An Important Combination

The ability to speak, to use words, and to understand their meanings is an absolutely necessary part of socialization. We use words to communicate, and even in an early childhood setting where children are presented with pictures instead of words, the pictures are related to words, and the words are attached to the picture. Language and communication are linked; likewise, socialization and language arts are linked.

In the second section of *Everyday Activities for Preschool*, you will find activities that allow children to explore language, communication, and word meaning in a real-life, relevant context.

This section exposes children to stories, poems, and music, giving them a substantial number of opportunities to be part of active, self-directed play where the words they hear immediately mean something concrete. Their participation in self-directed play makes them an involved and totally interactive part of their own socialization and language connection.

The Sections *(cont.)*

As illustrated by the crown diagram, language is the basis for communication and communication is the basis for socialization. Furthermore, language is the basis for learning, since learning requires an understanding of words as symbols for things, people, actions, and, later, ideas.

The activities in the second section highlight the following socialization concepts (Hendrick):

- ❖ fostering generosity
- ❖ fostering empathy
- ❖ fostering altruism
- ❖ fostering respect
- ❖ fostering compromise

Section Three: Mathematics and Order

Creating Order

As children begin to learn about the world around them, they desire to create order for themselves. They like to sort, to classify, to line things up and then scatter them, and to build things and then knock them down. All of this enjoyable and sometimes seemingly random behavior is actually a child's exploration of early learning in mathematics.

Number Fun

Most young children are interested in numbers. They have a natural curiosity about them. In this section, mathematical concepts are introduced in a way that gives children enhanced exposure to a variety of concepts. It is not important that a young child can count, sort, match, or add. What is important is that a young child be exposed to a world where these experiences are available and a part of his or her everyday world.

Remember, it is the enriched environment that sets the basis for later learning, not the mastery of the concepts. Children master concepts at their own paces, just like adults. An environment rich with opportunities to experience many different learning areas, including mathematics, begins the process by which children begin to find order in their worlds.

Section Four: Science and Curiosity

The World Around Them

This section gives children an opportunity to explore their own curiosity about the world around them. Later, this curiosity will become the basis for the kind of thinking skills that are needed for scientific investigation.

Children have a natural need to know. Any parent or early childhood educator is quite familiar with the question, "Why?" This question is the basis for all great achievements. Someone began with the simple question, "Why?"

The "Science and Curiosity" section celebrates young children's need to know why. Finally, the goal of each of the sections and all of the activities in this book is to create a "child-centered environment" that excites, pleases, and inspires children to play at learning. For when we play at learning, we make learning what it is meant to be—fun!

How the Book Works

Example Activity with Explanation of Each Section

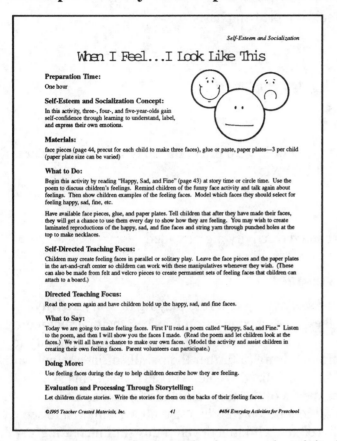

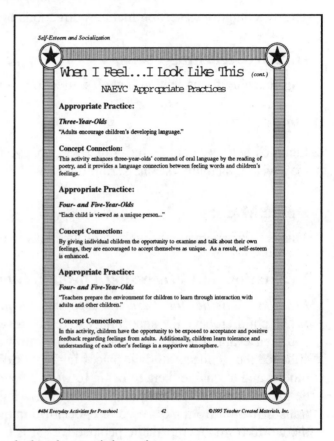

As you can see in the example above, each activity includes these mini-sections:

- ❖ Preparation Time
- ❖ Concept
- ❖ Materials
- ❖ What to Do
- ❖ Self-Directed Teaching Focus
- ❖ Directed Teaching Focus
- ❖ What to Say
- ❖ Doing More
- ❖ Evaluation and Processing Through Storytelling
- ❖ NAEYC Appropriate Practices
- ❖ Concept Connection

Preparation Time:

Because each activity is clearly labeled with the time it takes to prepare, it is possible to skim the book and find an activity that fits into your schedule.

Concept:

Because each section has a concept explained briefly, there is no guesswork.

Materials:

Because the materials needed are listed with page references to other sections (if needed), nothing is left to chance.

What to Do:

Included are simple preparation and presentation directions.

How the Book Works *(cont.)*

Self-Directed Teaching Focus:

This teaching focus section includes directions for self-directed emphasis.

Directed Teaching Focus:

This teaching focus section includes directions for directed emphasis.

What to Say:

Included here is a sample script that will give you an idea of how to direct the activity. Some teachers may wish to actually use the script; others will read it for review.

Doing More:

This is self-explanatory; quick and easy ideas to expand the activity are provided.

Evaluation and Processing Through Storytelling:

Everyday Activities for Preschool uses the concept of storytelling and role playing in every activity. When children have the opportunity to tell a story, they make a connection between their current reality and their evaluation of it. Encourage storytelling in your classroom to give children the opportunity to enhance their concept of their places in the world around them, to further their skills of interacting with others, and to enable them to begin to work as part of a socialized whole. (In later years, this skill will be part of the basis for cooperative learning.) Piaget speaks of the early childhood years as a time of transformation from a centered or egocentric mind set to a decentered one that allows children to see the world from an empathetic perspective. It is believed that children develop this skill increasingly during early childhood years, and the presence of nurturing and positive role models enhances the transition immensely. When children have an opportunity to describe and act out their daily experiences in narrative, they have an opportunity to synthesize and relate to what is happening around them. They also have in the context of the "social art of storytelling" an opportunity to connect with their classmates, hear the other children's perspective and begin to form the basis for what we believe are the principles of socialization.

Teaching the principles of socialization requires the following steps (Hendrick):

1. identifying and imitating an appropriate role model
2. encouragement from the role model

Each activity in this book gives students an opportunity to evaluate and process their own experiences, (just as they will be asked to do in later years) in a natural and self-directed manner that is proven to be an effective and progressive technique in early childhood education.

NAEYC Appropriate Practices:

This section provides age-appropriate concepts in keeping with current National Association for the Education of Young Children (NAEYC) philosophies.

Concept Connection:

Included are age-appropriate activities that support the NAEYC appropriate practices.

Centers

The activities in *Everyday Activities for Preschool* are specifically designed to make your existing learning centers also work as centers relevant to the themes in this book. Take a look at the illustrations below, which provide a sampling of some of the centers used in *Everyday Activities for Preschool*.

Puppet Theater

Dress Up!

READING CENTERS

Puppet Theater

Table of Contents: Self-Esteem and Socialization

Neat and Tidy

Preparation Time:

One afternoon

Self-Esteem and Socialization Concept:

This activity introduces three-, four-, and five-year-olds to the idea of self-esteem through body awareness, and it teaches personal grooming habits along with the concept of neatness versus messiness.

Materials:

plastic combs for each child, grooming center (ordinary bathroom facilities may be used with some minor additions), two dolls, messy and neat bulletin board (see example below)

What to Do:

This activity gives children an opportunity to learn about the importance of personal grooming and at the same time begin the lifelong habit of being neat and tidy. To create a neat-and-tidy center, use your already existing bathroom facilities. Be sure the bathroom area has the following: a mirror (full length is excellent but a standard mirror will work as well), tissues, paper towels, and soap for hand washing. You may wish to set up your center using the neat and messy bulletin-board signs on pages 17 and 18. Begin the activity by discussing the idea of grooming with your children. Give all the children their own labeled combs that they may store in their cubbies, and let each demonstrate its use. Next, talk about how important it is to be neat and tidy every day. Let children look at their neat-and-tidy center and discuss the use for each item (e.g., mirror, soap, towels, comb, tissues). Then model "neat" and "messy" using two dolls. Let children who are interested use dolls from the house center to illustrate both neat and messy and share with others.

Neat and Tidy *(cont.)*:

What to Do *(cont.)*:

To self-direct the activity maintain the neat-and-tidy center as a regular center in your classroom. Give children an opportunity to use the center at regular intervals during the day, or let them use it whenever they want to.

Directed Teaching Focus:

Have children take turns using the center and demonstrating their own ideas of neat and messy for the rest of the class. Let each child dress a doll both neatly and messily. Make enough copies of pages 17 and 18 for your class and have children color them.

What to Say:

Today we are all going to get a special new gift to keep in our cubbies to use every day. Who can tell me what this is? (Hold up a comb and discuss with the class its use; distribute a prelabeled comb to each child.) I have made our toilet area into a neat-and-tidy center. Let's all take a look at what I've done to this area and decide how we will use it. (Model the use of the center for the children and show them the bulletin board with the neat and messy labels.) Let's talk about what these words mean, and then let's take turns using our neat-and-tidy center.

Doing More:

Let children cut out pictures from old magazines of neat and tidy people to put on the neat-and-tidy section of the bulletin board.

Evaluating and Processing Through Storytelling:

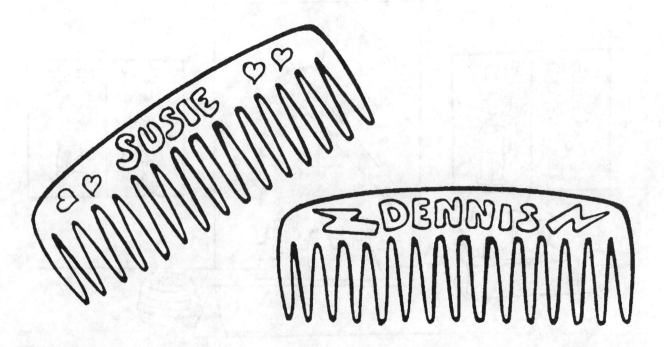

Neat and Tidy *(cont.)*

Neat and Tidy *(cont.)*

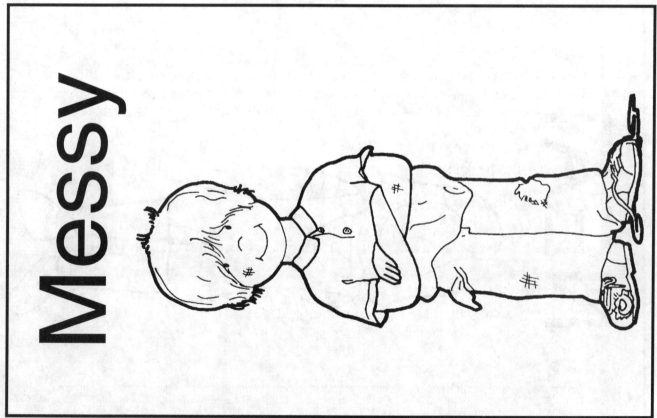

Neat and Tidy *(cont.)*

NAEYC Appropriate Practices

Appropriate Practice:

Three-Year-Olds

"Adults support three-year-olds' play and developing independence, helping when needed but allowing them to do what they are capable of doing and what they want to do for themselves (I can do it myself!)."

Concept Connection:

This activity allows children to have mastery over a number of real-life skills and provides them an opportunity for everyday, self-directed practice. Additionally, children benefit by the increased self-esteem associated with positive body image and the realization that they have personal control over their own bodies and how they choose to look.

Appropriate Practice:

Four- and Five-Year-Olds

"Teachers prepare an environment for children to learn through active exploration...with materials."

Concept Connection:

This activity lets children explore the concept of personal grooming by using a permanent center on a daily basis. The regular use of the center and the availability of the grooming materials allow children time to perfect their own ideas and attitudes regarding grooming.

Appropriate Practice:

Four- and Five-Year-Olds

"Children are provided many opportunities to see how reading and writing are useful before they are instructed in letter names… seeing classroom charts and other print in use."

Concept Connection:

Children make the connection between words and ideas by seeing the neat and messy bulletin board displays and learning the difference between neat and messy. Children are regularly exposed to the words and the ideas they convey each time they use the neat-and-tidy center.

Neat and Tidy *(cont.)*
Neat and Tidy Word Patterns

Messy

Neat

Funny Faces

Preparation Time:

30 minutes

Self-Esteem and Socialization Concept:

Children gain self-confidence, a sense of body awareness, and self-acceptance through learning about their own faces and feelings.

Materials:

painting supplies, several hand mirrors, an instant camera (optional), a video camera (optional)

What to Do:

This activity introduces children to the connection between expressions and feelings and the words that describe how people's faces look. Begin this activity by telling children that they are all going to get to play a funny mirror game. Next, talk with children about the idea of feeling words and what they mean. Let children share times they have felt happy, sad, afraid, or any other emotion. Draw the parallel between how people feel and what their faces look like. Ask children to remember when they have seen their brother or their sister or a friend look sad or happy, etc. Let children know that it is all right to feel their feelings and to show them on their faces. You may wish to draw simple circle faces to model the faces and the words about feelings that go with them or use the patterns on page 24.

Have children stand up and playact the feeling words as you call them out. For example, say "happy!" Children may laugh, smile, and jump up and down. Say "sad," and children may pretend to cry, etc. This game can be played often, as it gives children an opportunity to playact and utilize some energy while making them familiar with what emotions and feelings look like. Point out to children that there are many different ways to look happy or sad and let children show as many different ways as they can.

Funny Faces *(cont.)*

What to Do *(cont.)*:

Set up a painting center with the hand mirrors so children can paint their own faces while looking at the mirrors to see their expressions. Have older children work in pairs and mimic each other's funny faces.

Self-Directed Teaching Focus:

Let children use the painting center to make face pictures whenever they want to. Encourage children to paint pictures often to tell about how they feel. Have available copies of page 24 for children to paint or color.

Directed Teaching Focus:

Use an instant camera to have children make happy face pictures. Send these pictures home or mount them as part of a bulletin board display.

What to Say:

Today we are going to make funny faces. Have you ever noticed you can tell a lot about people and the way they are feeling by looking at their faces? (Discuss feelings and faces.) Now I am going to say some words about feelings, and I want everyone to play-act what they think these feelings mean. Let me show you. Who thinks they can make a happy face? (Students demonstrate.) Great! Now can someone make a sad face? Okay. Let's try it. (Have students demonstrate. Say a variety of words and give children time to playact and comment. You can pass out mirrors for children to use during this activity. Some word ideas might include the following: mad, angry, happy, glad, funny, excited, afraid, sad, bored, sleepy, crying. Give children an opportunity to think of others.)

Doing More:

Use a video camera and videotape children making funny faces. Let children view their funny faces video and guess the words that go with their faces.

Evaluating and Processing Through Storytelling:

After children paint pictures of their faces, let them dictate stories to go with their pictures about their faces.

Funny Faces *(cont.)*
NAEYC Appropriate Practices

Appropriate Practice:

Three-Year-Olds

"Adults know that children are rapidly acquiring language...and beginning to use language to solve problems and learn concepts."

Concept Connection:

This activity allows children to begin to use language to describe their own feelings and gives them a basis to begin to communicate how they feel.

Appropriate Practice:

Four- and Five-Year-Olds

"Experiences are provided that meet children's needs and stimulate learning in all developmental areas...including emotional."

Concept Connection:

In this activity children become aware of their own emotions in a safe, accepting manner and have the opportunity to explore each of their own emotions without judgement.

Appropriate Practice:

Four- and Five-Year-Olds

"Each child is viewed as a unique person with an individual pattern of timing of growth and development."

Concept Connection:

In this activity each child's uniqueness is reinforced by the act of examining his/her own emotions. Also, children begin to notice the emotions of others, which is a crucial step in socialization.

Funny Faces (cont.)
Patterns for Funny Faces

Happy

Mad/Angry

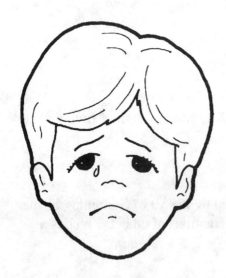

Sad

Excited

24

Costume Party

Preparation Time:
One hour (longer if your classroom does not have an already existing costume or dress-up center)

Self-Esteem and Socialization Concept:
This activity helps three-, four-, and five-year-olds foster their own creativity and enhances their self-esteem through personal expression.

Materials:
costume or pretend center with enough costume materials for each child to have a costume, paper costume mask for each child (page 26), party supplies (cookies, punch)

What to Do:
In this activity children select their own dress-up costumes and share the pretend characters they invent at a class costume party. This activity is an excellent one for parent and volunteer participation. If you have an already existing pretend center in your classroom, there is practically no set-up time for this activity. If not, use the parent letter to request donations of costume materials and build your own center (page 27).

Tell children that they will be attending a costume party. Hold a class discussion about when children have worn costumes before and what characters they were (e.g., Halloween). Next, give children plenty of time to explore the pretend center and choose their own costumes. Give the children masks so they can pretend to be anyone they want.

Finally, serve punch and cookies and let children sit in the storytelling or circle area and share who they are with the rest of their classmates. At the end of the party, let the children take off their masks and show their real faces again.

Self-Directed Teaching Focus:
Maintain a costume or pretend center in your classroom, so children may use it every day. For this activity, encourage students to choose their own costumes rather than deciding for them what they will be.

Directed Teaching Focus:
End the activity with organized sharing about the children's costumes and who they are pretending to be.

What to Say:
Today we are going to have a costume party! Can anyone tell me what a costume is? (Hold class discussion about costumes and when children have worn them and what characters they have chosen to be for the party.) I want everyone to spend some time in the costume center picking out a costume and deciding who to be. After you are ready, come to the circle area and we will have a party. All of you will get a chance to tell who you are and why you chose the costume you did.

Doing More:
At the party have children tell stories or act out something their characters might do.

Evaluation and Processing Through Storytelling:
Have parent volunteers help students dictate their own "Who Am I?" stories. Let children draw pictures to go with their stories.

Costume Party *(cont.)*
Paper Masks

Directions: Reproduce on heavy paper enough masks for each child in your class. If you wish, have children decorate with paint, crayons, glue, glitter, etc. Punch holes where marked and knot a 12-inch (30 cm) length of yarn through each. Tie a mask around each child's head.

Costume Party *(cont.)*
Parent Letter

Dear Parents,

To make your children's learning and play experiences more meaningful, I am creating a Costume and Pretend Center in our classroom. I am in need of any old costumes or old and used clothing that children can use for costumes and pretend dress-up activities. Anything our class cannot use will be donated to a local charity.

Please remember that you are always invited to be a guest at any time, and I always appreciate parent volunteers. If volunteering interests you, please return this note with your name and phone number, and I will contact you about how you can take part in your child's early-childhood educational experience.

In advance, I thank you for your help.

Sincerely,

❑   Yes, I will be able to donate costume supplies.

❑   Yes, I would like to volunteer. You may call me.

Name _____

Child's name _____

Phone number _____ Best time to call _____

Costume Party *(cont.)*

NAEYC Appropriate Practices

Appropriate Practice:

Three-Year-Olds

"Adults provide large amounts of uninterrupted time for children to persist at self-chosen tasks."

Concept Connection:

In this activity children have the opportunity to explore the costume and dress-up center and discover the kinds of costumes they would like and the kinds of characters they might choose to be.

Children gain autonomy and decision-making skills and have the opportunity to explore and discover in solo and parallel play situations.

Appropriate Practice:

Four- and Five-Year-Olds

"Children work individually or in small informal groups most of the time."

Concept Connection:

This activity lends itself to individual and informal group play. By allowing children plenty of time to plan and execute their own costume plans and discuss their ideas and share informally, children gain both self-esteem and socialization skills.

Appropriate Practice:

Four- and Five-Year-Olds

"Experiences are provided that meet children's needs and stimulate learning in all developmental areas...including social."

Concept Connection:

By attending a costume party, children have the opportunity to practice socialization skills such as respecting others, compromise, and sharing in a low-key manner.

Skip, Hop, Stop! ABC Game

Preparation Time:

30–60 minutes

Self-Esteem and Socialization Concept:

This activity helps three-, four-, and five-year-olds foster body awareness and self-esteem through active play.

Materials:

white or colored chalk, blacktop area (for outside play); reproduced letter patterns, tape, and floor space (for inside play)

What to Do:

This activity is an adaptation of the old favorite "Mother, May I?" game. In addition to body awareness and self-esteem through active play, children have the opportunity to develop thinking and motor skills and coordination.

Begin this activity by placing ABC patterns in a circle in the proper alphabetical order. (If you are playing outside, use chalk to draw the letters in a large circle.) Next, show children the letter circle and choose a leader. The leader stands in the middle of the circle. Have children pick a favorite alphabet letter to stand on. The leader chooses a movement word, and the children move around the circle, enacting that word. For example, Ashley says, "Jump!" Children then jump from letter to letter around the circumference of the circle. Then she says, "Hop!" Children hop. The leader chooses when to say "Stop!" Children then name the letters they are standing on. (Another variation is to have children sit down quickly when the leader calls out stop as in "Musical Chairs," and the last one down is out. In this manner, eventually a winner will be determined. However, you may prefer to focus the game in a way that does not exclude players.) The leader chooses a next leader and returns to the circle.

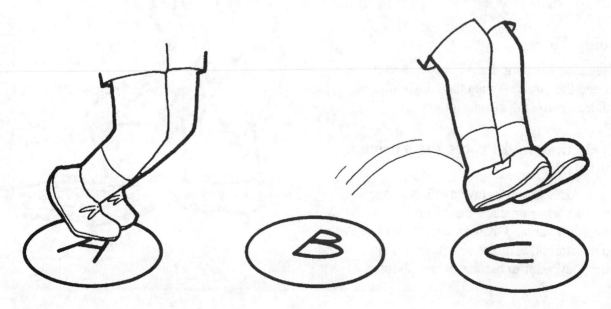

Skip, Hop, Stop! ABC Game *(cont.)*

Self-Directed Teaching Focus:

Encourage children to self-direct their own ABC games by leaving the alphabet circle available for self-directed play.

Directed Teaching Focus:

The teacher acts as caller, saying movement words to a group of children and leading letter recognition discussion.

What to Say:

Today we are going to play an ABC game called "Skip, Hop, Stop!" Before we start, I want everyone to practice skipping, hopping, and stopping. Okay, let's all get in a big circle. When I say skip, we will all skip around the circle. Ready? Skip! Good! Now let's all try to hop. Remember that we hop on one foot like this. (Model hopping.) Now let's try it again, and when I say "Stop!" everybody hold perfectly still like a statue. Ready to try it? (Model the activity several times with students.)

Now, take a look at our ABC circle. Don't these letters look nice? Let's all pick a letter to stand on. Now we're going to play "Skip, Hop, Stop!" and move from letter to letter. When you hear "Stop!" stop on the first letter you see, and then we will see if you can name the letter. I'll be the leader for the first game; then you can choose your own leaders to play the game. Let's begin!

Stop! Okay, now, Tom, what letter are you standing on? B? Great. Do you know a word that starts with B? Does anyone? "Banana" is a great choice. Can we think of any others? Wow! I am impressed with the way you know your letters!

Doing More:

Have children sing the ABC song and move around the circle. When the song ends, let children name the closest letters.

Evaluation and Processing Through Storytelling:

Make ABC stories. Have available paper with one letter on each sheet in the storytelling area. Or make extra copies of the letter patterns. Children may choose any letter they want to dictate stories about.

Skip, Hop, Stop! ABC Game *(cont.)*
NAEYC Appropriate Practices

Appropriate Practice:

Three-Year-Olds

"Adults provide plenty of space and time indoors and outdoors for children to explore and exercise their large muscle skills like running, jumping..."

Concept Connection:

This activity provides three-year-olds with an opportunity to exercise their large muscle groups, while also providing intervals for rest that are built into the game.

Appropriate Practice:

Four- and Five-Year-Olds

"Children are expected to be physically and mentally active."

Concept Connection:

In this activity, children combine both physical and mental activity, building their own sense of both physical and mental mastery and self-esteem.

Appropriate Practice:

Four- and Five-Year-Olds

"Children have daily opportunities to use large muscles by running, jumping, and balancing..."

Concept Connection:

Four- and five-year-olds have the opportunity to exercise large muscle groups in this activity. To enhance this opportunity further, play the game outside and spread the letters far apart.

Around-the-World Dance Party

Preparation Time:

None (provided dance music has already been gathered)

Self-Esteem and Socialization Concept:

In this activity children build a variety of socialization and self-esteem skills. This includes body awareness through movement, as well as understanding and empathy toward other people and cultures through use of multi-ethnic musical experiences.

Materials:

multicultural music tapes or CDs and player, dance floor area, scarves (optional), rhythm and musical instruments (optional)

What to Do:

This is a simple and easy everyday activity that you may wish to make available on an ongoing basis for your children. All that is needed is dance floor space and a variety of music. Some teachers may also wish to make rhythm instruments or scarves available to enhance children's creative expression during their daily musical experience. To set up your own creative movement or dance party area, see page 36.

After you have created your dance area, gathering the music can be an excellent opportunity for you to connect with the different parents and families of your children. To make a request of parents for music and explain about the children's dance party activity, see page 35.

There are many possibilities here. Some parents or family members from various cultures may wish to share traditional dances with the children during a dance party day. The main ingredients are a variety of multi-ethnic music and the opportunity for children to move to the music. Make children aware of the various places that certain pieces of music come from. Some teachers may wish to have a world map in the dance party area to show children where the music comes from. Encourage children to share their own dances or songs with other children in the class, building tolerance, understanding, and enjoyment of the music of many cultures from a very early age.

Around-the-World Dance Party *(cont.)*

Self-Directed Teaching Focus:

To self-direct this activity let children use the dance area during a certain part of each day as they choose. Regular and noncompulsory dance-party time will give children who wish to participate the opportunity to do so while other children doing other self-directed tasks will still be exposed to the multicultural music.

Directed Teaching Focus:

Direct the activity by featuring music that has specific movement or by having parent volunteers teach simple dances to the students.

What to Say:

We are going to do something new in our classroom. I want to show all of you our new dance party center. After I have shown you, we will all try it. Then every day we will have an opportunity to dance. Let's listen to some of the music at the center. You may also bring your favorite music to share with the class. I have written a letter to your parents inviting them to show us special dances and to have fun with us during our dance party!

(Turn on music and model activity. If children seem hesitant to dance, use a dance video in the center to give children dancing ideas. However, most children in a nonjudgmental and safe situation are more than willing to take part in dance and movement fun.) We also have some things to use while we dance. I have a big box of scarves here to twirl and swing while we dance, and I also have a big box of different kinds of rhythm instruments from other countries. (Model the use of various multicultural instruments such as castanets, maracas, etc.) Every day at this time we will turn the music on, and anyone who wants to dance may do so.

Doing More:

Use the parent invitation letter (page 35) to invite parents to share dances of different cultures.

Then schedule dance-party lessons.

Evaluation and Processing Through Storytelling:

Give children time to dictate stories of their dance party experiences. Allow them use of a tape recorder for this activity. Some children may prefer to make up songs about their dance party activity and sing into the tape recorder.

Around-the-World Dance Party *(cont.)*
NAEYC Appropriate Practices

Appropriate Practice:

Three-Year-Olds

"Adults read a story or play music with groups and allow children to enter and leave the group at will."

Concept Connection:

In this activity three-year-olds have the opportunity to choose to take part or not in the dance party activity, to leave and return as they feel comfortable and to take part on whatever level pleases them. This freedom allows them to gain self-confidence about their own decisions and a sense of mastery of themselves and their feelings and desires.

Appropriate Practice:

Four- and Five-Year-Olds

"Children develop understanding of concepts about themselves, others, and the world around them through....singing and listening to music from various cultures."

Concept Connection:

In this activity four- and five-year-olds have the opportunity to be exposed to the music and customs of a variety of different ethnic backgrounds in a relaxed and tolerant manner. In this way, children begin to see the world as a community and themselves as world citizens.

Appropriate Practice:

Four- and Five-Year-Olds

"Teachers work in partnership with parents, communicating regularly to build mutual understanding and greater consistency for children."

Concept Connection:

This activity allows teachers to bridge the gap in learning between home and school and to create an opportunity for children to bring their loved ones into their school environment in a happy and positive manner.

Around-the-World Dance Party (cont.)
Parent Invitation

Dear Parents,

As part of our focus on multicultural awareness, we are beginning a new, ongoing activity in our classroom. Our new activity will be called "Dance Party." During this activity, the children will be exposed to a variety of music and dance from other lands.

We are lucky to have a variety of different nationalities represented in our student population, and I would like to expose children to the dance and music from these cultures as part of our Dance Party activity. This is where you come in! I would like to invite all interested parents to share their special songs or dances with the class. Please plan to come in and demonstrate; hopefully, I hope we will involve the children in learning simple steps or portions of simple songs.

Almost anything goes. I would like to have all kinds of music and dance represented, from American rock-and-roll to the traditional dances of Africa, Southeast Asia, and Central and South America. I am very open to any suggestions you may have about sharing music and dance with the children. I am also interested in borrowing tapes or compact discs of culturally varied music.

Please return this form with your name and phone number and a simple description of the kind of music and/or dance you would like to share with our class. If you would like to take part but don't have a particular kind of dance or music to share with the class, that is fine. The children benefit from the presence of parent volunteers, and I am always happy when you can take part in your child's educational process.

I hope to hear from you soon!

Sincerely,

Name _____

Child's name _____

Phone number _____ Best time to call _____

Kind of dance or music you would like to share with the children _____

_____

Around-the-World Dance Party *(cont.)*

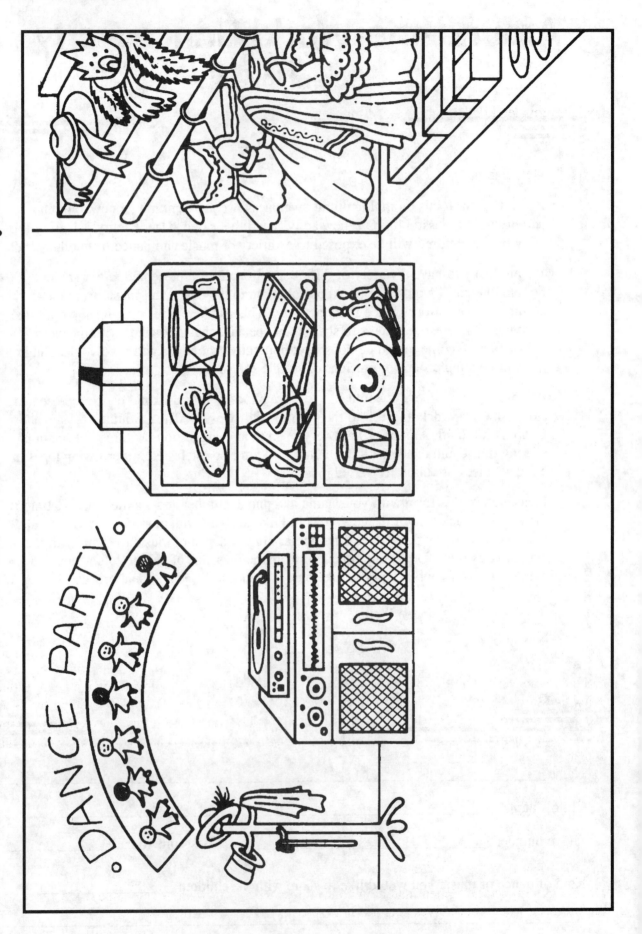

Kitchen Marching Band

Preparation Time:

None (provided kitchen supplies and music have already been gathered)

Self-Esteem and Socialization Concept:

In this activity three-, four-, and five-year-olds develop competency, creativity, and body awareness through creating their own kitchen marching band. Additionally, children build socialization skills like compromise and generosity by playing in a group and sharing kitchen instruments.

Materials:

pots, pans, wooden spoons, brooms and mops, coffee can drums or juice can shakers (See directions on page 40.)

What to Do:

Introduce this activity by reading "The Kitchen Marching Band" on page 38 to children. Ask children about the times they have seen marching bands or parades. Next, show students the kitchen instruments and ask them to pick a marching instrument. Use any marching or regular music with a march beat. (You may have already gathered enough music for use in your dance party center.) Turn on music and let children form a line and march around the classroom.

Self-Directed Teaching Focus:

To self-direct this activity in the dance party area, leave kitchen marching band materials for students to use.

Directed Teaching Focus:

Lead children on a march around the preschool or on a neighborhood march. Play music on a small tape player or have children sing and play at the same time.

What to Say:

Today we are going to form our own marching band. First, I am going to read you a poem called "The Kitchen Marching Band." (Read poem on page 38.) Now, let's talk about the marching bands and parades we have seen. (Have an informal discussion.) Look at all the items I have gathered for our own kitchen marching band. We will each choose an instrument, and then we will play some marching music so we can march. Let's try it.

Doing More:

Combine this activity with the costume party activity so children can march in costume.

Evaluation and Processing Though Storytelling:

Have children dictate kitchen marching band stories. You may wish to videotape this activity so children can watch themselves perform in their own marching band on TV.

Kitchen Marching Band *(cont.)*
The Kitchen Marching Band
by
Grace Jasmine

One day I saw a funny thing,
A sight so very grand,
I saw it right outside my door,
A Kitchen Marching Band!
Ten children played on pots and pans,
And tapped big spoons together.
I even saw one boy waving
A duster made of feathers!
There were
pie tins,
cake bowls,
brooms,
and
mops,
big wooden spoons,
and plates.
In all my life I never saw a marching band so great!
If ever you see one, you will really think it's grand!
So go ahead,
Why don't you make
Your own fine Kitchen Marching Band!

38

Kitchen Marching Band *(cont.)*

NAEYC Appropriate Practices

Appropriate Practice:

Three-Year-Olds

"Adults provide many experiences and opportunities to extend children's language and musical abilities."

Concept Connection:

In this activity three-year-olds are exposed to a variety of music and movement; at the same time, they become aware of a variety of real-life objects and the words and uses associated with them.

Appropriate Practice:

Four- and Five-Year-Olds

"Children have daily opportunity for aesthetic expression and appreciation through art and music."

Concept Connection:

In this activity four- and five-year-olds have an opportunity to create the kind of marching band they envision, and use their own creativity to self-direct their play.

Kitchen Marching Band (cont.)

Drums and Shakers

Drums and shakers are enjoyable to make. Simply follow the easy steps below.

Drums

Directions:

1. Collect old, clean coffee cans with plastic lids (or use oatmeal boxes for drums with no sharp edges.)

2. Paint, cover with construction paper, add glitter, or decorate in whatever way you wish.

3. Create a drum holder by tying the ends of 4' (1.22 m) lengths of rope or ribbon in knots, to form a circle. Glue the ropes around the bottoms of the cans, and also glue them to the sides of the cans. For additional support, cut 2" (5 m) wide strips of construction paper and glue those around the middles of the cans to hold the ropes in place. Have children wear the drums by placing the ropes around their necks.

4. Use hands, unsharpened pencils, or wooden spoons to beat on the drums. Practically anything will work. Enjoy making wonderful drum sounds!

Shakers

Directions:

1. Collect old juice cans, or small gift boxes. Anything small and easy to hold will do.

2. Fill with items that rattle. Use rocks, seeds, paper clips, buttons, or anything you have around that makes a nice sound.

3. Carefully secure the tops or lids to the boxes or cans with masking tape.

4. Decorate. Cover the seals with decorations so children will not be tempted to open the containers.

5. Shake, rattle, and roll!

When I Feel...I Look Like This

Preparation Time:

One hour

Self-Esteem and Socialization Concept:

In this activity, three-, four-, and five-year-olds gain self-confidence through learning to understand, label, and express their own emotions.

Materials:

face pieces (page 44, precut for each child to make three faces), glue or paste, paper plates—3 per child (paper plate size can be varied)

What to Do:

Begin this activity by reading "Happy, Sad, and Fine" (page 43) at story time or circle time. Use the poem to discuss children's feelings. Remind children of the funny face activity and talk again about feelings. Then show children examples of the feeling faces. Model which faces they should select for feeling happy, sad, fine, etc.

Have available face pieces, glue, and paper plates. Tell children that after they have made their faces, they will get a chance to use them every day to show how they are feeling. You may wish to create laminated reproductions of the happy, sad, and fine faces and string yarn through punched holes at the top to make necklaces.

Self-Directed Teaching Focus:

Children may create feeling faces in parallel or solitary play. Leave the face pieces and the paper plates in the art-and-craft center so children can work with these manipulatives whenever they wish. (These can also be made from felt and velcro pieces to create permanent sets of feeling faces that children can attach to a board.)

Directed Teaching Focus:

Read the poem again and have children hold up the happy, sad, and fine faces.

What to Say:

Today we are going to make feeling faces. First I'll read a poem called "Happy, Sad, and Fine." Listen to the poem, and then I will show you the faces I made. (Read the poem and let children look at the faces.) We will all have a chance to make our own faces. (Model the activity and assist children in creating their own feeling faces. Parent volunteers can participate.)

Doing More:

Use feeling faces during the day to help children describe how they are feeling.

Evaluation and Processing Through Storytelling:

Let children dictate stories. Write the stories for them on the backs of their feeling faces.

When I Feel...I Look Like This *(cont.)*

NAEYC Appropriate Practices

Appropriate Practice:

Three-Year-Olds

"Adults encourage children's developing language."

Concept Connection:

This activity enhances three-year-olds' command of oral language by the reading of poetry, and it provides a language connection between feeling words and children's feelings.

Appropriate Practice:

Four- and Five-Year-Olds

"Each child is viewed as a unique person..."

Concept Connection:

By giving individual children the opportunity to examine and talk about their own feelings, they are encouraged to accept themselves as unique. As a result, self-esteem is enhanced.

Appropriate Practice:

Four- and Five-Year-Olds

"Teachers prepare the environment for children to learn through interaction with adults and other children."

Concept Connection:

In this activity, children have the opportunity to be exposed to acceptance and positive feedback regarding feelings from adults. Additionally, children learn tolerance and understanding of each other's feelings in a supportive atmosphere.

When I Feel...I Look Like This (cont.)

Happy, Sad, Fine
by
Grace Jasmine

Sometimes I feel happy,
And I smile like this,
The corners of my mouth turn up!

I laugh, and I sing, and I do all kinds of things;
I feel happy and I look like this!

Sometimes I feel sad,
And I frown like this,
The corners of my mouth turn down!

I cry and I'm sad because I'm feeling bad;
I feel sad and I look like this!

Sometimes I feel fine,
And I look like this,
I don't have a smile or a frown.

I feel fine today, and I'm feeling okay;
I feel fine and I look like this!

When I Feel...I Look Like This (cont.)

Feeling Faces

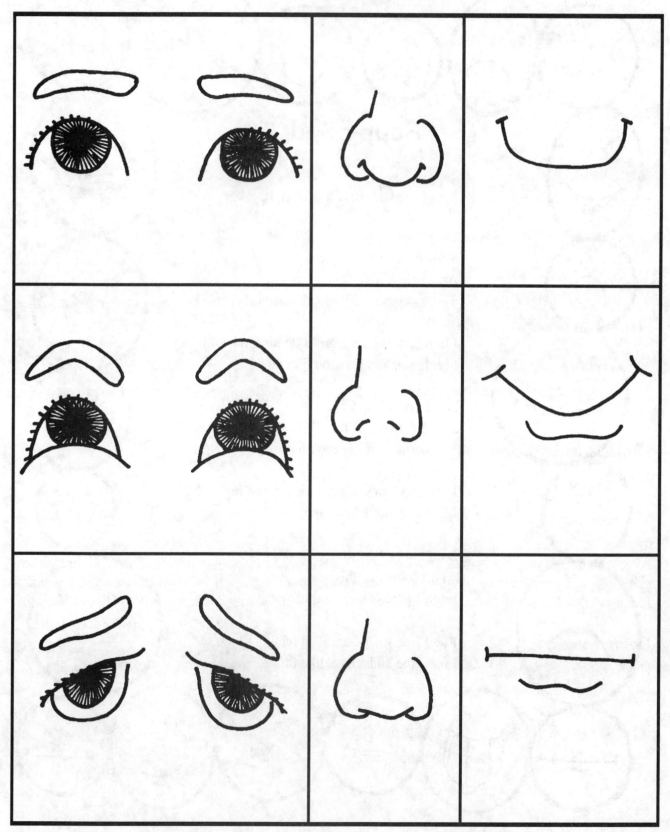

How Do I Feel Today?

Preparation Time:

None (if children have completed the "When I Feel...I Look Like This" activity)

Self-Esteem and Socialization Concept:

In this activity three-, four-, and five-year-olds gain self-confidence through awareness of their own and others' feelings.

Materials:

paper plate feeling faces, 3 for each child (See previous activity.)

What to Do:

This activity allows both children and teachers to become aware of how children are feeling on a daily basis. Remind children about the previous activity, and ask them to select a feeling face every day before they come to circle time or storytime. Then, in a group sharing situation, ask children to share how they feel and why.

Self-Directed Teaching Focus:

To self-direct this activity give children three feeling-face choices suspended on yarn chains like necklaces. Let them alter the feeling faces they are wearing as their feelings change through the day.

Directed Teaching Focus:

Use this activity as a regular and directed daily sharing in circle time.

What to Say:

Today we are going to put the feeling faces we made the other day in our cubbies. Every day we will be able to bring the faces that show how we are feeling to our circle and tell about how we are feeling and why. Let's try it now. Go to your cubbies and choose the feeling face that best tells how you are feeling. (Direct the children to their cubbies.) Now let's all sit in a circle and talk about our feelings.

Doing More:

Have children bring their feeling faces along to storytime. Ask them to hold up their feeling faces to indicate how the story makes them feel.

Evaluation and Processing Through Storytelling:

Have children dictate both sad and happy stories.

How Do I Feel Today? *(cont.)*

NAEYC Appropriate Practices

Appropriate Practice:

Three-Year-Olds

"Adults provide affection and support, comforting children when they cry and reassuring them when fearful."

Concept Connection:

This activity creates an opportunity for adult-child communication. Children are helped both to understand and to cope with their own emotional responses.

Appropriate Practice:

Four- and Five-Year-Olds

"Experiences are provided that meet children's needs in all developmental areas... (including) emotions."

Concept Connection:

This activity provides opportunities for children to share and to recognize the similarity of emotions among themselves and others.

Appropriate Practice:

Four- and Five-Year-Olds

"Interactions and activities are designed to develop children's self-esteem."

Concept Connection:

Children are given a method for expressing their emotions and dealing with daily problems through the use of symbols and language.

I Like Me

Preparation Time:

30 minutes

Self-Esteem and Socialization Concept:

In this activity three-, four-, and five-year-olds begin to form positive self-concepts based on thoughts of and verbal statements of what they like about themselves. Children also foster empathy, altruism, and respect by interacting with others concerning this topic.

Materials:

circle buttons, crayons, glue, glitter, safety pins or tape, painting supplies, paper

What to Do:

In this activity children think about what they like about themselves and create "I Like Me" buttons to wear in the classroom and at home. Begin this activity by reading "I Like Me!" (page 49) during story time. Then hold an informal discussion about the many things we like about ourselves. Next, model the activity by showing students already prepared buttons and telling them they will make one today. Place the buttons and supplies in the art center for students to use daily if they wish. Assist individuals and small groups with deciding what they like about themselves. Encourage students to decorate their buttons and wear them. (This activity is an excellent parent participation activity.)

Self-Directed Teaching Focus:

This activity can be set up for regular and self-directed use in your art center. For an additional self-directed activity, write "I like me because..." with a large felt marker across the tops of large pieces of paper for children to paint pictures illustrating what they like about themselves.

Directed Teaching Focus:

On a daily basis have children participate in a group sharing activity to discuss what they like about themselves. Also encourage children to share what they like about the other children.

What to Say:

Today I am going to read you a poem called "I Like Me!" Listen while I read this poem. Then we are going to make buttons to wear. (Model the button activity and help interested children select button slogans.) After we make our buttons, we can wear them, and you can make new ones every day. They will be in the art center for you to use.

Doing More:

Play "Button, Button, Who's Got the Button?" Have children take turns hiding their buttons and calling out "cold," "warm," or "hot" as others guess. After the button is found, read what it says and give children an opportunity to discuss whether they like this quality about themselves.

Evaluation and Processing Through Storytelling:

Have children dictate "I Like Me" stories.

I Like Me *(cont.)*

Circle Buttons

To make circle buttons, use any size circle you like. Use any kind of paper—cardboard, tagboard, or whatever is on hand. If you wish, use these patterns to reproduce and precut circle buttons!

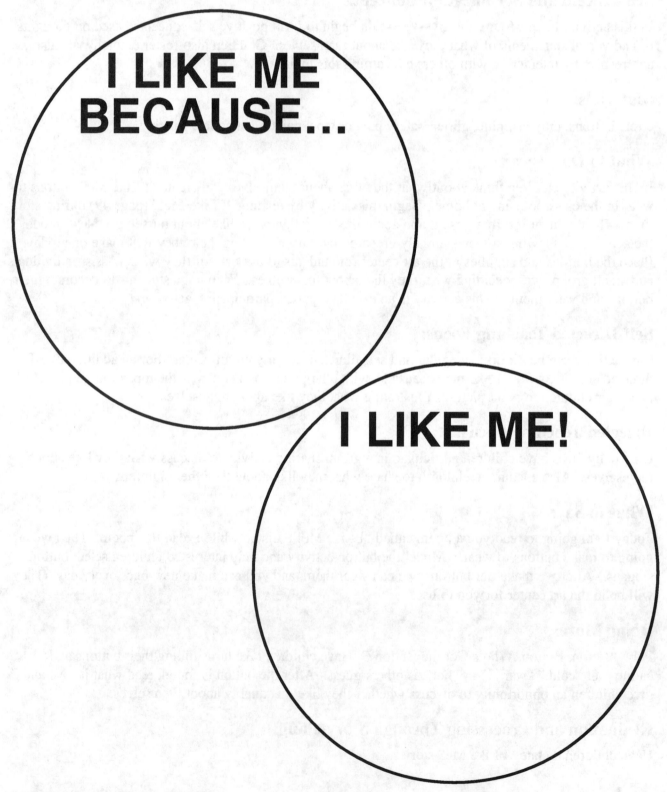

I Like Me! *(cont.)*

I Like Me!

by

Grace Jasmine

I like me!
I think I'm neat.
I think I'm cute and fun and sweet.
I like my face and hair and clothes.
I even like my mouth and nose!
I think I'm smart.
I think I'm kind.
You know I am a friend of mine!
I like myself.
You know it's true,
And guess what else?
I like you, too!

I Like Me *(cont.)*
NAEYC Appropriate Practices

Appropriate Practice:

Three-Year-Olds

"Adults provide large amounts of uninterrupted time for children to persist at self-chosen tasks."

Concept Connection:

Because circle buttons are part of a regular art center, children are encouraged to explore artistic mediums whenever they wish, thus reinforcing self-esteem concepts.

Appropriate Practice:

Four- and Five-Year-Olds

"Activities are designed to develop children's self-esteem."

Concept Connection:

This activity encourages children to celebrate everything they like about themselves; at the same time, it provides a positive and nurturing environment for children to appreciate others.

Appropriate Practice:

Four- and Five-Year-Olds

"Teacher accepts that there is often more than one right answer."

Concept Connections:

This activity focuses on each child's uniqueness; therefore, there is no incorrect way to complete it or to respond to it. Children see the wide variety of choices available to them and enhance their tolerance and empathy skills.

Laundry Line

Preparation Time:

One hour

Self-Esteem and Socialization Concept:

In this activity three-, four-, and five-year-olds gain self-esteem through mastering the names of common objects and gain increased body awareness through understanding the concept of dressing and clothing.

Materials:

variety of clothes for clothesline (these can be items from the costume box, assorted doll clothes, or donated clothes; clothes can also be purchased inexpensively at thrift stores), a rope or clothesline, clothespins (the straight unhinged wooden ones are best for little fingers), a play washing machine or one large cardboard box (see page 53 for instructions; these items will be used again in the math section of the book)

What to Do:

In this activity, children have the opportunity to be exposed to and to recognize the names and uses of common items of clothing. This activity will take several hours to prepare if you do not have an already existing house center. See page 53 for instructions about making your very own play washer. Next, near the house center, set up a basket of "washed" clothes. For each item of clothing you select for this activity, you will need to provide two clothespins. Next, make children aware of the new addition to their house center. Ask how many children have ever seen clothes hung on a clothesline. Explain to those who have dryers that some people choose to hang their clothes on a line to dry. Next, model how they can use the clothesline to pretend to hang out their wash to dry. As you model the activity, ask children for the names and uses of each piece of clothing. Let the child who can name the item have the fun of pinning it to the clothesline.

Laundry Line *(cont.)*

Self-Directed Teaching Focus:

Make the clothesline a part of regular, self-directed house center activity.

Directed Teaching Focus:

Ask each child to bring an old T-shirt to class. Have a T-shirt decorating party. Use non-toxic fabric glue and glitter to make beautiful wearable art.

What To Say:

Today we have a new game to play in our house center. How many people have clotheslines to hang their laundry on at home? (Class discussion.) Let me show you this new game. We will name each of these clothes and hang them on our new clothesline. Who can tell me what this is? (Hold up a shirt.) Right. The person who guesses the name of the clothing gets to pin it up on our new pretend clothesline. (Model the activity with other articles of clothing. Clothing list should include a variety of different nameable items like shirts, pants, underwear, T-shirts, hats, mittens, sweaters, sweatshirts, shorts, etc. The more items available, the more opportunities children will have for name recognition.)

Doing More:

Let children cut pictures of different articles of clothing out of old magazines and play a matching game. Hang one article of clothing on the line and have children find as many similar clothing pieces as possible during a day. For example, hang a shirt one day. Put out two laundry baskets, and the idea for that day is to sort all the shirts out of the laundry and place them together. This activity incorporates whole language and mathematical skills.)

Evaluation and Processing Through Storytelling:

Cut large pieces of butcher paper into the shape of shirts for children to decorate. Have children dictate stories about their shirts. Write their stories on their shirt pictures.

52

Laundry Line *(cont.)*
Cardboard-Box Washing Machine

Making a cardboard-box washing machine can be as simple or detailed as you wish. There is no "right" way, and any way you choose to make it for your classroom will work wonderfully!

Materials:

a large cardboard box, scissors or craft knife, marking pens, paint or contact paper, masking tape

Directions:

1. Decide where you want the clothes to drop in. (If it is a smaller box, the top works great; for larger boxes you may want a side opening.)

2. If you chose the side opening, cut out three sides of the square opening with scissors or craft knife. This allows you to open and close the washing-machine door.

3. If you desire, you can easily attach a panel of buttons and dials by drawing or painting them on excess cardboard and gluing to the machine, or you may want to draw the panel right on the machine. (See illustration.)

4. You may want to make two washing machines and store one. Once the other one gets worn by lots of use, simply discard it and bring out the new one.

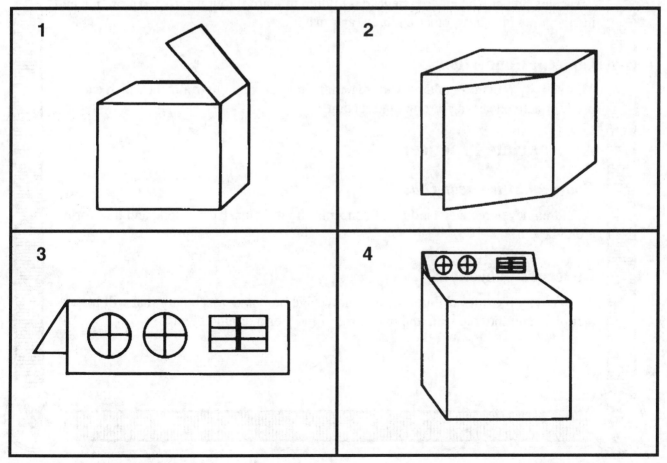

Laundry Line *(cont.)*
NAEYC Appropriate Practices

Appropriate Practice:

Three-Year-Olds

"Adults provide opportunities for children to demonstrate and practice their newly developed self-help skills... Adults know that children are rapidly acquiring language...and beginning to use language to solve problems and learn concepts."

Concept Connection:

This activity provides opportunities for children to put new skills into practice as they identify, name, and sort articles of clothing, and it increases self-esteem with the resulting mastery.

Appropriate Practice:

Four- and Five-Year-Olds

"Teachers prepare the environment for children to learn through active exploration and interaction with adults, other children, and materials."

Concept Connection:

This activity provides children with materials in a relevant environment which can be used for active learning through interaction.

Appropriate Practice:

Four- and Five-Year-Olds

"Children develop understanding of concepts about themselves, others, and the world around them."

Concept Connection:

This activity provides children with a knowledge base and vocabulary that will help them feel comfortable with and in control of the world around them.

Kids' Olympics

Preparation Time:

One hour

Self-Esteem and Socialization Concept:

In this activity three-, four-, and five-year-olds have the opportunity to gain a variety of socialization skills, including respect and compromise, competency, creativity, and positive body awareness.

Materials:

outdoor playing area, whatever equipment you choose for activity (e.g., tricycles, balls, etc.), video or movie featuring Olympics or athletic events, participation awards (page 56)

What to Do:

In this activity children participate in an athletic or outdoor activity of your choice, ending with an Olympic ceremony in which everyone is a winner (use awards on page 56). Choose whatever kind of event will work best with your children. Anything is possible. Consider:

- ❖ running, jumping, or hopping races
- ❖ riding bikes, trikes, scooters, wagons or anything else you have at your facility
- ❖ ball toss or basketball shooting
- ❖ pitching and catching baseballs or footballs
- ❖ sack races, water-balloon toss, or any other picnic game

Begin this activity by letting children view a sporting event on TV or, even better, a tape of an Olympic event. Next, let children be part of the decision-making process to help decide what kind of activities they would like to have for their Olympics.

Self-Directed Teaching Focus:

Set up a variety of self-directed play stations and let children play at each for a certain length of time. Then have them rotate to the next play center.

Direct Teaching Focus:

Organize actual running races. Choose a child to start the race and others to watch the finish line.

What to Say:

Today we are going to watch a video about the Olympics. Then we'll be planning our own Olympic games to play outside. (Model the activity idea and ask children to decide what Olympic events they would like to have in their Kids' Olympics.) Okay, let's go start the races. After we are done, we will have our own Olympic ceremony. Everyone will get an Olympic medal!

Doing More:

Have a regular weekly Olympic event on Fridays. Ask for parent volunteers who have special athletic abilities to demonstrate and help.

Evaluation and Processing Through Storytelling:

Have children dictate their Olympic stories into a tape recorder, or video the Olympic event and have children interview each other on camera.

Kids' Olympics *(cont.)*
Kids' Olympics Awards

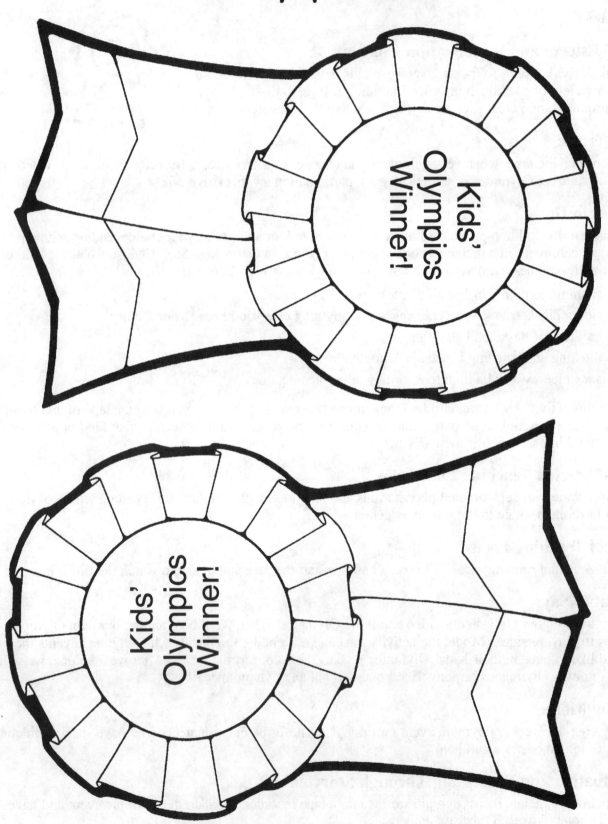

56

Kids' Olympics *(cont.)*
NAEYC Appropriate Practices

Appropriate Practice:

Three-Year-Olds

"Adults provide plenty of space and time indoors and outdoors for children to explore and exercise their large muscle skills like running, jumping, galloping, riding a tricycle, or catching a ball, with adults close by to offer assistance as needed."

Concept Connection:

This activity provides three-year-olds with an opportunity to apply and practice large muscle skills in a supportive and motivational environment.

Appropriate Practice:

Four- and Five-Year-Olds

"Children are expected to be physically active...Children have daily opportunities to use large muscles...Outdoor activity is planned daily..."

Concept Connection:

This activity provides children with a planned opportunity to be physically active and to gain in self-esteem through participation in large-muscle athletic events where everyone receives a medal.

Appropriate Practice:

Four- and Five-Year-Olds

"Children are provided many opportunities to develop social skills..."

Concept Connections:

This activity provides children with an opportunity to try out their social skills in a pleasant and motivating way.

I Can Help

Preparation Time:

One hour

Self-Esteem and Socialization Concept:

In this activity three-, four-, and five-year-olds build self-confidence through mastery of simple in-class and at-home chores.

Materials:

"I Can Help" charts for home and school (pages 61–64), stickers or stars, parent letter on page 60

What to Do:

In this activity children have the opportunity to gain self-discipline and mastery by performing simple chores and taking responsibility for helping at home and/or at school. To begin this activity, use the patterns on pages 61–64 to make a classroom chart and an at-home chart for each child. Begin this activity by deciding what are appropriate chores in the classroom for your children. This will depend upon the skill levels and the ages of the children in your classroom. The key here is to give children chores that they can complete without too many problems in order to ensure success. The success, then, translates into a self-esteem- building experience.

During circle time, hold a discussion with children to decide which classroom chores will be part of the weekly chore list. Then explain that children will take part in a game called "Put It Back." Each day at the end of playtime, every child will put back as many things as possible to make the room look neat. Everything should be in its place. Each week there will be several children assigned to each center. Children must put back objects that belong in their assigned centers. Show children the classroom chart and explain that every day after the "Put It Back" game is completed successfully, each group of helpers will get stars or stickers by their names.

		M	T	W	T	F
Shelly	Water	☆	☆	☆		
Kevin	Feed Pet	☆				
Dalton	Pick Up	☆	☆	☆	☆	
Ron	Help Others	☆	☆			
Lowan	Be Polite	☆	☆	☆		

I Can Help *(cont.)*

Self-Directed Teaching Focus:

After modeling this activity, children will be self-directed to complete their chores daily. At the end of the day, mention that it is "put it back" time.

Directed Teaching Focus:

Work with individual children to help them dictate the chores they would like on their home charts. Include these charts with the parent letter you send home.

What to Say:

Today we are going to talk about how we can help around our classroom and at home. How many of you help your parents? What do you do at home to help? (Have a class discussion.) Now let's talk about what we need to do here every day to keep our classroom neat. (Have a class discussion.) I have made a chart that we are going to hang on the wall. Every day we are going to play a pick-up game called "Put It Back." When I say that it's "put it back" time, we will all put things back where they belong. That way when we return to class in the morning, everything will be neatly stored and ready for us to enjoy.

Doing More:

Have children share in groups or at circle time how their chores are going at home or how they are doing with "put it back" time. Ask whether they have any concerns.

Evaluation and Processing Through Storytelling:

Have children dictate "The Biggest Chore" stories. "What I Like About Helping" is another good story topic.

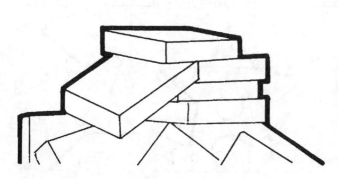

I Can Help *(cont.)*
Parent Letter

Dear Parents,

As part of my emphasis on developing children's socialization and self-esteem skills, I am adding some activities to our daily routine that center around responsibility. I have several small and achievable chores that the children are responsible for in the classroom. Manageable responsibilities and acknowledgment for achieving these responsibilities build children's sense of mastery and self-confidence. Consequently, as the children become more confident, they feel good about themselves. I have included a Home Chores Chart so you can continue this idea at home with your child. The idea is to choose simple chores that your child can achieve or to simply use this form to keep a positive record of your child's already existing chores. I hope this small addition to your home life will be enjoyable for both you and your child and that you will use it as a way to instill greater confidence in your child.

Please feel free to contact me regarding this letter or if you have any other concerns or questions. As usual, you are always invited to drop in to visit and take part in our day's activities.

Sincerely,

Please call me.

Name _____

Child's name _____

Phone number _____   Best time to call _____

I Can Help *(cont.)*

Classroom Chore Chart

We Help

	Monday	Tuesday	Wednesday	Thursday	Friday
Paste Chore Card Here					
Paste Chore Card Here					
Paste Chore Card Here					

I Can Help *(cont.)*
Classroom Chore Cards

Water Plants

Feed Class Pet

Lost & Found Helper

Pick Up Inside

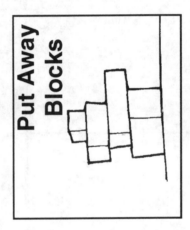

Put Away Blocks

Put Away Toys

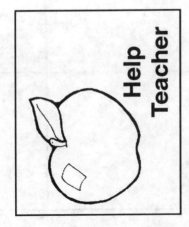

Help Teacher

Pick Up Center

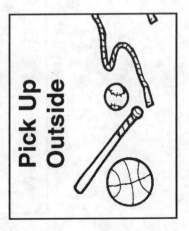

Pick Up Outside

I Can Help *(cont.)*

Home Chore Chart

I Help

	Paste Chore Card Here	Paste Chore Card Here	Paste Chore Card Here
Monday	Paste sticker or star here.		
Tuesday			
Wednesday			
Thursday			
Friday			

I Can Help *(cont.)*
Home Chore Cards

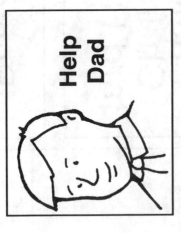

Help Dad

Water Plants

Bring In Paper

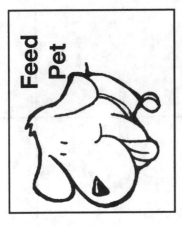

Feed Pet

Weed

Help Mom

Pick Up Toys

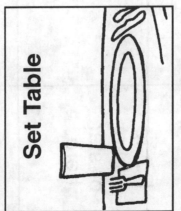

Set Table

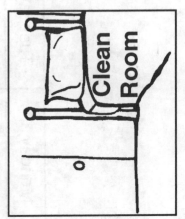

Clean Room

I Can Help *(cont.)*
NAEYC Appropriate Practices

Appropriate Practice:

Three-Year-Olds

"Adults provide opportunities for three-year-olds to demonstrate and practice their newly developed self-help skills."

Concept Connection:

By providing children with ways of helping that are within reach and designed for success, children become more confident about their self-help skills.

Appropriate Practice:

Four- and Five-Year-Olds

"Teachers' expectations match and respect children's developing capabilities."

Concept Connection:

Both the Classroom Chore Chart and the Home Chore Chart are designed to meet the actual capabilities of children rather than to set unattainable or unrealistic expectations.

Appropriate Practice:

Four- and Five-Year-Olds

"Children are provided many opportunities to see how reading and writing are useful before they are instructed in letter names, sounds, and word identification."

Concept Connection:

By the use of a picture chart, children are exposed to the usefulness of words and reading. To combine words and pictures without emphasizing the words helps children make a stress-free and natural correlation.

Multicultural Family Puppets

Preparation Time:

Several afternoons

Self-Esteem and Socialization Concept:

In this activity three-, four-, and five-year-olds have the opportunity to gain self-esteem, empathy, and respect through the use of multicultural puppet families.

Materials:

multicultural puppets (pg. 68); puppet-show theater (pg. 69)

What to Do:

In this activity children have the opportunity to create dramatic puppet plays based on multicultural families. To prepare for this activity, see page 68 to make your own multicultural puppets. After you have prepared your puppets, you will need to select an area for your puppet theater. You can make a puppet theater easily by turning over two chairs or a bench and throwing an old sheet or a blanket over them. (Or see page 69 to make an easy cardboard puppet theater.)

Introduce children to the family puppet area and provide time for them to explore the puppet theater and play with the family puppets. Let children know that anyone may present a family puppet show to the class.

Self-Directed Teaching Focus:

To self-direct this activity, leave the puppet area set up for puppet play.

Directed Teaching Focus:

To direct this activity set a time every day for interested children to prepare puppet shows and present them to the class. Or give children family situations to act out with their puppets. For example, say, "Let's pretend it's dinner time at the puppet family's house" or "Let's pretend the puppet family is going on a picnic."

What to Say:

Today we have a wonderful new group of puppets and a puppet theater to play with. Let's take a look. (Introduce activity area and show children the variety of family puppets. Demonstrate how they are not sets but may be combined any way the children wish.) We will be presenting family puppet shows. We have puppets that can be daddy and mommy puppets, children puppets and grandparent puppets, even aunt and uncle puppets. We can use these puppets to be anyone we want them to be in our make-believe families. Later we can show each other our puppet shows.

Doing More:

Have children use the puppet theater on a regular basis.

Evaluation and Processing Through Storytelling:

This activity already incorporates storytelling. However, children may dictate stories about the puppet theater shows.

66

Multicultural Family Puppets *(cont.)*
NAEYC Appropriate Practices

Appropriate Practice:

Three-Year-Olds

"Adults provide plenty of materials and time for children to explore and learn about the environment, to exercise their natural curiosity."

Concept Connection:

By using multicultural family puppets, children learn about their own and other children's families and begin to explore the idea of tolerance and understanding of others, which leads to increased socialization.

Appropriate Practice:

Four- and Five-Year-Olds

"Children develop understanding of concepts about themselves, others, and the world around them through observation, interacting with people and real objects, and seeking solutions to concrete problems."

Concept Connections:

Multicultural puppet plays give children an opportunity to explore real-life situations in the context of play and give them the opportunity to interact with other children, enhancing socialization skills. Additionally, children can explore their everyday family concerns and problems in a safe context that allows them to examine choices.

Appropriate Practice:

Four- and Five-Year-Olds

"Children's natural curiosity and desire to make sense of their world are used to motivate them to become involved in learning activities."

Concept Connection:

Children see themselves and their own situations in the multicultural puppet activity. It stimulates their involvement with other children and with learning.

Multicultural Family Puppets *(cont.)*
Making Multicultural Puppets

Making sock puppets is easy and enjoyable. Even if you have not done it before, the concept is so easy that it will be no problem to make your puppets in an afternoon or two. These multicultural puppets should be made to represent the variety of ethnic backgrounds you feel are relevant for the children in your preschool. Most teachers choose to represent Anglo, Black, Asian, and Hispanic cultures, as these are the largest national populations. Feel free to add any other cultures represented in your classroom so children will be comfortable with the activity by seeing their own cultures represented.

Materials:

- ❖ a variety of different skin-tone colored socks (black, brown, tan, beige, white)
- ❖ thread
- ❖ large buttons
- ❖ felt
- ❖ glue
- ❖ scissors
- ❖ yarn
- ❖ bows, ribbon, or old ties to cut up

Directions:

1. Select socks. Try these on your hand first to decide the best placement for ears, hair, and mouth area.

2. Create the face. Buttons or felt pieces work well. Some teachers use indelible markers or fabric paint. Make sure the paint you use is nontoxic, and secure all buttons to ensure they will not be pulled off or swallowed. (Some teachers prefer felt or fabric paint for this reason.)

3. After constructing the face, select the hair. Secure hair by sewing rather than gluing. In most cases, this will be more effective than gluing. However, to make sure hair stays on securely you may wish to both glue and sew.

4. Be as creative as you wish. You can add glasses, ears, even hats or hair bows. Just remember that you want to represent family members—mommies, daddies, grandmas, grandpas, brothers, sisters, etc. Create both males and females, and the children will decide who they are in their puppet families.

Multicultural Family Puppets *(cont.)*
Making a Puppet Theater

Making a puppet theater is not difficult. It should take you no longer than an afternoon or two.

Materials:

❖ large cardboard box (refrigerator or large appliance)
❖ poster paint
❖ scissors
❖ old material or sheets or old short kitchen curtains
❖ staple gun
❖ clothesline
❖ needle
❖ thread

Directions:

1. Select and position a large cardboard box. Remember that children will need a way to get in and out, so cut a stage opening in the box.

2. Paint the puppet theater. You may want to let this dry overnight.

3. Prepare curtain. Use an old one, or simply sew a casing in the material and string it on a length of clothesline or rope that has been measured to match the length of the curtain.

4. Staple the curtain to the theater. (See illustration.)

5. Enjoy your puppet theater!

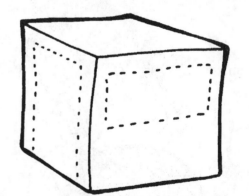

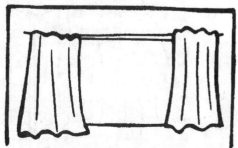

Family Scrapbook

Preparation Time:

One hour

Self-Esteem and Socialization Concept:

In this activity three-, four-, and five-year-olds gain self-esteem skills through an understanding and awareness of family roles and the differences and similarities in families.

Materials:

one large scrapbook with paper pages upon which pictures can be pasted or glued; old magazines, advertisements, and newspapers with pictures of people

What to Do:

In this activity, children have an opportunity to cut out pictures of families or select precut ones and make a scrapbook of families. To prepare this activity, you will need a large scrapbook with paper pages that can be used with paste. Next, gather a variety of pictures of different possible family groups. Remember to gather a variety of possibilities and stress non-traditional as well as traditional family units. The idea here is to make sure that children have exposure to many different kinds of family groups besides their own. A list of possible combinations that you will want to make available to children to see as families are:

❖ family units that include mother, father, children

❖ family units that include grandparents living with family

❖ single-father family unit

❖ single-mother family unit

❖ racially-mixed family units

❖ a variety of multi-ethnic combinations: Anglo, Hispanic, Black, Asian, etc.

❖ handicapped members in a family unit

Family Scrapbook *(cont.)*

What to Do *(cont.)*:

This activity should provide children with exposure to families (and people) and their differences, which will begin to help them learn tolerance and understanding. When presenting the different kinds of families possible, emphasize empathy and respect for others' situations. Building a foundation of personal respect and regard for others is something early childhood educators can accomplish.

Begin this activity by sharing the "Families" story on page 72. Then set up the scrapbook family center so children can look through the available pictures and add family pictures.

Self-Directed Teaching Focus:

Make the family scrapbook a permanent addition to one of your regular centers. The storytelling center is an obvious choice. Let children add to the family scrapbook whenever they feel like it.

Directed Teaching Focus:

Help each child find a picture of a family he or she likes and ask why the picture was chosen.

Use this picture to prompt storytelling.

What to Say:

Today we are going to talk about families. We all have families. Families are the people we live with and who love us. There are many different kinds of families. I am going to read a story about families, and then we will talk about it. (Read story and model activity.) We will all get a chance to find pictures of families, and then we will all be able to look at these pictures and add to them whenever we want to.

Doing More:

Ask children to share their favorite family times, what they did with their families over the weekend, or tell why they love their families.

Evaluation and Processing Through Storytelling:

Have children dictate stories like "I love my mommy (or daddy) because...." or "I love my aunt (or uncle) because..."

Family Scrapbook *(cont.)*
Families

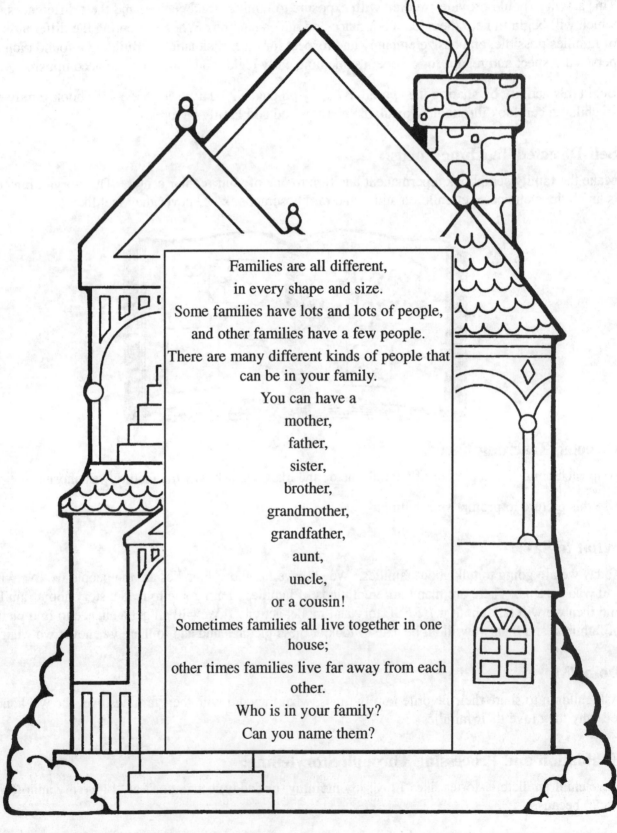

Families are all different,
in every shape and size.
Some families have lots and lots of people,
and other families have a few people.
There are many different kinds of people that
can be in your family.
You can have a
mother,
father,
sister,
brother,
grandmother,
grandfather,
aunt,
uncle,
or a cousin!
Sometimes families all live together in one
house;
other times families live far away from each
other.
Who is in your family?
Can you name them?

72

Family Scrapbook *(cont.)*
NAEYC Appropriate Practices

Appropriate Practice:

Three-Year-Olds

"Adults know that children are rapidly acquiring language, experimenting with verbal sounds, and beginning to use language to solve problems and learn language."

Concept Connection:

Children have the opportunity in this activity to be exposed to a number of family words and see their meanings in pictures, enhancing their understanding of language of things in their everyday world.

Appropriate Practice:

Four- and Five-Year-Olds

"Children develop understanding of concepts about themselves, others, and the world around them through observation, interacting with people and real objects, and seeking solutions to concrete problems."

Concept Connection:

This activity allows children to gain understanding about their own and other children's families, to see a variety of different kinds of families, and to learn about families other than their own.

Appropriate Practice:

Four- and Five-Year-Olds

"Children's natural curiosity and desire to make sense of their world are used to motivate them to become involved in learning activities."

Concept Connections:

Children learn about other kinds of families and begin to develop understanding, respect for others, and a sense of community.

Family Words

Preparation Time:

Several hours

Self-Esteem and Socialization Concept:

In this activity children gain mastery and self-confidence about themselves and their place in the world through exposure to the words related to families and to the meanings of these words.

Materials:

tape recorder and tape cassette

What to Do:

In this activity children will listen to the words related to families and use the scrapbook called "Families" (created in the previous activity) to match words to pictures. To prepare this activity, you will need to make a family word tape for your children's sound center. Ask children to help with this. During circle time, show children pictures from the family scrapbook and decide with them who could be fathers, mother, sisters, brothers, babies, grandparents, cousins, aunts, or uncles. Let children from different cultures share their words for these. Have each child record family words. When the children hear their own voices, they will be more interested in listening to the tape, and the repetitiveness of the tape will be helpful.

Self-Directed Teaching Focus:

To self-direct this activity, leave the tape and the scrapbook in the sound center for children to use as they wish.

Directed Teaching Focus:

To direct this activity have children learn the family words in different languages by listening together to the tape and repeating the different words during circle time.

What to Say:

Let's take the big family scrapbook we made and look at the pictures of families and name the people. (Model the names of the people in the pictures.) Now let's learn these names in all the different languages in our classroom. I know we have several students who speak Spanish. Can you tell me how to say "mommy" in Spanish? How about "daddy"? (Ask for all the different languages represented.) Now we are going to say all the family words again and make a tape recording of the words. When we are finished, we will put the tape in our sound center.

Doing More:

Have children make similar tapes of different words. For example, ask them to name all the things in the kitchen center to make a kitchen tape, etc.

Evaluation and Processing Through Storytelling:

Let each child tell a story about his or her mommy or daddy or any other family member. They may prefer to record it or act it out with puppets.

Family Words *(cont.)*
NAEYC Appropriate Practices

Appropriate Practice:

Three-Year-Olds

"Adults know that children are rapidly acquiring language, experimenting with verbal sounds, and beginning to use language to solve problems and learn concepts."

Concept Connection:

In this activity, children have the opportunity to hear a variety of words and sounds, which helps them enhance their command of their own language and gain exposure to the native languages of their classmates.

Appropriate Practice:

Four- and Five-Year-Olds

"An abundance of...activities is provided to develop language and literacy through meaningful experience..."

Concept Connection:

Children begin to see the relationship between sounds and words and letters and words in a context that is relevant and important to them.

Appropriate Practice:

Four- and Five-Year-Olds

"The curriculum and adults' interaction are responsive to individual differences in ability and interests."

Concept Connection:

As this activity is an ongoing activity that can remain at a self-directed center, children have the opportunity to use it again and again, based on their individual preferences, interests, and abilities.

Table of Contents for Language and Socialization Arts

My Favorite Breakfast

Preparation Time:

Several afternoons (Begin this activity preparation several weeks in advance to allow time for parent volunteers to bring in pretend food supplies.)

Language Arts and Socialization Concept:

In this activity three-, four-, and five-year-olds gain self-esteem and mastery skills by using oral language, listening, and decision-making skills and by exercising personal choice.

Materials:

pretend foods (See parent assistance letter); breakfast patterns (pages 82–84) paper plates, art supplies, recipe card pattern for parent gift

What to Do:

In this activity, children become familiar with the idea of breakfast and breakfast foods and have an opportunity to select the kinds of food they would like to eat for breakfast in a pretend kitchen center. (To prepare for all the activities in this unit, send the parent assistance letter home to parents to request food boxes, cartons, and packages to use for pretend food. See appendix).

Begin this activity by reading the first of three Billy Bartholomew stories on page 81. (The Billy stories run throughout this unit and introduce each meal and meal activity: breakfast, lunch, and dinner.) After reading "Billy Bartholomew's Big Beautiful Breakfast," encourage children to explore their kitchen center and choose food they would like to have for breakfast. Stock the kitchen area with what children feel they will need to make breakfast. Encourage children to play making breakfast whenever they want to, as part of self-directed play. Make paper plates available in the art center for children to cut out pictures of breakfast food (patterns, pages 82–84), color, and glue on the plates, or they can draw breakfast food right on the plates to use when they pretend in their kitchen center.

Self-Directed Teaching Focus:

Make the kitchen and breakfast center a part of regular self-directed play.

Directed Teaching Focus:

Have children select their very favorite pretend breakfast foods to share during circle time. Have children pick their very favorite foods weekly and bring in real samples for an enjoyable breakfast snack.

My Favorite Breakfast *(cont.)*

What to Say:

Today we are going to hear a story about a little boy who loved breakfast. His name is Billy Bartholomew. After we hear the story, we will talk about what we like for breakfast. When do we eat breakfast? (Discuss with children the idea of breakfast.)

Now, let's all look at all the pretend food for breakfast we have gathered here. We can all pick what our favorite breakfast is and pretend to eat it anytime here in the pretend kitchen. In the art center there are lots of paper plates on which to draw pictures of breakfast. When we are finished with our pictures, we can use them for breakfast in our kitchen center. We can also take pictures out of magazines to use in the kitchen center.

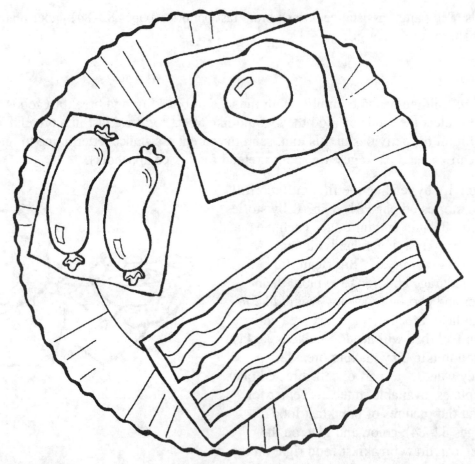

Doing More:

Have children begin the activity by drawing their favorite food from the Billy story on a paper plate. Let children put their plates in a special place in the kitchen center to use again.

Evaluation and Processing Through Storytelling:

Have children dictate descriptions of how to make their favorite breakfasts. You may wish to write these stories on their breakfast-food paper plates. This activity makes a clever parent-present recipe book, too. (See recipe book cover and recipe card pattern on pages 79 and 80 to make a parent gift, if desired.)

My Favorite Breakfast *(cont.)*

Favorite Recipes

Parents love reading children's very creative recipes. Let children create a recipe and dictate it to you. Write their recipes on the recipe cards (page 80). Then, make enough copies of all the children's recipes and of the book cover pattern on this page for everyone in class. The parents will enjoy this keepsake.

School

Favorite Recipes

My Favorite Breakfast *(cont.)*

Child _____

Name of Recipe

_____

Ingredients

_____

_____

_____

_____

_____

How to make it

_____

_____

_____

_____

_____

_____

_____

_____

My Favorite Breakfast (cont.)

Billy Bartholomew's Big Beautiful Breakfast

by

Grace Jasmine

Billy Bartholomew was a very hungry boy.

Breakfast was his very favorite time of the day.

All night long he dreamed about the wonderful food he would eat for breakfast.

He dreamed about cereal with fresh strawberries on top.

He dreamed about bananas and grapefruit and cantaloupe with cottage cheese.

He dreamed about fresh, hot pancakes and yummy maple syrup, and eggs scrambled and fried and over easy.

He dreamed about doughnuts. He dreamed about sweet rolls.

He dreamed about bacon and ham and sausages.

He dreamed about crunchy granola and fruity, sweet yogurt and big, cold glasses of milk and hot chocolate.

In the morning Billy's mommy said to Billy, "Why aren't you eating?"

"Well," said Billy, "I ate so much in my dream last night that I feel full."

Billy and his mother laughed and laughed when Billy told her all the things he dreamed he ate.

"Well, Billy, tonight I think you had better dream about something else, or you won't want your big beautiful breakfast!"

My Favorite Breakfast (cont.)
Breakfast Patterns

82

My Favorite Breakfast (cont.)
Breakfast Patterns (cont.)

My Favorite Breakfast *(cont.)*
Breakfast Patterns *(cont.)*

84

My Favorite Breakfast *(cont.)*
NAEYC Appropriate Practices

Appropriate Practice:

Three-Year-Olds

"Adults provide plenty of materials and time for children to explore and learn about the environment."

Concept Connection:

This activity provides lots of hands-on opportunities for children to explore their real world in a pretend context. Children become increasingly familiar and comfortable with common everyday objects.

Appropriate Practice:

Four- and Five-Year-Olds

"Children are provided many opportunities to develop social skills such as cooperating, helping, and negotiating."

Concept Connection:

In the context of a kitchen/house center, children have the opportunity to invent, to role-play, to assign roles, and to communicate, thus increasing socialization skills.

Appropriate Practice:

Four- and Five-Year-Olds

"Children select many of their own learning activities from among a variety of learning areas."

Concept Connection:

In a self-directed center, children may again and again "select, cook, and serve" breakfast, exploring the words and choices provided in the activity.

Our Very Own Restaurant

Preparation Time:

Several afternoons

Language Arts and Socialization Concept:

In this activity three-, four-, and five-year-olds gain experience in using listening and comprehension skills by reacting to and using the information in a story they hear read aloud.

Materials:

menus, pre-colored and laminated (pages 90–91); chef and server hats (pages 88-89); assorted restaurant play foods; lunch patterns (pages 93–95); plates and eating utensils (page 87); aprons

What to Do:

To begin this activity, first set up a part of your classroom that will serve as a restaurant center.

Use the parent request letter on in the appendix to request parents to send in necessary items if you do not already have these. The idea is to create a restaurant center where children can have the fun of modeling restaurant play after hearing "Billy Bartholomew Goes Out to Lunch." Begin the activity by reading this story on page 92. Then show children their new restaurant center and model how they may use it. Let small groups play together in the restaurant center in self-directed play. Be available to help children make decisions, when necessary. Remember this activity is more interactive than most, and some children will tire of it quickly based on the development of their own interactive skills.

Self-Directed Teaching Focus:

Make the restaurant center part of your regular center setup for as long as children enjoy playing the game.

Directed Teaching Focus:

Have children color and paint their favorite menu items (pages 93–95) after looking at the laminated menus. Later, use these plates of food in your restaurant center.

What to Say:

Today we are going to hear another story about Billy Bartholomew. After we hear it, we all going to play in our new restaurant center I have set up. (Read story and model the restaurant center.) This center will be here for all of us to play restaurant.

Doing More:

Have children make paper-plate pictures of food for the restaurant center.

Evaluation and Processing Through Storytelling:

Let children dictate and share their own "When I Went Out to Eat" stories. Give children an opportunity to hear each others' experiences and discuss proper restaurant manners, etc.

Our Very Own Restaurant *(cont.)*

Plate and Eating Utensils

If you do not wish children to use real forks, knives, etc., you can make copies of this page and precut the items. Or copy the page, laminate it, and let children use it as a place mat.

Our Very Own Restaurant *(cont.)*
Chef's Hat

Insert string or rubber bands to tie it on.

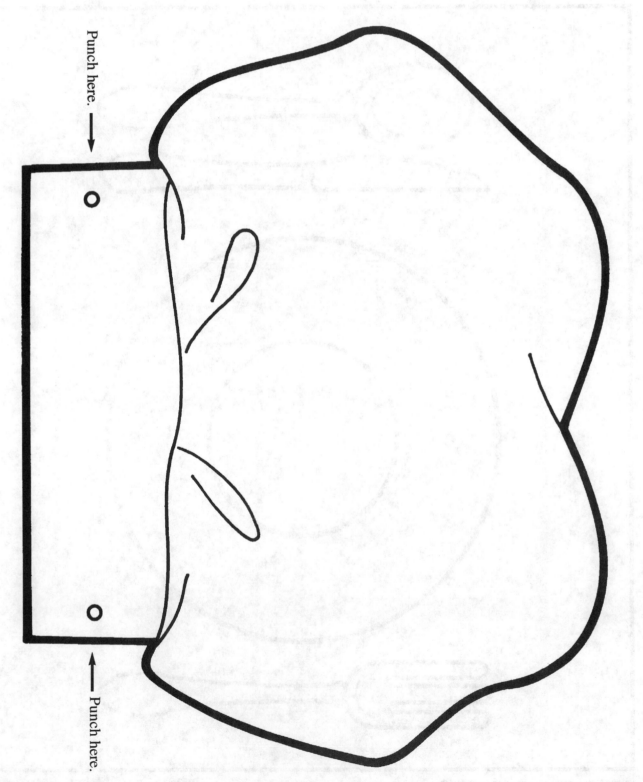

Punch here.

Punch here.

Our Very Own Restaurant *(cont.)*

Server's Hat

1. Fold a piece of 8 ½" x 11" piece of paper.
2. Place dashed line on fold.

3. Cut around solid edges.
4. Tape the bottom sides together to make hat.

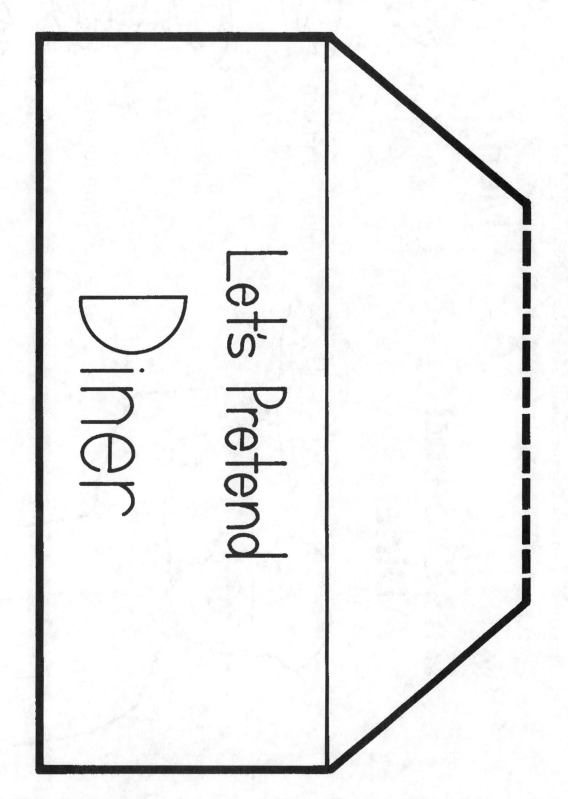

Our Very Own Restaurant *(cont.)*

Menu

Tuna Salad

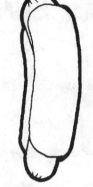

Turkey Sandwich

Hot Dogs

Hamburgers

French Fries

Let's-Pretend Diner

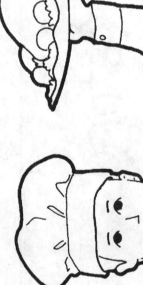

Our Very Own Restaurant *(cont.)*

Menu *(cont.)*

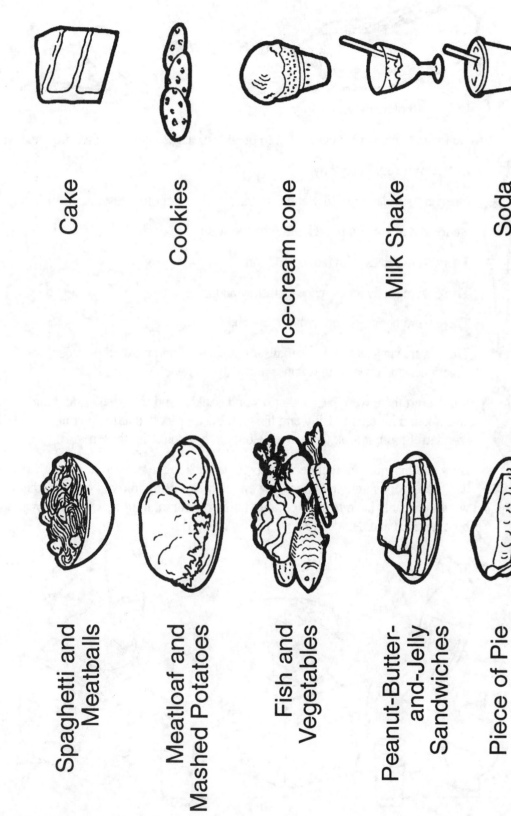

Cake

Cookies

Ice-cream cone

Milk Shake

Soda

Spaghetti and Meatballs

Meatloaf and Mashed Potatoes

Fish and Vegetables

Peanut-Butter-and-Jelly Sandwiches

Piece of Pie

Our Very Own Restaurant *(cont.)*

Billy Bartholomew Goes Out to Lunch
by
Grace Jasmine

Billy Bartholomew was a very hungry boy.

He loved to eat very much. Next to breakfast, his second very favorite meal was lunch.

Billy was a very lucky boy.

One very special day, Billy and his grandmother went to a restaurant for lunch.

He looked at a menu to pick out what he wanted to eat.

There were salads with lettuce and tuna.

There were sandwiches made of turkey and ham.

There were hot dogs and hamburgers and French fries.

There were spaghetti and meatballs, and meatloaf and mashed potatoes, and fish and vegetables and even peanut-butter-and-jelly sandwiches.

For dessert there were pies and cakes and cookies and milkshakes, and pudding and custard, and ice cream. Billy and his grandmother looked at the pictures of all the wonderful food. It took them a very long time to make up their minds.

Billy and his grandmother decided to come back to the restaurant once a week until they had tried every single item they saw on the menu. Billy told his grandmother that they would probably have to keep coming to the restaurant until he was all grown up. They both laughed and decided to have pie for dessert!

92

Our Very Own Restaurant *(cont.)*
Lunch Patterns

Our Very Own Restaurant (cont.)
Lunch Patterns (cont.)

Our Very Own Restaurant *(cont.)*
Lunch Patterns *(cont.)*

Our Very Own Restaurant *(cont.)*

NAEYC Appropriate Practices

Appropriate Practices:

Three-Year-Olds

"Adults provide plenty of material and time for children to learn about the environment...complex dramatic play props (for playing work and family roles)."

Concept Connection:

A pretend restaurant center allows children to role-play "work and family roles" and creates an opportunity for children to increase awareness and knowledge of the world around them.

Appropriate Practices:

Four- and Five-Year-Olds

"Children are provided concrete learning activities with materials and people relevant to their own life experiences."

Concept Connections:

In this activity, children role-play in a situation that is both interesting to them and relevant to their lives.

Appropriate Practices:

Four- and Five-Year-Olds

"Learning...is integrated through meaningful activities."

Concept Connection:

In this activity, children are involved in a meaningful activity that is relevant to their lives. This, in turn, enhances learning in a variety of content areas including reading readiness, language arts, and socialization.

Dolls' Dinner Party

Preparation Time:

Several hours (This activity can be done on several separate days or as an ongoing self-directed activity.)

Language Arts and Socialization Concept:

In this activity three-, four-, and five-year-olds have the opportunity to use listening skills and oral language to plan and give a party.

Materials:

pretend food plates that children have constructed; stuffed animals and toys (You may ask children to bring their favorites to the party or use the existing dolls and stuffed animals at your center.); tables, chairs and/or floor space; large, old bedspread for a tablecloth

What to Do:

In this activity, children have the opportunity to plan their own stuffed animal and doll dinner party. Begin this activity by reading the third installment of Billy Bartholomew, "Billy Bartholomew's Dolls' Dinner Party." After children hear the story, tell them they will have a chance to have their own dinner party for their dolls and stuffed animals. (Prior to this, decide whether or not you are going to ask children to bring their own stuffed animals from home for this activity.) Another option for your classroom is to encourage children to have "on-site" dolls or stuffed animals that remain in their cubbies for rest time or whenever they feel they want something with them that is a "friend from home." If each child has a stuffed animal or doll that remains at your facility, it will avoid the hassle of children bringing and forgetting favorite dolls, etc.

Provide children with a variety of paper plates and art materials to create their dolls' meals. You may wish to provide old magazine and newspaper food sections and possibly old cookbooks for interesting food pictures. Children may make food whenever they feel like it as part of a self-directed activity.

Schedule a time for the dolls' dinner party. You may wish to provide real snacks for children to eat at the party.

Dolls' Dinner Party *(cont.)*

Self-Directed Teaching Focus:

The best results in an activity like this one are achieved by providing the setting and letting children take part in it at will. Depending upon the children in your classroom, this activity will be a regular favorite or something that children do only sometimes. In the self-directed format, children are required to use their own imaginations.

Directed Teaching Focus:

Set a specific time for the dinner party to take place, and assist children in preparing for the event by creating food plates, etc. Use the dinner patterns on pages 101 and 102.

What to Say:

Today we are going to hear the third story about Billy. Let's think about the other stories we have heard about Billy Bartholomew. First, he dreamed about a big, big breakfast. Then he went out to lunch with his grandmother. This third story is called "Billy Bartholomew's Dolls' Dinner Party." Let's read it and then we will all have a chance to participate in a doll dinner party. (Read the story and model the activity.)

Now, let's all look over here. I have put together all the things we will need to make our own dolls' dinner party. Anyone who is interested can make food plates for the dinner party, using these supplies in the art center. Now we have to decide where we want our dolls to have their party. (Give children the opportunity to plan as many of the elements of this activity as they are able. In some cases this activity will take little or no direction from you. Simply providing the supplies and standing back will be enough.)

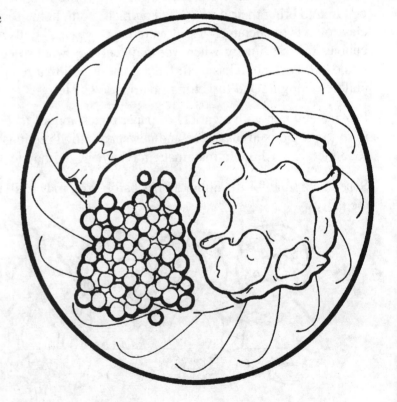

Doing More:

Use the parent invitation letter on page 100 to invite parents to attend this activity. Cut it out on the dashed lines and fold to create the invitation.

Evaluation and Processing Through Storytelling:

Let children dictate their own "Billy" stories, such as "What Does Billy Do Next?" or their own "Favorite Dinner" stories.

Dolls' Dinner Party (cont.)

Billy Bartholomew's Dolls' Dinner Party

by
Grace Jasmine

Billy Bartholomew was a very hungry boy.

Next to breakfast and lunch, dinner was his very, very most favorite meal of the day.

One day when it was raining outside and he had nothing to do, he decided to make for his dolls and stuffed animals their very own special dinner party.

He decided he would make pictures of all the food he wanted to serve them to eat and they could have pretend food.

He thought and he thought about what his dolls might like for dinner, and this is what he decided.

He drew pictures of big green salads and warm, steamy dinner rolls; steak and hamburger; fish, chicken, and pork chops; turkey and ham; roasts and stew and lasagna and tostadas; tacos and enchiladas and spaghetti; and casseroles full of steamy, tasty treats.

He drew peas and carrots, and spinach and broccoli, and mashed potatoes, and baked potatoes and French fries.

He drew chocolate cake and apple pie and ice cream and candies.

His dolls and stuffed animals all sat down to dinner, very excited and hungry, and they ate and ate until they were all so full they had to go straight to bed.

Dolls' Dinner Party (cont.)
Parent Invitation

ᴚƎNNIᗡ ,Ꙅ⅃⅃Oᗡ
ʎ⊥ᴚ∀d

Please help us celebrate
more learning fun
by joining your
child's class.

*From*_____

*To*_____

*On*_____

*R.S.V.P.*_____

Dolls' Dinner Party (cont.)
Dinner Patterns

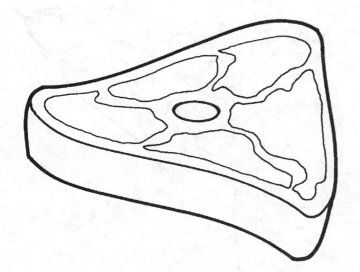

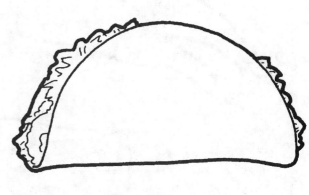

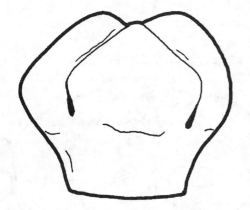

Dolls' Dinner Party *(cont.)*
Dinner Patterns *(cont.)*

102

Dolls' Dinner Party *(cont.)*

NAEYC Appropriate Practices

Appropriate Practice:

Three-Year-Olds

"Adults provide large amounts of uninterrupted time for children to persist at self-chosen tasks."

Concept Connection:

As a self-directed and ongoing activity, the dolls' dinner-party theme allows children to enjoy this activity again and again in solitary or parallel-play situations.

Appropriate Practice:

Four- and Five-Year-Olds

"A variety of art media is available for creative expression."

Concept Connection:

As children prepare the "dinner" for their dolls' dinner party, they have the opportunity to work with a variety of art materials.

Appropriate Practice:

Four- and Five-Year-Olds

"Children are provided concrete learning activities with materials and people relevant to their own life experiences."

Concept Connection:

Children have the opportunity to play with things that are meaningful to them, favorite toys and stuffed animals, and have the fun of taking part in a familiar activity that they recognize from their own lives.

Our Own Movie Theater

Preparation Time:

A few afternoons

Language Arts and Socialization Concept:

In this activity three-, four-, and five-year-olds gain self-confidence through mastery of autonomy and personal choice. The children increase their visual-knowledge base by acquiring mental pictures to go with the words in their expanding vocabularies.

Materials:

television, VCR, a variety of videotapes, comfortable seats like pillows or small beanbag chairs, movie tickets (page 106)

What to Do:

In this activity children use an existing movie theater center to view a variety of videos in a self-directed manner. To begin this activity you will need a VCR and television and an area that can be used as a space for a "theater." This area is best utilized when it remains an active and regular center. Before beginning this center you may wish to let parents know which videos you will be using. A suggested list is given on page 107.

Introduce children to the area of a self-directed video center and instruct and model the use of the TV and VCR to children. (Most children are very familiar with TV and VCR equipment from toddlerhood on.) Place a variety of previewed and appropriate videos in reach of the TV and VCR area. The key here is to make the movie theater a self-directed environment. Decide ahead of time how you will determine which children may use the center daily. In some preschools, this will be a favorite activity and children will have to take turns. One easy way to do this is to give out laminated movie tickets (see page 106) on a daily/rotating basis. Children with tickets have the use of the movie theater that day.

You will need to set up simple viewing rules for the children to follow to make watching videos fun. For example, if more than one child is in the viewing area at once, the children will need to compromise and come to an agreement about which film to watch. Some teachers choose to supply a "daily feature movie," thereby avoiding situations in which children would have to agree on movies. When necessary, facilitate the process of decision making by standing near the center and providing help and suggestions as needed. Most children with siblings have to come to agreement at some time or another about what to watch on TV. This is one of the first ways we learn socialization skills in our TV culture.

Our Own Movie Theater *(cont.)*

What to Do *(cont.)*:

Be sure to preview any video that you use in your preschool from start to finish, especially if it is a home-recorded copy. You will avoid any unwelcome surprises.

This activity, used in a self-directed and daily manner, will give children a time for relaxed and quiet play and an opportunity to wind down in a way that is both appropriate and in keeping with the subject area of your current curriculum. (This activity is especially valuable for the visual learner who can be overlooked in classrooms that concentrate on accommodating auditory and kinesthetic learners.)

Self-Directed Teaching Focus:

This activity works best as a regular part of your center setup. Children will only need to be made aware of the basic rules and will use the center with ease.

Directed Teaching Focus:

Talk with children daily at sharing or circle time about the videos they watch. Reinforce the concepts that relate to what is currently happening in your preschool and give children time to share their thoughts.

What to Say:

We have a new center that I think you will all enjoy. It is our very own movie theater. Let's all take a look at it, and I will tell you how we will use it. First of all, I need to know how many of you know how to operate a TV and a VCR. Many of you probably have these at home. (Model the operation of TV and VCR.) Now we are going to have a chance to use the movie theater. How many of you would like to use it? I will give out movie tickets each day. If you have a movie ticket, you may use the movie theater. We will take turns every day so that we all get a chance to look at videos. Okay, now let's talk about the rules for our new center. (Hold a class discussion.) Each day, we will have a special movie to watch. Then, during circle time, we will talk about how we liked it.

Doing More:

Let children select their own favorite videos or ask them to bring appropriate videos from their private collections to share with classmates..

Evaluation and Processing Through Storytelling:

Help children make their own videos by videotaping them as they act out stories. Add these videos to your video movie theater so children may view themselves.

Our Own Movie Theater *(cont.)*
Movie Tickets

These tickets can be printed on colored paper and laminated. Give them to the children to designate daily movie-theater turns.

Our Own Movie Theater (cont.)
Video List

Self Esteem and Socialization

Sesame Street—*I'm Glad I'm Me*. Random House Home Video, 1992.

Sesame Street—*Dance Along*. Random House Home Video, 1992.

Sesame Street—*Bedtime Stories*. Random House Home Video, 1992.

Sesame Street—*Sing, Hoot, Howl*. Random House Home Video, 1992.

Sesame Street—*Big Bird Visits the Hospital*. Random House Home Video, 1992.

The Berenstain Bears—And The Truth. Random House Home Video, 1992.

The Berenstain Bears—In The Dark. Random House Home Video, 1992.

The Berenstain Bears—And The Messy Room. Random House Home Video, 1992.

Barney—Caring Means Sharing. The Lyons Group/Time Life Video, 1992.

Richard Scarry's Busy People. Random House Home Video, 1993.

Socialization/Language Arts

Barney's Birthday—Barney. Lyons Group, 1992.

Barney's Alphabet Zoo—Barney. Lyons Group-Barney Home Video, 1994.

Let's Pretend—Barney. Lyons Group-Barney Home Video, 1993.

Sesame Street—Elmo Sing Along Guessing Game. Random House Home Video, 1992.

Sesame Street Rock and Roll. Random House Home Video, 1992.

The White Seal. Family Home Entertainment, 1975 Chuck Jones Enterprises. Redistributed 1986.

Dr. Seuss ABC's. Random House Home Video, 1992.

Ricki Tiki Tavi. Family Home Entertainment 1975 Chuck Hones Enterprises. Redistributed 1986.

Richard Scarry's ABC's. Random House Home Video, 1992.

Mother Goose Rhymes—Barney. Lyons Group, 1992.

Mathematics/Science and Curiosity

Clifford The Red Dog Series. Family Home Entertainment, 1988 Scholastic Productions, Inc.

Richard Scarry's Counting Video. Random House Home Video, 1992.

One Fish Two Fish—Dr. Seuss. Random House Home Video, 1992.

Sesame Street—Learning About Numbers. Random House Home Video, 1992.

Sesame Street—Learning To Add and Subtract. Random House Home Video, 1992.

Frosty The Snowman. Family Home Entertainment. Redistributed 1989.

Our Earth Our Home—Barney. Lyons Group, Time Life Video, 1992.

Where's Spot?—Disney. Walt Disney Home Video, 1992.

Rock with Barney—Barney. Lyons Group, 1991.

Our Own Movie Theater *(cont.)*

NAEYC Appropriate Practices

Appropriate Practice:

Three-Year-Olds

"Adults guide three-year-olds to do restful activities periodically throughout the day."

Concept Connection:

This activity lends itself to the quiet time that three-year-olds need throughout the day; it is also enjoyable and relaxing.

Appropriate Practice:

Four- and Five-Year-Olds

"Children work individually or in small informal groups most of the time."

Concept Connection:

The movie theater activity allows children to be involved in parallel activity with a small group.

Appropriate Practice:

Four- and Five-Year-Olds

"Experiences are provided that meet children's needs..."

Concept Connection:

Each child needs an opportunity to rest and relax throughout the day. This activity allows children time to regroup to prepare for more interactive activities.

Race Track

Preparation Time:

Several afternoons

Language Arts and Socialization Concept:

In this activity three-, four-, and five-year-olds gain mastery of cooperation and compromise and have the opportunity to practice safety skills. Children also expand their ability to recognize useful words in context.

Materials:

cardboard boxcars, one per child (See pages 115.); car detail patterns (See pages 116–118.) traffic signs (See pages 111-114.); space for a car race track or city-street course

What to Do:

In this activity children use pre-made cardboard boxcars to "drive" around a track and take part in a "Stop, Go, Fast, Slow" listening-and-directions game. To begin preparation for this activity, you will need a cardboard box for each car you intend to make. See the car-making directions on page 115. Also see pages 111-114 for traffic sign patterns and pages 116-118 for car detail patterns. After making cars and signs, decide what kind of a car track or street setup will work for your classroom. You may wish to use large blocks or chairs to make dividers; or, if you have an outdoor space, it is quite easy to draw a car track or streets in colored chalk.

To begin this activity with your children, you may want to discuss the different kinds of cars they have seen or take a walking tour of your own parking lot to look at the different kinds of cars there. Be sure to point out the various parts of the cars (e.g., the steering wheel, the headlights, the doors, the tires, etc.). On your walking tour, ask children to share any information they already know about cars. (You may wish to discuss cars by using toy cars as models.) Also, encourage children to notice the sounds that cars make and ask them to imitate these sounds.

Next, show children the play cars and provide plenty of time to try on the cars and drive around the room. Show children the car track and introduce them to the traffic signs. (You may choose to use only the "Stop" and "Go" signs, as most children have some awareness of these signs.)

Have children driving pretend-cars model the meanings of stop, go, fast, and slow. Use the traffic signs for a variety of car driving games.

Self-Directed Teaching Focus:

After children are familiar with the pretend cars, leave the cars available for playtime fantasy fun.

Let children direct traffic using the traffic signs.

Race Track *(cont.)*

Directed Teaching Focus:

Use the car games as an opportunity to talk with children regarding safety, crossing the street, and using hand signals. During your walking tour, have children practice good safety habits by looking left and right before crossing any part of the parking lot.

What to Say:

Today we are going to talk about cars, and then I have some brand-new cars I made for us. First, though, let's all walk out together to our parking lot and look at the cars we see there. (Ask aides or volunteers to help you lead a walking tour to the parking lot to inspect the different kinds of cars.) Now look at our new play cars. Let's all put these on and try them out. What kinds of car noises can we make? Who can honk? Who can beep? Who can make the sound of a motor running or a car starting? (Children will probably also make a variety of car-crashing noises. This is all part of play, and the simple reminder to be safe drivers will lead children in the right direction if you feel it is becoming a problem.) Now let's all try stopping and going and then driving fast and driving slowly. Ready? Good. These cars will be here for us to use whenever we want to. Let's all remember to take good care of them. Why don't we decide where we will have our car garage. (Decide with children where they will store the cars.)

Doing More:

Have parent volunteers who use trucks or cars for work bring them for a car show-and-tell. Children will also be interested in seeing a police car or a fire engine. Some police departments will send an officer over to pay a visit and show the police car to the children. Children find this particularly interesting.

Evaluation and Processing Through Storytelling:

Have children dictate stories into a tape recorder and add their own car sound effects. Let children paint pictures of fantasy cars and use these to inspire storytelling.

Race Track *(cont.)*
Traffic Sign Patterns

Race Track *(cont.)*
Traffic Sign Patterns *(cont.)*

Race Track *(cont.)*
Traffic Sign Patterns *(cont.)*

Race Track *(cont.)*
Traffic Sign Patterns *(cont.)*

Race Track *(cont.)*

Cardboard Boxcars for Race Track

Making cardboard boxcars can be fun. Allow several afternoons or get your older children or family members involved in a weekend project!

Materials:

cardboard boxes (one for each child); car detail patterns (pages 116–118); art supplies; rope, cord or ribbon; paper plates (one per child); scissors; glue; masking tape

Directions:

1. Cut tops and bottoms off of cardboard boxes so children can fit them over their bodies.

2. Punch holes and attach a 40" (100 cm) length of rope or cord. (See illustration.)

3. Paint.

4. Reproduce pages 116–118, making enough copies so that each car will have a set of headlights, a set of taillights, and four wheels. You may want children to color these before you attach them. Glue on car details.

5. Attach a paper-plate steering wheel, or simply give each child a Frisbee or any other round object to use as a wheel.

6. If you wish, have children add more decorations to their cars to personalize them.

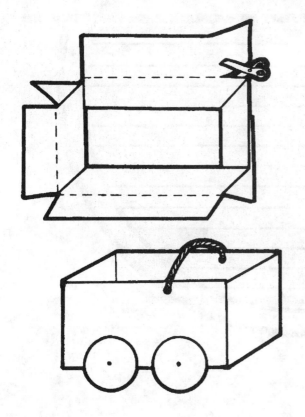
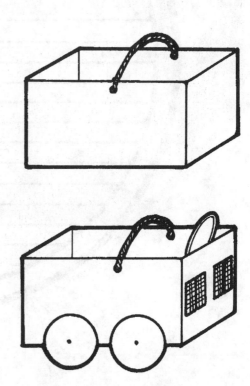

Race Track *(cont.)*
Car Detail Patterns

Headlights – Make Two.

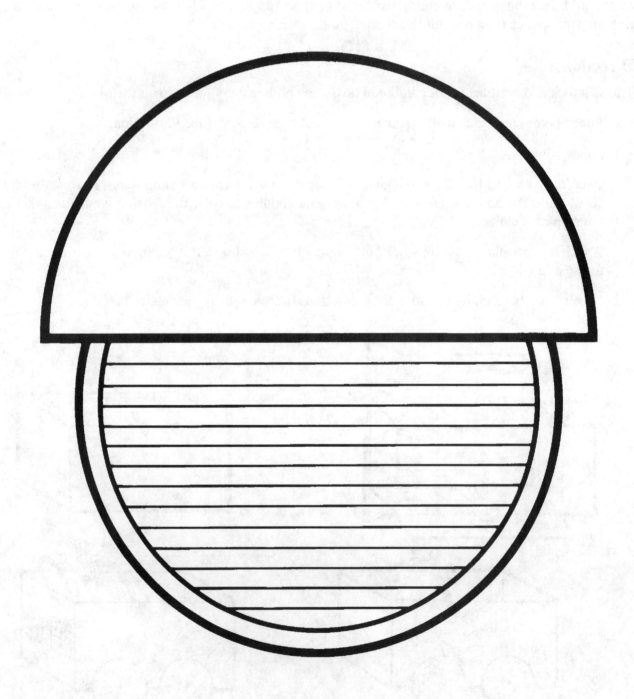

Race Track *(cont.)*

Car Detail Patterns *(cont.)*

Wheel – Make One

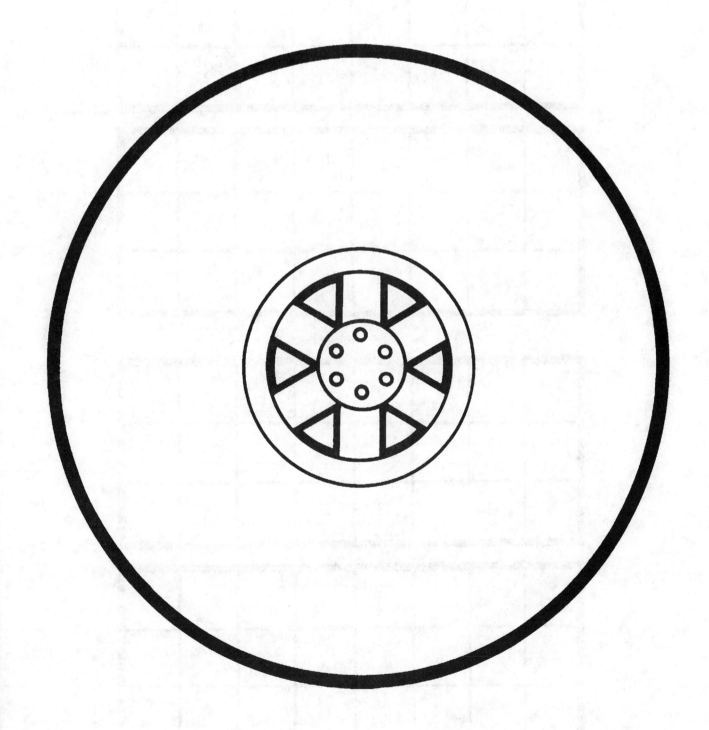

Race Track *(cont.)*

Car Detail Patterns *(cont.)*

Taillights

Race Track *(cont.)*

NAEYC Appropriate Practices

Appropriate Practice:

Three-Year-Olds

"Adults provide large amounts of uninterrupted time for children to persist at self-chosen tasks...adults know that children are beginning to use language to solve problems and use concepts."

Concept Connection:

This activity affords children the opportunity to practice skills at their own paces and relate these skills to their developing grasp of language.

Appropriate Practice:

Four- and Five-Year-Olds

"Children are provided many opportunities to see how reading and writing are used...an abundance of these types of activities is provided to develop language and literacy through meaningful experience."

Concept Connection:

This activity provides a meaningful context in which children can begin to recognize and apply the meanings of useful words.

Appropriate Practice:

Four- and Five-Year-Olds

"Children are provided concrete learning activities with materials and people relevant to their own life experiences."

Concept Connection:

This activity is designed to give children an opportunity to practice real-life skills in a play situation.

Yummy Mud Buckets

Preparation Time:

One-two hours

Language Arts and Socialization Concept:

This activity introduces three-, four-, and five-year-olds to the idea of following sequential directions.

Materials:

small, disposable heat-resistant containers (Small plastic cups shaped like small pails will work.), one for each child ; chocolate pudding, enough for ½ to ¾ of a cup (125 mL to 180 mL) for each child; several pounds of gummy worms; two boxes of graham crackers; plastic spoons; two boxes of chocolate sandwich cookies

What to Do:

In this activity children help make their own edible mud buckets. wormy pudding treats only a child could love! Children will learn to follow sequential directions, make models, and learn about nature—all while preparing a "wormy" pudding treat! To prepare for this activity you will need to ensure you have a bucket and a work space for each child. While you can prepare your own pudding at school from a package or make a large bowl of it at home, it is also possible to buy prepared chocolate pudding from a regular grocery store or a restaurant supply store.

To begin this activity, talk with the children about things that live in the earth. Hold a class discussion regarding all the insects and animals that live in the earth. Mention worms, grubs, ants, moles, groundhogs, squirrels, snakes, mice, etc. Next, model the mud-bucket activity for children and let them create their own pudding buckets with assistance. Children will love to drop in the "worms." Expect lots of laughter! Following are the steps to prepare a mud bucket:

❖ Use a clean bucket or cup.

❖ Put in a ½ cup (120 mL) of chocolate pudding.

❖ Drop in several gummy worms.

❖ Add more pudding.

❖ Squish several more "worms" down in the pudding soil.

❖ Crunch up a handful of graham crackers. Sprinkle on top.

❖ Crunch up a handful of chocolate cookies. Sprinkle on top.

Yummy Mud Buckets *(cont.)*

Self-Directed Teaching Focus:

Activities in which students create food are not appropriate for complete self-direction. In order to add a self-directed teaching focus, let children create mud buckets according to their own plans, providing each with the materials to do so. Be available to assist individual children.

Directed Teaching Focus:

Give step-by-step instructions and let each individual child have the opportunity to experience the idea of following directions.

What to Say:

Today we are going to have a lot of fun! We are going to make something different that is good to eat. Can anyone tell me what these are? (Hold up gummy worms.) Yes, these are gummy worms. They aren't real worms, are they? Real worms live in the ground. Let's try to think of as many animals and bugs as we can that live in the ground. (Have a class discussion.) Now, let's all look at the yummy treat we will make. These are called mud buckets. They are made with chocolate pudding and gummy worms and graham crackers and chocolate sandwich cookies. We will make it look like we have a bucket of worms! Won't that be funny? Let me show you how to make it, and then we will each get a chance to make our own.

Doing More:

Let children make play dough or clay worms. Set out clay or play dough materials and leave several worm models for children to look at.

Evaluation and Processing Through Storytelling:

Have children tell about their experiences making mud buckets, or have them dictate stories about how they have cooked, or how they have helped their parents prepare food, at home.

Yummy Mud Buckets (cont.)
NAEYC Appropriate Practices

Appropriate Practice:

Three-Year-Olds

"Adults encourage children's developing language by speaking clearly and frequently to individual children."

Concept Connection:

Adults and children have many opportunities to communicate in this activity, because making and eating mud buckets stimulates much conversation!

Appropriate Practice:

Four- and Five-Year-Olds

"Teachers prepare the environment for children to learn through active exploration and interaction with adults, other children, and materials."

Concept Connection:

Children love to explore food, and this activity allows them to share their experiences with other children and adults.

Appropriate Practice:

Four- and Five-Year-Olds

"Experiences are provided that meet children's needs and stimulate learning in all developmental areas."

Concept Connection:

This activity enhances numerous learning areas, including sequential order, small-motor coordination, and listening.

Sharing Cube

Preparation Time:

One hour or less

Language Arts and Socialization Concept:

In this activity three-, four-, and five-year-olds gain mastery of sharing, an important aspect of the idea of generosity. Children also gain self-confidence through understanding the limits of sharing and from the knowledge that they are able to set their own personal limits.

Materials:

sharing-cube faces (page 124); square box, approximately 6" (15 cm) square or larger (Look at craft stores, or you can even use a shoe box, if necessary.)

What to Do:

To prepare for this activity, copy, color, and glue the sharing-cube faces to a square box to use during oral sharing at circle time. The sharing cube will create a directed sharing atmosphere (you may choose to have children share about whatever they would like). The sharing cube may be used intermittently as a way of changing topics or as a way to create a topical theme based on what is happening in your children's lives, moods, etc. For example, if the children are upset about a world or local event or an event in a classmate's life, use the sharing cube to give children an opportunity to express their feelings and to enhance their ability to come to terms with real-life situations.

Self-Directed Teaching Focus:

The moods depicted on the cube can be selected by the children as they use the cube, thus creating a format for self-direction in a directed activity.

Directed Teaching Focus:

Use only one of the faces daily at sharing time and direct children to share about something that makes them "smile, laugh, feel sad or angry," etc. Be prepared to listen to their responses and offer support and feedback when needed.

What to Say:

Today we are going to be using our new sharing cube during circle time. Let's talk about what these faces mean and how we can use our new sharing cube. (Model use of the cube, asking children to describe the meanings of the faces on it. You may wish to model an event from your own life in response to each of the faces.) Now let's give it a try. When we pass the cube, each child may tell about something that makes him or her feel like the face he or she sees on the cube.

Doing More:

Alter subjects on a regular basis. Base them on books that are being read in class, experiences children are going through, or even current events or holidays.

Evaluation and Processing Through Storytelling:

Oral sharing is an important skill in the concept of language and oral storytelling. Encourage students to dictate their sharing as a combination storytelling/sharing activity.

Sharing Cube (cont.)
Sharing-Cube Faces

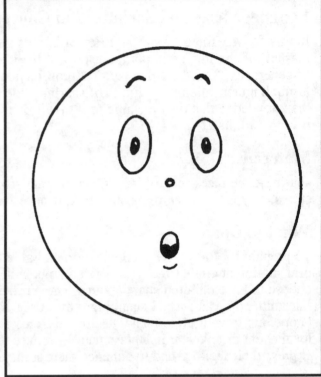

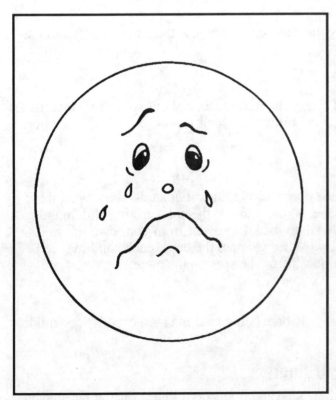

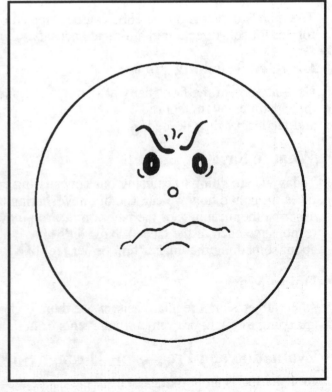

Sharing Cube *(cont.)*

NAEYC Appropriate Practices

Appropriate Practice:

Three-Year-Olds

"Adults recognize that, to three-year-olds, talking may be more important than listening."

Concept Connection:

In this activity children have an opportunity to talk to an interested adult and share their feelings.

Appropriate Practices:

Four- and Five-Year-Olds

"Experiences are provided that meet children's needs in all developmental areas...emotional.

Concept Connection:

By allowing children to look at and express their feelings they gain an increased sense of self awareness and self-esteem.

Appropriate Practice:

Four- and Five-Year-Olds

"Teachers accept that there is often more than one right answer."

Concept Connection:

This activity has no right answer. Each child is encouraged to explore how they feel, and is accepted for their expression of those feelings.

Finders Keepers

Preparation Time:

Half-hour

Language Arts and Socialization Concept:

In this activity three-, four-, and five-year-olds learn a variety of socialization skills—altruism, empathy, generosity, respect for people's property, and the increased self-esteem that comes from being honest and responsible—through the idea of being responsible for the belongings of others. They also have a chance to practice oral language skills.

Materials:

large, sturdy box for lost-and-found items

What to Do:

To prepare this activity, all that is necessary is a large, sturdy box or container in which to store lost-and-found items. Clearly label this box "Lost and Found" and place it in a regular and accessible place in your preschool.

At circle time, introduce the children in your preschool to the lost-and-found box and instruct children to place items that others have lost in the box so that they can find them there at the end of the day. Explain to the children that each day a child will get to hold up the items in the lost-and-found box, and everyone can help find the owners. (This will stress oral language skills as well as the variety of socialization skills listed above.) Additionally, you may wish to read the label to the children, showing them the connection between words and their meanings and stressing pre-reading skills of letter and sound recognition.

Finders Keepers *(cont.)*

Self-Directed Teaching Focus:

The lost-and-found box will become a part of regular everyday activity for the children. You and your aides can model correct behavior regarding lost-and-found items every day by attempting to find the owner of every lost item. In doing so, you will reinforce the concepts of honesty and responsibility for the children in your classroom.

Directed Teaching Focus:

To direct this activity, make a regular event of choosing a lost-and-found monitor and having a regular time each day when the monitor holds up lost items so the rest of the children can "find" them. Rotate the job of monitor so that each child in your classroom has a chance to be the monitor.

What to Say:

Children, this morning, I want to show you something I have made for us. It is a lost-and-found box. Does anyone know what it is for? (Model and discuss the concept of lost and found with children. Include a situation when you lost something and someone returned it to you.) Now, sometimes we all lose things. It is responsible and caring to return anything that is lost and found. If we lose anything in this classroom, we are all going to be caring and good friends to each other and give back what we found to whomever lost it. If we find something and we don't know who it belongs to, we will put it in our new lost-and-found box. Every day (or every week) we will take a look at all the items in the box and figure out to whom they belong. I will pick someone every day to hold up the things in the box and help find out whom they belong to. Let's give it a try.

Doing More:

Talk about the other kinds of lost and found. For example, you can talk about when a child loses a kitten or pet or when a child gets lost in a supermarket. Discuss with children the proper procedure for reporting to an official or an adult. Find out if every child in your classroom knows his/her first and last name. Have children tell their first and last names every day at circle time.

Evaluation and Processing Through Storytelling:

Have children dictate lost-and-found stories about something they lost or found.

Finders Keepers (cont.)
NAEYC Appropriate Practices

Appropriate Practice:

Three-Year-Olds

"Adults encourage children's developing language by speaking clearly and frequently to individual children and listening to their responses."

Concept Connection:

In this activity children have a daily opportunity to talk to other children and adults and listen to their responses.

Appropriate Practice:

Four- and Five-Year-Olds

"Children are provided many opportunities to develop social skills such as cooperating, helping, negotiating, and talking with the person involved to solve interpersonal problems."

Concept Connection:

The concept of helping others find things encourages empathy and understanding and altruism in children; three important factors in the development of socialization skills.

Appropriate Practice:

Four- and Five-Year-Olds

"An abundance of these types of activities is provided to develop language and literacy through meaningful experience....dictating stories...participating in dramatic play and other experiences requiring communication, talking informally with other children and adults..."

Concept Connection:

The lost-and-found theme encourages children to interact with each other in a cooperative and problem-solving manner. This interaction increases language ability and word knowledge, the basis for later literacy.

Even Steven!

Preparation Time

One hour

Language Arts and Socialization Concept:

In this activity three-, four-, and five-year-olds gain generosity, empathy, respect, and compromise skills. They are given practice in listening to directions and following steps to complete a rather complicated procedure.

Materials:

one dividable treat for each two children (If the treat will need to be cut, children will need assistance using a blunt cutting tool like a plastic knife; however, the best choice is a treat that can be broken in half.)

What to Do:

To prepare for this activity, all that is necessary is a dividable treat for each two children in your classroom. Depending on the philosophy of your preschool, this will be either a sweet treat such as a cookie or candy of some kind or a fruit snack like an orange that can be easily divided.

To begin this activity, talk with children about the idea of sharing treats and dividing them equally. Most children have had the opportunity to try this at home, especially if they have siblings. Next, give each two children a treat to share. Be nearby to assist with ideas of how they might choose to divide this. Lend support and encouragement and model appropriate interaction behaviors.

Self-Directed Teaching Focus:

To self-direct this activity, have available treats to share on a regular basis (like a bowl of fruit or small packages of chewable fruit snacks). Allow children to help themselves at snack time.

Directed Teaching Focus:

Talk about what it means to share something "even Steven!" Let children practice taking turns being the person who divides the treat and then the person who chooses first.

What to Say:

Today we are all going to have a tasty treat to share during snack time. How many of you have shared a cookie or a piece of candy or fruit with your brother or sister or a friend? When we divide a cookie to share, we try to give each person the same amount. That is called being fair and generous.

Even Steven! *(cont.)*

What to Say *(cont.)*:

Now, find a partner (or assign each child a partner). I'm going to give each pair of you a candy bar (or whatever your choice is) to share. Please divide it evenly. If you have trouble doing that, I will help you. Remember, one person divides and the other person chooses first. Okay? Let's try it!

Doing More:

Use this game concept when giving groups of children toys, or anything else they may want, to share. As far as taking turns is concerned, the best way to make children comfortable with the idea of taking turns is to ask children to use whatever they are using until they are tired of it, and then ask them to find the next person who wants it, rather than limiting the length of time a child has with an item.

This procedure will give children a sense of safety and comfort with their own abilities to control their environment and a feeling that they are not rushed. Be sure to orally acknowledge the way a child remembers to give the item to the next child to use.

Evaluation and Processing Through Storytelling:

Have children dictate stories about things they like to share and things they do not like to share. Let children know that they don't have to share everything. Explain the idea of personal possessions and how children can feel that their personal possessions are theirs to share or not.

Even Steven! *(cont.)*

NAEYC Appropriate Practices

Appropriate Practice:

Three-Year-Olds

"Adults encourage children's developing language by speaking clearly and frequently to individual children and listening to their responses."

Concept Connection:

This activity encourages children to interact with other children and adults and exposes children to a simple problem to solve with the assistance of an adult, if needed.

Appropriate Practice:

Four- and Five-Year-Olds

"Children are provided many opportunities to develop social skills such as cooperating, helping, negotiating, and talking with the person involved to solve interpersonal problems."

Concept Connection:

By dividing a treat, children begin to learn a variety of important socialization skills like sharing and cooperation. Children begin to see communication and interaction as important and valuable.

Appropriate Practice:

Four- and Five-Year-Olds

"An abundance of these types of activities is provided to develop language and literacy through meaningful experience: dictating stories, participating in dramatic play and other experiences requiring communication, talking informally with other children and adults..."

Concept Connection:

Children gain experience in communicating to solve a pleasant problem in this activity and eat the results of their success!

Birthday Party Fun: We Make It!

Preparation Time:

Several afternoons

Language Arts and Socialization Concept:

In this activity three-, four-, and five-year-olds gain self-esteem through creativity, competency, and socialization skills such as generosity. They are given the opportunity to learn and practice the language associated with birthdays and gift giving.

Materials:

gift materials (will vary based on the "present" stations you decide to set up); birthday chart (pages 137 and 138); "How Old Am I" birthday songs on page 135

What to Do:

In this activity children will each make a present to give at a group birthday party. (This activity is followed by two corresponding activities. See pages 139–147 for wrapping gifts and giving the gifts at a group birthday party.)

The idea is for children to each make a gift to present to another child at the group birthday party. Begin this activity by discussing birthdays. Use the birthday chart on pages 137 and 138 to make an attractive birthday chart for your classroom. Ask each child if he or she knows when his/her birthday is. (Remember to have class records available for those children who are not aware of when their birthdays are.)

You may wish to discuss with children how old they will be on their next birthday and begin to teach the "How Old Am I?" birthday songs on page 135.

Self-Directed Teaching Focus:

To self-direct this activity, decide beforehand on several activity centers in which children can make simple presents (see page 134 for several gift-making ideas) Set up the stations so children can choose which ones they are interested in. It's wise to keep the activity somewhat unstructured so there is no "right" way to make a present. Presents are a gift of caring.

Directed Teaching Focus:

To create a directed activity, lead a group gift-making session and choose only one gift for children to make.

What to Say:

Next week, we are going to have a big birthday party for all of us. We will all get to celebrate our birthdays! How many of you have ever had a birthday party? Let's talk about what happens at a birthday party.

Birthday Party Fun: We Make It! *(cont.)*

What to Say *(cont.)*:

(Hold a group discussion regarding birthdays—be sure to give children ample time to share and compare their experiences.)

Now we're going to watch a video about a birthday party. (There are several good birthday videos available. "Barney's Birthday" is cute and covers many of the birthday concepts here; "Spot" has an excellent birthday party scene.) We are each going to make a birthday present for someone else. Let's talk a little bit about giving presents. Why is it fun to give presents to someone else? Why do you give presents?

Some possible points regarding gift giving that you may want to focus on are:

It's fun to give a gift because the person who gets the gift is happy.

Giving makes the giver feel good inside.

Giving is a way to say "I love you" or "I like you."

Doing More:

Have children practice their birthday songs according to their ages. They will sing the songs at the birthday party (see page 135).

Evaluation and Processing Through Storytelling:

Have children dictate their favorite gift stories. Let them use ribbons and bows and wrapping paper scraps left over from the wrapping table to decorate their stories. (See activity on page 139.)

Birthday Party Fun: We Make It! *(cont.)*

Gift Making Ideas

Children love to make gifts! Consider making the projects enjoyable and easy; gifts that are too difficult to make or too fragile will only leave you frustrated. Use this list for some quick ideas. It's sure to jog your memory and get you thinking creatively! Enjoy the gift making process!

- ☆ pictures, clay animals

- ☆ clay change holders, vases, etc.

- ☆ hand prints in sand

- ☆ edible goods like cookies, muffins, etc.

- ☆ pipe-cleaner flowers

- ☆ holiday-theme crafts

- ☆ knickknacks of any kind

- ☆ clay or papier-mache jewelry

- ☆ self-portraits

- ☆ portrait of person who will receive the gift

- ☆ "I love you" cards

- ☆ illustrated stories

- ☆ material painting

- ☆ voice recordings

- ☆ valentines

    134

Birthday Party Fun: We Make It! *(cont.)*
"How Old Am I?" Birthday Songs

Sing these three songs to the tune of "Row, Row, Row Your Boat."

Three-Year-Olds

I was one,
And then was two,
And right now I am three—
And I am very, very happy,
As happy as can be!

Four-Year-Olds

I was two,
And then was three,
And right now I am four!
I'm so happy it's my birthday,
No one could ask for more!

Five-Year-Olds

I was three,
And I was four,
And right now I am five!
I'm so happy it's my birthday,
It's great to be alive!

Birthday-Party Fun: We Make It! *(cont.)*
NAEYC Appropriate Practices

Appropriate Practice:

Three-Year-Olds

"Adults provide many experiences and opportunities to extend children's language and musical abilities. Adults know that children are rapidly acquiring language, experimenting with verbal sounds, and beginning to use language to solve problems and learn concepts."

Concept Connection:

In this activity children have the opportunity to learn simple and amusing songs, increasing their language ability and experimenting with verbal sounds through music.

Appropriate Practice:

Four- and Five-Year-Olds

"Teachers prepare the environment for children to learn through active exploration and interaction with adults, other children, and materials."

Concept Connection:

The birthday-party theme encourages children to interact with other children in a context that is relevant and important to them. Additionally, the materials in this activity are interesting and important to children and increase their understanding of their own environment.

Appropriate Practice:

Four- and Five-Year-Olds

"Interactions and activities are designed to develop children's positive feelings toward learning."

Concept Connection:

The fun of a birthday party creates an atmosphere of learning that is exciting to children.

Birthday Party Fun: We Make It! *(cont.)*

Birthday Chart

September	October
November	**December**
January	**February**

Birthday Party Fun: We Make It! *(cont.)*
Birthday Chart *(cont.)*

March	April
May	June
July	August

Birthday-Party Fun: We Wrap It!

Preparation Time:

Several hours

Language Arts and Socialization Concept:

In this activity three-, four-, and five-year-olds increase fine-motor skills and gain creativity experience, as well as respect, empathy, and compromise.

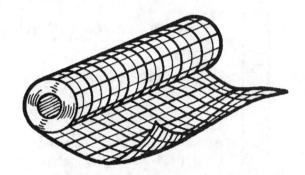

Materials:

wrapping paper materials: bows, ribbons, tape, blunt scissors, wrapping paper (See page 141 for potato-print paper.); wrapping-station area; small boxes for gifts; gift tags (See page 142.)

What to Do:

In this activity children wrap the gifts they made in preparation for the group birthday party. To prepare this activity, first decide what kinds of wrapping materials you would like to use. You can use leftover Christmas wrapping paper, colored Sunday funnies, and/or potato-print wrapping paper. (See page 141 for design ideas.)

Self-Directed Teaching Focus:

Set up wrapping center for children to use after they have completed their gifts. Be sure there is a colorful variety of interesting wrapping materials and provide help with scissors and tape as needed.

Directed Teaching Focus:

Have children work together in a directed activity to make potato-print wrapping paper.

What to Say:

Today we are going to wrap the presents we made for our group birthday party. Over here I have set up a center filled with wrapping materials: paper and bows and gift tags and tape and scissors.

(Model use of center by wrapping a present.) You will be able to use this center to wrap the presents you made. Use your imagination to make your presents beautiful. Who would like to try it first? I will help you write your names on the gift tags.

Doing More:

Display wrapped gifts on shelves and window sills around your preschool so the children can admire each other's work and become familiar with the way the children's names look on the gift tags.

Evaluation and Processing Through Storytelling:

Have children describe their gift wrap at circle time. They can talk about why they chose the colors and materials they used and how they feel about their finished wrapping.

Birthday-Party Fun: We Wrap It! *(cont.)*
NAEYC Appropriate Practices

Appropriate Practice:

Three-Year-Olds

"Adults provide many materials and opportunities for children to develop fine motor skills. Art is viewed as creative expression and exploration of materials."

Concept Connection:

Children have an opportunity to work with a variety of wrapping materials, thus increasing mastery of their fine-motor skills.

Appropriate Practice:

Four- and Five-Year-Olds

"Children are provided concrete learning activities with materials and people relevant to their own life experiences."

Concept Connection:

Wrapping a present is something that children take pride in doing and find exciting because it is relevant to their own lives.

Appropriate Practice:

Four and Five-Year-Olds

"Teachers move among groups and individuals to facilitate children's involvement with materials and activities."

Concept Connection:

By creating a wrapping center as part of an existing art center, children become involved in the excitement of the birthday party planning. The teacher can enhance children's feelings of competence by allowing them to make choices and self-direct their own wrapping jobs.

Birthday-Party Fun: We Wrap It! *(cont.)*

Potato-Print Designs

Children can make interesting wrapping paper by dipping cut potatoes into tempera paint and stamping them onto butcher paper. Follow these simple instructions:

1. Cut potato in half.

2. Draw the pattern you have chosen on the surface of the cut side of the potato.

3. With a knife, cut an outline of your shape on the potato about ¼" (.6 cm) deep. Use the knife to chip away all the other parts around the shape. Do not cut into the design. The design should protrude about ¼" (.6 cm) above the surface of the potato.

4. Have children dip the potatoes in tempera paint and stamp the prints on butcher paper.

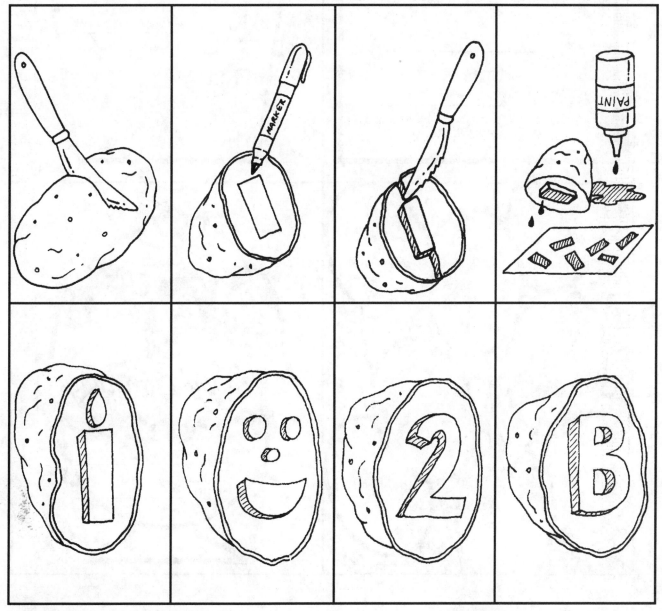

Birthday-Party Fun: We Wrap It! *(cont.)*
Gift Tags

Birthday-Party Fun: We Give It!

Preparation Time:

Several hours

Language Arts and Socialization Concept:

In this activity three-, four-, and five-year-olds are exposed to a number of situations that increase feelings of compromise, mastery, creativity, altruism, respect, and generosity. The children will also have a chance to use oral language as they take part in the celebration, conversing with the other children and with invited adults.

Materials:

name cake or cupcakes with candles (See page 145.), party hats (See page 147.), paper plates, napkins, punch, paper cups, paper towels, presents (from previous activity), balloons and/or any other party supplies you wish

What to Do:

In this activity children take part in a whole-class birthday party. To prepare, you will need a sheet cake for the class or a cupcake for each child. You may wish to write the name of each child on a frosted cupcake or a section of a sheet cake with ABC cereal letters. This gives children the fun of finding their own names or having exposure to the letters in their names.

Next, prepare your classroom for a birthday party. Anything goes, but remember that the more festive the atmosphere and the more attractively arranged the room is, the more likely children will be enthused about taking part. (See party decoration ideas on page 145 for quick and low-cost party ideas.) Prepare and decorate a present table for the gifts the children have made. Also add to the birthday theme by having music. (By now, you have set up a listening area in your music center, and it is simple to use this area for a party dance floor and music area.) Each child should be presented with a party hat when he/she arrives for the day. These are easy to make from the pattern on page 147, and children will love to wear them.

You may also wish to use this party opportunity to invite parent volunteers and participants or visitors. Some parents may want to take part; there are many ways you can let them be part of the fun. Parents can bring supplies, provide entertainment by playing a guitar or other instrument; and/or just enjoy the party with their children.

Let children exchange gifts by having them take turns picking one out of the gift bag without looking, or choose whatever method you decide would be best for your children. Decide beforehand on one or two simple party games and provide small gifts for participants. An old standard that children love is Pin the Tail on the Donkey. Musical Chairs is also enjoyable and will bring music into the occasion.

Birthday-Party Fun: We Give It! *(cont.)*

Self-Directed Teaching Focus:

This activity, by its very nature, will have moments that are self-directed, as at any party, and also directed moments when children are organized, such as in a sing-along. To lend a self-directed focus to the event, do not be overly concerned about what the children should do. In other words, do not require that they perform a song for their parents, but let them mingle and enjoy as adults also like to do at a birthday party. Let children choose their own cupcakes, and use ABC letters to decorate them for a self-directed twist.

Directed Teaching Focus:

Organize a time when children can sing the birthday songs they learned on page 135. Also remember to let children make wishes and blow out candles on their cupcakes, or have a group wish if you use a sheet cake instead of cupcakes.

What to Say:

Welcome to our class party. Each of you will get to wear a party hat, play games, have cake, and receive a present. Let me show you how everything is set up, and then we will decide what we will do first.

Doing More:

Let children get into the party mood several days before the event by reading or telling stories about birthdays.

Evaluation and Processing Through Storytelling:

Have children dictate birthday party stories or stories about the fun they had at the group birthday.

Birthday-Party Fun: We Give It! *(cont.)*
Party Ideas

Cupcakes with ABC Names

Buy or make frosted cupcakes and purchase ABC letter cereal. You may wish to place these letters out in bowls so each child can put letters on his or her own cupcake, or you can work with individuals and help them find the letters for their names. Let children use their own gift name tags as guides to see how their own names are spelled.

Decoration Ideas

A classroom party should be easy, inexpensive, and fun. Anything colorful can add pizazz to the festivities. Following are some ideas.

+ Use old colored sheets in prints and patterns to cover tables.
+ Use children's artwork to create a colorful touch.
+ Decorate with balloons. They are always great, and kids love to take them home; just having bunches of balloons can be all you need.
+ You can pin the tail on any animal, not just a donkey .
+ Set up dolls and stuffed animals for decoration, but only if you will let children play with them; otherwise it is too frustrating for them.
+ Streamers can be made from gluing paper chains together. (Children can help with this.)
+ Use colored construction paper for placemats.
+ Cover tables with butcher paper and put crayons at each table so children can color the tablecloths.

These ideas will help you get started or jog your memory about things you have done in the past that worked for you!

Birthday-Party Fun: We Give It! *(cont.)*
NAEYC Appropriate Practices

Appropriate Practice:

Three-Year-Olds

"Adults provide opportunities for (children) to demonstrate and practice their newly developed self-help skills."

Concept Connection:

This activity allows children to practice a variety of skills that enhance their feelings of competence and autonomy: selecting a gift, selecting refreshments, taking part in party games, etc.

Appropriate Practice:

Four- and Five-Year-Olds

"Experiences are provided that meet children's needs and stimulate learning in all developmental areas—physical, social, emotional, and intellectual."

Concept Connections:

A party atmosphere provides real experiences on a variety of levels for children, including emotional, intellectual, physical and social.

Appropriate Practice:

Four- and Five-Year-Olds

"Children are provided concrete learning activities with materials and people relevant to their own life experiences."

Concept Connection:

The birthday party theme is one that children are familiar with and enjoy taking part in. Children have a sense of mastery and competence by taking part in an activity that they are already familiar with.

Birthday-Party Fun: We Give It! *(cont.)*

Birthday Party Hats

Make enough copies of this page for each child in your class. Cut out the hats and punch the holes. Then fold and glue. Attach rubber bands or string ties to hats so children can wear them. If you wish, children may color and decorate the hats before you cut them out.

We Have Friends, a Name Game

Preparation Time:

One hour

Language Arts and Socialization Concept:

In this activity three-, four-, and five-year-olds will gain socialization skills by taking part in an activity that fosters friendship.

Materials:

paper name strip (one for each child), thick marking pens, masking tape

What to Do:

In this activity children have an opportunity to interact by learning one another's names and getting to know individual children better. To prepare for this activity, each child's first name should be written out on a large, easy-to-read strip of construction paper. Next, place tape loops on the back of each strip so it can adhere to a child's clothing. Hand each child the name of a classmate; each child must find the classmate written on the strip and name him or her when you say "Go!" Children will need help reading the names of their classmates. However, this will give each child an opportunity to become aware of his/her own name and how it is spelled and, further, to begin to be able to recognize and spell his or her own name.

Self-Directed Teaching Focus:

Create a name center by taking an instant picture of each child, clearly labeling each picture with the child's first name, and attaching all pictures to a bulletin board. Then prepare a large box of duplicate name strips, and let children who are interested match name strips to the names on the bulletin board and stick these name strips on a name wall.

Directed Teaching Focus:

Repeat this activity often. Ask children who find each other (it works well if you do this in pairs) to look at their names and see if they have any matching letters, or if they can name all the letters in their names. For teachers who do not wish to stress letters, take a picture of each child. Hand each child a picture of a classmate and play "Find Your Friend!"

What to Say:

Today we are going to play a name game. We will all get a chance to learn one another's names and see how our names are spelled. Our names are all made from letters of the alphabet. Each of us will get a name strip. When I say "Go!" we will try to find that person, and when we do we will stick the name strip on the person! Ready? Go!

Doing More:

Make the name strips and picture strips. These will be easy for nonreaders.

Evaluation and Processing Through Storytelling:

Let children write stories about their own names and why they like them.

We Have Friends, a Name Game

(cont.)

NAEYC Appropriate Practices

Appropriate Practice:

Three-Year-Olds

"Adults support children's beginning friendships."

Concept Connection:

This activity gives children an opportunity to interact directly with other children and learn their names.

Appropriate Practice:

Four- and Five-Year-Olds

"Children are provided many opportunities to develop social skills."

Concept Connection:

The name-game format gives children an organized and enjoyable way to get to know each other in a nonthreatening manner, and it allows them to practice their beginning socialization skills.

Appropriate Practice:

Four- and Five-Year-Olds

"Different levels of ability, development, and learning styles are expected, accepted, and used to design appropriate activities."

Concept Connection:

Children can redo this activity as part of self-directed play; based on their individual ability and learning style, they may choose this or a variety of other activities that appeal to them.

Painting My Friend's Picture

Preparation Time:

One hour

Language Arts and Socialization Concept:

In this activity three-, four-, and five-year-olds build socialization and friendship skills as well as self-esteem and respect skills through painting friends' portraits.

Materials:

painting materials: brushes, paper, paints, easels

What to Do:

In this activity children have the opportunity to paint a picture of one classmate and tell in a dictated story why they like the person they chose to paint. To prepare for this activity, all that is necessary is your already existing painting area.

Begin this activity by talking with children about friends. Then pair the children and have each child sit or stand across from the child he or she is painting. After each child has finished a picture of a friend, let each dictate to you what he or she likes about that person or why being with that person is fun. Give them a starter such as, "Being with Billy is fun because..."

Remember that children who are three, four, and five will not always give you an answer that makes sense to you, but that isn't the point. The point is to give them an opportunity to express themselves both creatively and artistically.

Self-Directed Teaching Focus:

Leave the painting supplies in your painting area and let two children who wish to paint each other's pictures do so whenever they wish.

Directed Teaching Focus:

To direct this activity, have every student share his/her picture during sharing and tell a story about the picture.

What to Say:

Today we are going to talk more about friends. It's nice to have friends, and a good place to make friends is in school. Today we are going to paint one another's pictures, and then we will get to tell a story about why our friend is fun. (Model activity and give example. After painting is finished, work with individual students to let them dictate their stories. The stories can be written directly on the portraits.)

Doing More:

Make talking about friends a part of everyday activity. Use the language of friendship daily. For example, say, "You are being a really good friend to Billy when you let him use your truck."

Evaluation and Processing Through Storytelling:

The storytelling section of this activity is really built in, but give children a chance to act out or record their stories or tell them in puppet play.

Painting My Friend's Picture *(cont.)*
NAEYC Appropriate Practices

Appropriate Practice:

Three-Year-Olds

"Adults provide materials (such as art materials) and opportunities for children to develop fine-motor skills."

Concept Connection:

In this activity children have the opportunity to gain fine-motor skills through the use of painting with equipment such as brushes.

Appropriate Practice:

Four- and Five-Year-Olds

"Children are provided many opportunities to develop social skills."

Concept Connection:

Painting friends' pictures allows children to interact and communicate.

Appropriate Practice:

Four- and Five-Year-Olds

"Children work individually or in small informal groups most of the time."

Concept Connection:

This activity makes it fun for small informal groups to interact and may be used again and again as a self-directed activity by children who are interested in playing "portrait painters."

Come Back Cards

Preparation Time:

Several hours

Language Arts and Socialization Concept:

In this activity three-, four-, and five-year-olds gain experience in a variety of socialization concepts including generosity, empathy, and altruism.

Materials:

construction paper; art supplies including crayons, colored felt pens, glue, stickers, glitter, etc.

What to Do:

In this activity children make cards to be used when children are absent from school because of illness or some other reason. This is an ongoing activity that will reinforce children's caring about others and their sensitivity and empathy regarding their peers. Also this activity will reinforce the cognitive and developmental concept of remembering things, people, or events—an important part of learning to think.

To prepare for this activity, all that is needed is the variety of art supplies that you currently have in your preschool. Anything a child can use to make cards will be fine, and children will use a variety of art materials and let their own creativity be their guides if they are given a chance.

Make cards by simply folding construction paper into a fold-out card. Regular 8 ½" x 11" (22 cm x 28 cm) paper will work well for this activity.

Begin this activity by explaining to students that when they are absent, it is nice for the rest of the class to think of them. Ask them if they have ever received a card for their birthdays or when they were sick, and explain it makes people feel good when they are thought of.

Next, let children make a variety of brightly colored and decorated cards. Let children decide when to send these. They can also be sent to anyone else children think they would like to send a card to. (Remember to keep envelopes and postage on hand so children will get to see the process of their cards being mailed. Walking to a nearby mailbox to mail cards is an enjoyable trip.)

Self-Directed Teaching Focus:

Set up a regular card-making area. Excite children about keeping the card area well stocked, thinking of people to send cards to, and discovering occasions for sending cards. Let children make and send cards for friends' and relatives' birthdays.

Come Back Cards *(cont.)*

Directed Teaching Focus:

During circle time decide as a class to whom to send a card weekly. Make an event of preparing and mailing these cards.

What to Say:

Today we are going to make cards to send people. I have brought some cards for us to look at.

Can anyone tell me what this one is? (Show birthday card.) Yes, it's a birthday card.. Has anyone here ever received a birthday card on his\her birthday? We give cards to people to let them know we are thinking about them and that we care about them.

We are going to create a special place for us all to make cards that we can send to whomever we would like. In fact, let's think about who we would like to send a card to today. (i.e. How about Mrs. Smith? She broke her foot. It would be nice if we sent her cards telling her that we care and we miss her. Would you all like to do that for her?) Let's start now!

Doing More:

Use cards as self-esteem builders. You can mail cards to children in their cubbies; draw on them happy faces or, cats or balloons or whatever the children might like. This activity can also be geared to Valentines Day or the winter holidays.

Evaluation and Processing Through Storytelling:

Let children tell about a time that they wanted to make someone feel better. Or, use the cards to let children dictate what they would like to say to recipients as a storytelling experience.

Come Back Cards *(cont.)*
NAEYC Appropriate Practices

Appropriate Practice:

Three-Year-Olds

"Adults support children's beginning friendships."

Concept Connection:

Children begin to foster a variety of socialization skills such as empathy, understanding, and consideration through this activity.

Appropriate Practice:

Four- and Five-Year-Olds

"Children are provided many opportunities to develop social skills."

Concept Connection:

In this activity children begin to understand the concept of caring for another, and they practice the social skills required to convey caring and empathy.

Appropriate Practice:

Four- and Five-Year-Olds

"Children are provided many opportunities to see how reading and writing are useful."

Concept Connection:

This activity is such that children can easily see how useful it is to be able to write, to tell people things when they are not there, to address a letter or card, etc.

Shoe Hunt Game

Preparation Time:

None or little

Language Arts and Socialization Concept:

This activity introduces three-, four-, and five-year-olds to the idea of using similarities and differences to identify like objects.

Materials:

the children's shoes masking tape or labels, pen (optional)

What to Do:

In this activity children play a shoe-hunt game to reinforce the idea of using similarities and differences to identify like objects (in this case, pairs of shoes). To prepare for this activity, all you need are children with shoes on! You may wish to put a name label on the sole of each child's shoe if you thinking finding the original owner might be a problem, but this is not really necessary.

Have each child take one shoe off and put it in a pile. Blow a whistle and have everyone grab a shoe from the pile. Tell children to match (find one that looks the same as) the shoe they are holding to another shoe that someone is wearing. You may wish to give children who find the other shoe first a sticker or some other prize. Or just have everyone clap when everyone is finished and try it again. Use the words—pairs, alike, matching, same, and different—to reinforce concepts.

Self-Directed Teaching Focus:

Have children bring things that are pairs to school for sharing, or collect a box of pairs for children to play with and leave as part of a center.

Directed Teaching Focus:

This activity works well as a directed activity.

What to Say:

We are going to play a game called Shoe Hunt. First, I want all children to look at their own feet. Take a really good look at your shoes. Think to yourself about how they look and what color they are. They are a matched pair. A pair means there are two of them that go together. Now we are going to have a shoe hunt. How many of you ever lose your shoes at home and can find only one? You have to look to find the other one. This is kind of like the game we will play. I want all of you to put one of your shoes in this pile. When I say "Go!" (or blow a whistle), grab a shoe and look for the person it belongs to. Tell me when you have found the person and you have made a set of two shoes. Ready? Let's try!

Doing More:

This game will also work with mittens if you do not want children to take their shoes off.

Evaluation and Processing Through Storytelling:

Ask children to tell stories about something they lost.

Shoe Hunt Game *(cont.)*

NAEYC Appropriate Practices

Appropriate Practice:

"Adults encourage children's developing language."

Concept Connection:

The ability to recognize similarities and differences is a basic skill needed for reading readiness; this activity provides exposure to this skill in the context of an exciting game.

Appropriate Practice:

Four- and Five-Year-Olds

"Teachers prepare the environment for children to learn through active exploration and interaction with adults, other children, and materials."

Concept Connection:

This activity gives children a perfect opportunity to gain exposure to a reading readiness concept while participating in active play.

Appropriate Practice:

Four- and Five-Year-Olds

"Children are expected to be physically and mentally active."

Concept Connection:

This activity provides a creative mix of physical and mental activity that will involve the young child.

Alphabet Matching

Preparation Time:

One to two hours

Language Arts and Socialization Concept:

This activity introduces three-, four-, and five-year-olds to the concept of matching. It reinforces logic, language arts, and reading-readiness skills.

Materials

alphabet-letter pattern (in appendix—make several set of these); several, large colored tubs, baskets, boxes, or buckets

What to Do:

In this activity children match letters to identical letters, colors to colors, letters to objects, and upper-case letters to lowercase letters. Each of the exercises within this activity reinforces language arts skills.

To prepare for this activity, first decide how you want children to be able to match letters. There are many possibilities. Some are:

- ✦ Matching letters to a duplicate. (You will need at least two complete sets for this.)
- ✦ Matching colors. (You will need to copy your letter patterns on a variety of colors for this.)
- ✦ Matching upper and lower case letters. (You will need at least two complete sets. See appendix.) It is helpful to laminate these letter cards, as they will last much longer if laminated. After preparing your sets of letters, put each set in its own bucket (or other container).

 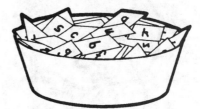

Begin this activity by talking with children about the ABCs. You may wish to teach them the alphabet song. Most children love to sing this song and think it's fun to learn the letters. Talk with children about matching sets or putting things together that look alike. One good example to model is shoes. (See Shoe Hunt Game on pages 155–156.)

Model the exercise by holding up matching letters. Ask whether they are the same or different or whether they match.

Self-Directed Teaching Focus:

Leave the letter buckets out for children to play with. Let them match all the blue cards, match all the letters from two sets, or find all the w's in these sets, etc.

Alphabet Matching *(cont.)*

Directed Teaching Focus:

Play "Same or Different?" Hold up two letters and say, "Are these the same or different? Does anyone know what letter this is? This is an A."

What to Say:

Today we are going to play with letters. I have made us several sets of ABC letters. Let's all sing the ABCs. Ready? (Sing ABC song with class.) Now let's see if we can match a letter in this bucket with the same letter in the other bucket. Let's try. See this A? It matches this A. They are the same letter. They match.

Now let's try another matching game. Let's put all the cards that are blue over here. Who can tell me which is blue? (Hold up two cards, one blue and one another color.) Great. This is the blue one. Can we think of anything else that is blue? Yes, the sky is blue. The sky matches this card. Now let's find all the blue cards.

Doing More:

Have children find matching things outside. They can find leaves that match, flowers that match, even bugs that match.

Evaluation and Processing Through Storytelling:

Have children tell stories about the activity or act out something that starts with a letter for alphabet charades.

Alphabet Matching *(cont.)*
NAEYC Appropriate Practices

Appropriate Practice:

Three-Year-Olds

"Adults provide many experiences and opportunities to extend children's language abilities."

Concept Connection:

In this activity children are exposed to letters as the components of a game, an exposure that will make younger children feel like part of the older children's world.

Appropriate Practice:

Four- and Five-Year-Olds

"Children are provided with many opportunities to see how reading and writing are useful."

Concept Connection:

In this activity the ABCs are an enjoyable part of a matching game in which students become familiar with not only the various way to match letters but also the concept of similarities and differences.

Appropriate Practice:

Four- and Five-Year-Olds

"Different levels of ability, development, and learning styles are expected, accepted, and used to design appropriate activities."

Concept Connection:

This activity gives children at all different levels access to the letters of the alphabet which can then be processed at the pace of the individual child.

Rhyming Words

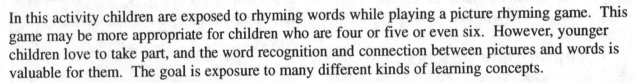

Preparation Time:

One hour

Language Arts and Socialization Concept:

In this activity three-, four-, and five-year-olds experience increased skill in the following areas of language arts: word recognition, rhyming, and word/object connection.

Materials:

rhyming flash cards (See appendix.)

What to Do:

In this activity children are exposed to rhyming words while playing a picture rhyming game. This game may be more appropriate for children who are four or five or even six. However, younger children love to take part, and the word recognition and connection between pictures and words is valuable for them. The goal is exposure to many different kinds of learning concepts.

Have children sit in a circle. Pass out the cards. Ask someone to stand up and tell what is on his or her picture. Next, look for a rhyming word. There are 40 different cards and 20 different rhymes. Have children that have matching cards find each other and say the words that they see in the pictures; they will be exposed to rhyming words. You may wish to read a poem that rhymes and talk about how people sometimes use rhyming words to make poems.

Self-Directed Teaching Focus:

Make double-card sets where a rhyming pair is together. Place these where children can play with them at self-directed times, and children will have exposure to the concept of rhyming through pictures.

Directed Teaching Focus:

This game lends itself to circle time and can be used a directed exercise.

What to Say:

Today we are going to play a game where we look at pictures. It's called a rhyming game. Let's all sit in our circle and look at our pictures. Now who has the picture of a cat? Great. Tim has it. Stand up, Tim. Who has a picture of a hat? Perfect. Mark has the picture of a hat. Those words rhyme. They end the same. Now let's try some more. Pretty soon, we will all be good rhymers!

Doing More:

Older children can have fun thinking of as many words as possible to rhyme with their picture words (e.g., cat, bat, sat, mat).

Evaluation and Processing Through Storytelling:

Let children write poems and dictate them to you.

Rhyming Words *(cont.)*
NAEYC Appropriate Practices

Appropriate Practice:

Three-Year-Olds

"Adults provide many experiences and opportunities to extend children's language abilities."

Concept Connection:

This activity gives three-year-olds an entertaining introduction to rhyming in the context of a picture game and provides exposure to a concept that will become more important to them as time goes on.

Appropriate Practice:

Four- and Five-Year-Olds

"Children's natural curiosity and desire to make sense of their world are used to motivate them to become involved in learning activities."

Concept Connection:

Children are introduced and exposed to the idea of rhyming in this activity.

Appropriate Practice:

Four- and Five-Year-Olds

"Different levels of ability, development, and learning styles are expected, accepted, and used to design appropriate activities."

Concept Connection:

This activity includes elements that can appeal to and satisfy the needs of children at many different levels of ability, development, and learning styles.

Table of Contents for Mathematics and Order

Look Who's on TV!

Preparation Time:

One hour

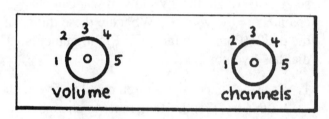

Math Concept:

This activity will introduce three-, four-, and five-year-olds to the concepts of number recognition and counting. (This activity also enhances oral language and self-expression through imaginary play.)

Materials:

a large box, two pieces of cardboard for the dials, scissors, felt pens or paint, brads

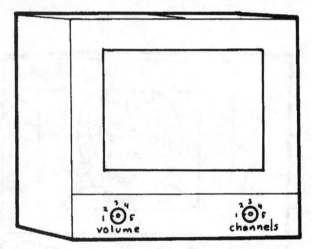

What to Do:

While this activity requires a bit more construction time, it can remain in your classroom as part of a regular learning center. A refrigerator or large appliance box works best. The idea is to create a "play TV." The construction of the TV can be as detailed or simple as you wish. Some teachers might spend a Saturday using paint and contact paper and getting creative, while another teacher will cut out a TV screen square, attach numbered dials (perhaps one for volume and one for the channels) with the brads, and let the children's imaginations take over. Either way is appropriate, and both ways will create positive results. Rather than utilizing an actual TV dial for number recognition, a play TV entices children to use their imaginations to create play situations while enhancing oral language and social skills. When introducing the play TV to the children, emphasize the numbered dials and ask them to name a number on the dial. You may wish to start this exercise by introducing children to the numbers one through five. Allow children to have an opportunity to "play TV." Facilitate the process by watching "TV programs" and helping children to select a channel or increase the volume, all the while helping them with number names and recognition.

Look Who's on TV! *(cont.)*

Self-Directed Teaching Focus:

After introducing the "play TV," leave it in one of the centers for self-directed play. Children may wish to put on shows for themselves, for other children, or for an audience of toys. Encourage children to use items from the pretend center to enhance creative play.

Directed Teaching Focus:

Make this a directed activity by reading a story during a circle time and letting children take turns acting out the story as a TV puppet show.

What To Say:

Today we have something really exciting to do. We are going to pretend we are on TV! I've made us a pretend TV. Here, let me show you. Here is the screen. Here are the TV dials so you can change channels or the volume. What are these things on the dial? (Point to numbers.) Right, numbers. This dial has five numbers.

1...2...3...4...and 5. Can you count to five with me? Let's try. Good. Remember to change the channel or the volume to the right number when you play. We are going to leave the play TV right here so everyone will have a chance to pretend to be on TV. (At this point, facilitate the playing and watch the children, responding positively to their imaginary programs, possibly providing puppets or other props to enhance play. You can also enhance number awareness and recognition by asking what channel the TV is on, what volume it is set on, what this number is, etc.)

Doing More:

Give children art paper and have them draw pictures about who they played on the pretend television or what they saw on the play TV. Then listen to children's descriptions and write them on paper.

Evaluation and Processing Through Storytelling:

Ask each child to pretend to be his/her favorite number and tell how that number feels. Write the stories down as they are dictated.

Look Who's on TV! *(cont.)*
NAEYC Appropriate Practices

Appropriate Practice:

Three-Year-Olds

"Adults provide plenty of materials and time for children to explore and learn…to exercise their natural curiosity (through using) complex dramatic play props (for playing work and family roles)."

Concept Connection:

This activity allows three-year-olds to use a usually noncreative interactive tool, a TV, to explore imaginary role-playing and play. Because the exercise utilizes a pretend rather than a real TV, children have an opportunity to use their imaginations and take an active rather than passive part in play, all the while using an object of common experience.

Appropriate Practice:

Four- and Five-Year-Olds

"Children select many of their own activities from among a variety of learning areas the teacher prepares, including dramatic play, blocks, science, math, games, and puzzles, etc."

Concept Connection:

This activity, while introducing number recognition in a relevant way, also lends itself to dramatic play. Children are free to create the "TV show" in their imaginations, while developing oral language and social skills.

Appropriate Practice:

Four- and Five-Year-Olds

"Teachers move among groups and individuals to facilitate children's involvement with materials and activities by asking questions, offering suggestions or adding more complex materials or ideas to a situation."

Concept Connection:

This activity provides many opportunities for the teacher to move around and interact with groups as well as individual children in order to facilitate and validate dramatic play. Adding puppets and/or costumes would stimulate more complex situations and ideas.

Finger-Counting Pals

Preparation Time:

Several hours

Math Concept:

This activity introduces three-, four-, and
five-year-olds to the concepts of counting and
number recognition.

Materials:

finger puppets, one set per child (See page 169 for finger puppet patterns.)

What to Do:

In this activity children enjoy playing with finger puppets while becoming familiar with the numbers
1–10 and counting. To prepare for this activity, you will need to make sets of finger puppets for each
child who will be taking part in the activity. These are simple to make and children will love to keep
them in their cubbies to play with at their leisure.

To begin this activity, give each child a set of ten finger puppets. Have children practice naming the
numbers and then see if they can count from one to ten. Next, have children try the finger puppets on.
See if they can put them on in order. See page 168 for finger-puppet rhyme. Be sure to hold up the
numbers as you model this activity.

Self-Directed Teaching Focus:

To self-direct this activity, have children store their finger puppets in their cubbies for solitary play.
Encourage children to play often with their finger puppets.

Directed Teaching Focus:

Teach children the finger-puppet verse on page 168. This is enjoyable for them to learn and reinforces
number vocabulary. It will also reinforce small-muscle and eye-hand coordination.

What To Say:

We have something fun to do today! I have made number finger-puppets for all of us. Before we look
at them, let's see how high we can count. Ready, let's try. (Count with the children as high as possible.) Wow! That is great. Okay, now let's look at our finger puppets. Who can find one that has a one
on it? Great. Now let's look for the two. Now the three (and so on.) Let's listen to a little rhyme we
can learn to recite with our puppets.

Doing More:

Children can also introduce their finger puppets in finger puppet plays. Any time children are around
numbers, they will pick up necessary math concepts they will use later.

Evaluation and Processing Through Storytelling:

Let children tell stories about their favorite numbers or their favorite number puppets.

Finger-Counting Pals *(cont.)*
NAEYC Appropriate Practices

Appropriate Practice:

Three-Year-Olds

"Adults read books…recite simple poems, nursery rhymes and finger plays."

Concept Connection:

In this activity children learn a finger play that also exposes them to numbers and counting.

Appropriate Practice:

Four- and Five-Year-Olds

"Children have daily opportunities to develop small-muscle skills."

Concept Connection:

This finger play allows children to develop fine-motor skills and eye-hand coordination.

Appropriate Practice:

Four- and Five-Year-Olds

"Learning about math can be integrated through meaningful activities."

Concept Connection:

Children enjoy learning rhymes and poetry, and the use of numbers in this finger play makes mathematical concepts more relevant by presenting them in a meaningful context.

Finger-Counting Pals *(cont.)*

Finger-Counting Pals

One little finger pal stands all alone.
He finds a friend, and now there are two.
Two little finger pals play pat-a-cake.
They find a friend, and now there are three.
Three little finger pals dance in a circle,
They find a friend, and now there are four.
Four little finger pals have a tea party,
They find a friend, and now there are five.
Five little finger pals count on one hand
1...2...3...4...5!
They add one more, and now there are six!
Six little finger pals go to the zoo.
They find a friend, and now there are eight.
Eight little finger pals listen to stories.
They find a friend, and now there are nine.
Nine little pals learn how to count.
They find a friend, and now there are ten.
1...2...3...4...5...6...7...8...9...10
Ten little finger pals march home to bed
Shhhhhh! They're sleeping!

Finger-Counting Pals *(cont.)*

Finger Puppets

Make enough copies of this page so that each child in your class has a set of ten finger puppets. Have children color and decorate their puppets. Then cut out and tape or glue the tabs around the children's fingers.

Kid Counting

Preparation Time:

Thirty minutes

Math Concept:

This activity introduces three-, four-, and five-year-olds to the practical reasons for learning to count, and it provides practice in number recognition and awareness, estimation, and logic.

ATTENDANCE RECORD

Materials:

numbers (See number patterns on pages 374-384.)

What to Do:

In this activity children find out how many children are present every day, and they see the practical uses for counting on a regular and repetitive basis. To prepare for this activity, simply make thick paper or laminated copies of the number patterns on pages 374-384. See page 171 for a bulletin board idea.

To begin this activity, tell children that they are going to get to start helping you take attendance. Explain that attendance is something you do every day to figure out which students are at school. Next, have children try to guess whether anyone is missing. Demonstrate how to count the whole class for the children, and let interested children count as far as they can with you. Tell children that every day you will all figure out how many people are present and then place the correct number on the "Kid Counting" bulletin board.

Self-Directed Teaching Focus:

Delegate the responsibility for attendance to any interested children. Children will feel a sense of self-confidence and mastery from taking on this responsibility.

Directed Teaching Focus:

Make this a directed morning activity by having children help you take attendance on a regular basis and then decide which number should go on the bulletin board.

What to Say:

Today I am going to ask everyone to help me. I want to figure out how many children are here today. We call this taking attendance. It's helpful to be able to count, and it becomes useful when you want to find out things like how many children are here today. There are twenty children in our class. Let's see how many are here today. Let's begin counting. (Count with the children.) Oh, only eighteen children are here. Let's put the number 18 on our Kid Counting bulletin board.

Doing More:

Show children other opportunities where a counting ability is useful. Have children count the pieces to games and toys in the class to see whether they can tell if there are any missing.

Evaluation and Processing Through Storytelling:

Kid Counting (cont.)
Bulletin Board Idea

Kid Counting *(cont.)*

NAEYC Appropriate Practices

Appropriate Practice:

Three-Year-Olds

"Adults provide opportunities for three-year-olds to demonstrate and practice their newly developed self-help skills and their desire to help adults."

Concept Connection:

Children take pride in being able to help adults, and this daily attendance count will give children an increased sense of mastery.

Appropriate Practice:

Four- and Five-Year-Olds

"Experiences are provided that meet children's needs and stimulate learning in all developmental areas."

Concept Connection:

This activity gives children exposure to numbers and counting while enhancing their socialization and self-esteem skills.

Appropriate Practices:

Four- and Five-Year-Olds

"Children are provided concrete learning activities with materials and people relevant to their own life experiences."

Concept Connection:

This activity is especially meaningful because children can see that it has a real-life purpose and that they are being helpful each day through their participation.

Sound Patterns

Preparation Time:

One hour

Math Concept:

This activity introduces three-, four-, and five-year-olds to the concept of patterns through the use of sounds, rhythm, and music.

Materials:

drums and shakers (from Kitchen Marching Band on page 40); rhythm instruments

What to Do:

In this activity children become aware of patterns by being part of rhythm, music, and movement exercises. To prepare for this activity, make sure that each child has some kind of rhythm instrument. Cereal-box drums are easy to make, and children will love to use them again and again. It is possible to simply clap hands to create sound patterns or pat hands on a table, or even knock on a door. The key to this activity is to give children an opportunity to become aware of patterns and the mathematical relationship of numbers to patterns.

To begin this activity, simply have all children take a rhythm instrument of some kind and tell them that they will be playing follow the leader. Lead your children by reproducing simple rhythm patterns and having them try to imitate the patterns. (Even a two-year-old has fun clapping her hands and saying "One!" with gusto) Try a variety of patterns and have children create some as well. For example, hit your drum while saying "One, two, three, four," and have children imitate the pattern.

Continue this "Follow the Leader" game by having children take turns being the leader.

Sound Patterns *(cont.)*

Self-Directed Teaching Focus:

To self-direct this activity, add a variety of musical tapes that feature rhythm and percussion and drums to your sound center. Let children listen to these tapes whenever they want and pretend they are drummers.

Directed Teaching Focus:

This activity can be done frequently as a listening-and-patterns exercise. A child who begins this kind of exercise in listening to and hearing patterns will have a far easier time hearing and following directions in first and second grades. Remember that the key here is not mastery but experience and exposure to a concept.

What to Say:

Today we are going to play a new kind of "Follow the Leader" game. I'm going to hit my drum, and I want all of you to do just what I do. Let's give it a try. Listen to this pattern. (Hit drum and say "one!")

Try to match the sound and the word. That was good. Let's try some more, and then we can take turns being the leader.

Now let's listen to this music and use our drums to keep time. Ready! Isn't this fun?

Doing More:

Make listening to patterns a regular part of your sound center. Encourage children to play with and use a variety of simple musical instruments. Some children will want to perform. Have a talent show where they can perform their musical pieces.

Evaluation and Processing Through Storytelling:

Let children make music and rhythm a regular part of their acting out of their stories. Encourage students to make up songs which you write down for them. Or use a tape recorder to preserve your students' "jam" sessions.

Sound Patterns (cont.)
NAEYC Appropriate Practices

Appropriate Practice:

Three-Year-Olds

"Adults provide many experiences and opportunities to extend children's language and musical abilities. (They) encourage children to sing songs and listen to recordings and provide simple rhythm instruments."

Concept Connection:

Children gain exposure to mathematical concepts like patterns and counting while enhancing musical and language experience.

Appropriate Practice:

Four- and Five-Year-Olds

"Children experiment and enjoy various forms of music."

Concept Connection:

This activity gives children an opportunity to experiment with making their own rhythm and music, while enhancing mathematical concept awareness.

Appropriate Practice:

Four- and Five-Year-Olds

"Learning about math (can be) integrated through meaningful activities."

Concept Connection:

Creating music and sound is something important to young children; through this activity they begin to have exposure to mathematical patterns and counting.

Pattern Jewelry

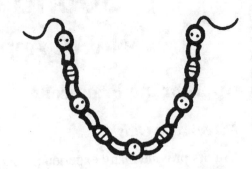

Preparation Time:

Several hours

Math Concept:

This activity introduces three-, four-, and five-year-olds to the concept of patterns through making bead pattern jewelry.

Materials:

an 18" (46 cm) string (thick) or one shoelace per child, large beads of assorted colors (Check out craft stores for a variety or see page 178)

What to Do:

In this activity children will become aware of patterns by making their own bead jewelry. To prepare for this activity, you will need to decide on the kinds of beads you will use and prepare them. Make sure you have a variety of bead shapes and colors available so children can be creative with their choices. (See bead-making suggestions on page 178.)

Model this activity for children by showing them how to string beads and talking with them about all the different color combinations and patterns they can make. After the necklaces are made, compare them and discuss with children how they differ.

Self-Directed Teaching Focus:

Make your bead pattern activity part of your regular craft center. Children may want to make play jewelry on a regular basis. Every time they string beads a new way, they are creating patterns and becoming aware of the concept of patterns.

Directed Teaching Focus:

Make pattern necklaces for Mother's Day or another gift time. Let each child wrap his/her own gift, with assistance, and take home to give to a family member.

What to Say:

Today we are going to make our own jewelry. Look at these pretty necklaces I've made. Can anyone tell me the two colors I've used on this necklace? Yes, red and yellow. See how first I strung one red bead and then I added a yellow bead? I made a pattern by alternating the beads— red, yellow, red, yellow. Let's all make necklaces, and then we can look at all the colorful patterns we have made.

Doing More:

Make children aware of patterns in everyday activities. Use blocks to make patterns, or use other pieces of toys or games. Take children outside and spend a few minutes looking at cloud patterns or patterns on leaves.

Evaluation and Processing Through Storytelling:

Have children enclose cards with their jewelry gifts. Let them dictate messages for their cards.

Pattern Jewelry *(cont.)*

Bead Pattern Jewelry
NAEYC Appropriate Practices

Appropriate Practice:

Three-Year-Olds

"Adults provide many materials and opportunities for children to develop fine-motor skills."

Concept Connection:

Making jewelry gives children an opportunity to fine tune their small-motor skills while undertaking an enjoyable task.

Appropriate Practice:

Four- and Five-Year-Olds

"Children have daily opportunities to develop small-muscle skills through play activities."

Concept Connection:

Stringing beads develops small-muscle control and eye-hand coordination.

Appropriate Practice:

Four- and Five-Year-Olds

"Learning about math (can be) integrated through meaningful activities."

Concept Connection:

Children enjoy making presents and find this activity meaningful. By creating jewelry they are learning about number patterns.

Pattern Jewelry *(cont.)*

Try some of these ideas to make beads.

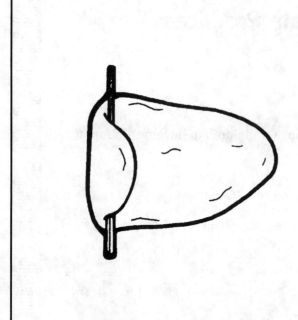

❖ rolling clay or play dough around a toothpick to dry (Grease toothpick with oil ahead of time.)

❖ using plain macaroni or one of the colored vegetable varieties

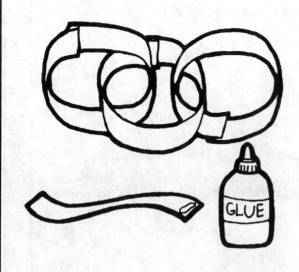

❖ using paper chains instead of beads

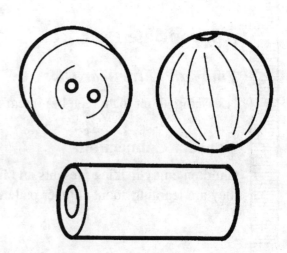

❖ using buttons (Ask parents to donate unused buttons.)

Rainbow Pattern Art

Preparation Time:

None

Math Concept:

This activity introduces three-, four-, and five-year-olds to the concept of patterns through the creation of color patterns.

Materials:

a variety of colors of paint, already existing painting center

What to Do:

To prepare for this activity, make sure your painting center is stocked with all the usual necessities, especially a variety of colors of paint. Begin this activity by discussing rainbows. Ask children if they have ever seen a rainbow after it rains. Discuss the color patterns in a rainbow and show pictures of rainbows to your children. Next, let children paint rainbows. Do not instruct the children to paint rainbows a certain way, for the less structured the rainbows are, the more patterns you will have to demonstrate to your class.

After children have finished painting, put the rainbows on a bulletin board and comment on all the different patterns you see.

Self-Directed Teaching Focus:

Let children paint rainbows whenever they want to. Encourage them to make as many different rainbows as they can.

Directed Teaching Focus:

Direct this activity by having children duplicate a rainbow sample or a picture of a real rainbow. You may read *Barney's Color Book*, which stresses rainbows. Another excellent book is called *Rain* written by Robert Kalan and illustrated by Donald Crews. The words and ideas are simple, and the rainbow at the end is beautiful.

What To Say:

Today we are going to paint rainbows. How many of you have seen a rainbow after it rains? We are going to paint our own rainbows, and then we will put them up and look at how different and pretty they all are. (Model and assist with this activity, stressing the different patterns and why the patterns are different.)

Doing More:

Have children make square patterns. Make a checkerboard design on painting paper and ask children to fill in the checkerboard however they wish. Use a real checkerboard as an example of a checkerboard pattern.

Evaluation and Processing Through Storytelling:

Have children tell about when they saw a rainbow or what they think it would be like if they ever saw one.

Rainbow Pattern Art *(cont.)*

NAEYC Appropriate Practices

Appropriate Practice:

Three-Year-Olds

"Adults provide plenty of materials and time for children to explore and learn about the environment."

Concept Connection:

Children learn about number patterns while also learning about the natural environment and weather conditions.

Appropriate Practice:

Four- and Five-Year-Olds

"Children are provided concrete learning activities with materials relevant to their own life experiences."

Concept Connection:

Rainbows and other gifts of nature are life experiences that all children treasure. Children enjoy creating rainbows because they are meaningful to them.

Appropriate Practice:

Four- and Five-Year-Olds

"Teachers accept that there is often more than one right answer."

Concept Connection:

The children will create a variety of rainbows, all of them lovely and all of them perfect.

Washing the Socks

Preparation Time:

Thirty minutes

Math Concept:

This activity introduces three-, four-, and five-year-olds to the concepts of one-to-one correspondence, sets, counting by twos, probability, and patterns.

Materials:

a large cardboard box with lid (an appliance box, for example), paint, markers, three pairs of socks or six socks cut from colored paper

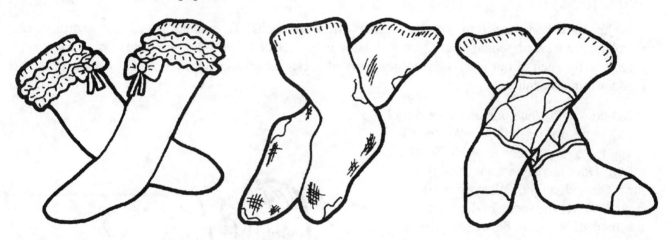

What to Do:

This activity is simple and enjoyable. Children are invited to "wash the socks" and take part in a family role-play, all while being introduced to one-to-one correspondence, sets, counting by twos, estimation, and patterns. A large cardboard box with lid and six socks are all the necessary materials. You may wish to decorate the box as a washing machine, or you may prefer to ask your children to use their imaginations. Six socks can be collected easily from home, or you may cut them out of colored paper.

Have children put the socks in the wash, take them out, and sort them into matching pairs of two that are the same color. Vary the activity by removing one sock and having one sock missing its mate. Talk with children about how socks come in pairs because we need one for each of our feet, etc.

This exercise also is a prompt for children to discuss real-life situations, such as not being able to find both socks, and explore logical conclusions and solutions based on "what ifs." This activity can also remain in a learning center area for individual play.

Washing the Socks *(cont.)*

Self-Directed Teaching Focus:

Leave the washing machine and socks set up in your house center for self-directed fun. You may also create a variety of counting challenges by putting in a number of mismatched socks or varying numbers of different colors and then changing them weekly.

Directed Teaching Focus:

Lead children in counting by twos. Use socks to demonstrate the concept. (While younger children may not join in at first, it is interesting for them to hear other children count. Later they may decide to join in with their own number verbalizations.)

What to Say:

Who knows what I have in my hands? Right! These are socks. How many people are wearing socks today? I see a lot of people wearing socks. How many socks do we wear at a time? We wear two at a time, one for each of our feet. I have three pairs of socks here, and I have a box that I made into a pretend washing machine.

What do we do when our socks are dirty? That's right, we wash them. We are all going to have a chance to wash the socks today. Does someone want to do it with me? Okay, Jennifer. What do we do first? We put the socks in the washing machine. Then what do we do? (Base your comments on the individual child's experiences and imagination.)

Let's take them out. Hmm, which ones go together? That's right, these two with the dots go together, and these green ones go together, and these black ones go together. That was great. Now our socks are all clean.

Doing More:

Use doll socks and let children choose clean socks to put on a doll. Discuss household chores and how the children help around the house.

182

Washing the Socks *(cont.)*
NAEYC Appropriate Practices

Appropriate Practice:

Three-Year-Olds

"Adults support three-year-olds' play and developing independence, helping when needed, but allowing them to do what they are capable of doing."

Concept Connection:

This activity allows three-year-olds to work independently. The teacher acts as a facilitator, listening and responding to the existing knowledge the three-year-old shares about his/her own experience, and offering ideas that gently guide the child into math ideas, such as pairs, matching, and counting by twos.

Appropriate Practice:

Four- and Five-Year-Olds

"Teachers prepare the environment for children to learn through active exploration."

Concept Connection:

This activity can be used in a variety of ways, including being part of an existing learning area in which children can explore at will, encouraging math concepts through creative play.

Appropriate Practice:

Four- and Five-Year-Olds

"Teachers recognize that children learn from self-directed problem solving and experimentation."

Concept Connection:

This activity is set up to be self-directed. Children can use their experiences and imaginations to solve the problem of "washing the socks." And though children will have many different interpretations of the activity based on their own experiences and environments, each child will experience math concepts and number relationships by experiencing the activity.

Big and Small

Preparation Time:

None

Math Concept:

This activity introduces three-, four-, and five-year-olds to the concepts of measurement, greater than and less than, and sorting.

Materials:

available materials in your classroom, "big and small" bulletin board (optional)

What to Do:

This activity can be done a variety of ways, based on your facility and the space and time available. Divide a bulletin board into two sections and label them "Big" and "Small." Cut out pictures of common small and big objects from magazines and place them accordingly for children to look at. Ask children to give some examples within your classroom. Ask children to point to something big in the classroom and then to something small. Children may also pick two objects in the classroom and tell you which is bigger and which is smaller. Another way to establish a relevant context for big and small is to label two toy boxes—one "Big" and one "Small." At clean-up time, children will naturally gain awareness of these number concepts. You may wish to begin this activity by reading the big and small story provided for you in the "What to Say" section. After reading the story, facilitate the activity by moving among groups and individuals to guide the discovery process.

Self-Directed Teaching Focus:

Mark a basket or box "small" and announce that this box will be for small pieces of games or toys that need to be sorted.

Directed Teaching Focus:

Play a big and small game every day at circle time. Let each child pick something that is big and something that is small.

What to Say:

I am going to read you a little story about big things and small things. Then, after I am done, we can talk about it. Story: "I look around me every day. I see big things like trees. I see small things like ladybugs. I see big things like buildings. I see small things like pennies. I see big people like grown ups. I see small people like babies. Every day I see things that are big and things that are small." Now, let's all find something big and something small. You may talk with the other children around you about big and small if you would like to.

Doing More:

Have children take turns comparing heights and deciding who is bigger and who is smaller. Or have children bring something small from home to share with the rest of the group.

Big and Small *(cont.)*
NAEYC Appropriate Practices

Appropriate Practice:

Three-Year-Olds

"Adults encourage children's developing language by speaking clearly and frequently to individual children and listening to their responses."

Concept Connection:

This activity is set up to promote individual interaction between teacher and child.

Appropriate Practice:

Four- and Five-Year-Olds

"Children are provided concrete learning activities with materials and people relevant to their own lives and experiences."

Concept Connection:

By building math concepts into the everyday routine of children's lives—having children sort big and small toys into the appropriately labeled boxes—children begin to realize the connection between learning and real-life activities.

Appropriate Practice:

Four- and Five-Year-Olds

"Children are provided many opportunities to develop social skills such as cooperating (or) helping."

Concept Connection:

By creating a math activity in which children can feel good about helping, not only are mathematics skills enhanced, but self-esteem is also.

Vegetable-Tasting Party

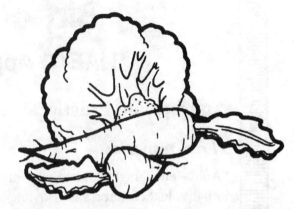

Preparation Time:

A few hours

Math Concept:

This activity introduces three-, four-, and five-year-olds to the concepts of taste and flavors, observation and investigation, and processing sensory input. Children will sort vegetables by taste and color.

Materials:

a variety of vegetables, plates, napkins, paper towels (If you do not prepare the vegetables at home, add knives, a colander, a peeler, etc.)

What to Do:

In this activity children have the opportunity to taste different vegetables, compare their tastes, and sort them according to a variety of characteristics such as taste and color. (Some children may end up liking vegetables they have never thought about eating before.) To prepare this activity, decide upon a variety of vegetables and prepare them in bite-sized portions. (Make sure that these pieces are easily eaten by small children.)

Explain to children that they will be taking part in a taste test. They will want to try as many different kinds of vegetables as they can to see the different ways they taste. They do not have to take more than a bite of any vegetable unless, of course, they want to. Encourage children to decide which they like best, which is their least favorite, and why.

Self-Directed Teaching Focus:

Prepare a different vegetable every day and provide these as snacks. Use as many different kinds as possible to give children exposure to different sensory experiences. (Even a negative reaction to something is a sensory experience, and their not liking something does not make the activity a failure.)

Directed Teaching Focus:

Have children sort vegetables by taste and then by color. Talk about how they made their decisions.

What to Say:

Today we are going to have a taste test. We have a lot of different kinds of vegetables here, and we are going to try them and see what we think of them. You can have as much or as little of each one as you want. Try to taste them all so you can tell us what you think.

Doing More:

Have clay or play dough available for children to use in making models of vegetables. They can make them true-to-life or experiment with blue tomatoes and pink broccoli.

Evaluation and Processing Through Storytelling:

Let children dictate stories to be illustrated later or to go with their clay models. Topics could include "Why I Like Carrots" or "Pink Broccoli Tastes Funny."

Vegetable-Tasting Party *(cont.)*
NAEYC Appropriate Practices

Appropriate Practice:

Three-Year-Olds

"Children are encouraged to "taste" in small portions with the possibility of more servings if desired."

Concept Connection:

A vegetable-tasting party is the perfect way to let children sample and taste many nutritious snacks without any expectation for them to try more than a taste.

Appropriate Practice:

Four- and Five-Year-Olds

"Teacher moves among groups and individuals to facilitate children's involvement with materials."

Concept Connection:

This activity is a perfect opportunity for a teacher to model a positive attitude toward trying new things and to show by example how much fun it is to investigate and experiment with vegetable tastes.

Appropriate Practice:

Four- and Five-Year-Olds

"Teacher's expectations match and respect children's developing capabilities."

Concept Connection:

This activity will be different for every child. The teacher can create an attitude of acceptance about each child's individual tastes and attitudes by supporting each child's choices.

Out of My Window

Preparation Time:

Fifteen minutes

Math Concept:

This activity introduces three-, four-, and five-year-olds to the geometric concept of shapes. (This activity also highlights language arts, speaking skills, and artistic exploration.)

Materials:

plain white paper or construction paper, crayons, a fine-tip felt pen

What to Do:

This activity introduces children to geometric shapes. Start by holding an informal discussion about what you can see from the window at your preschool. You may wish to have each student look out the window and tell what he/she sees. Next, discuss children's homes and what they can see from the windows at home. Be sure to mention that windows come in all kinds of shapes, and have students think about the shapes of the windows they look out of at home.

Work with individual students, helping each to draw a "window" or shape and then tell you what can be seen outside the window. Write their descriptions on the paper; then let them complete their window pictures by coloring or decorating with art materials. Display the finished windows or let children take them home.

Self-Directed Teaching Focus:

After introducing the "window" idea, encourage children to draw what they see from the classroom window whenever they wish. They can also draw what they see from a window at home and bring it to class to share.

Directed Teaching Focus:

Each day at circle time, ask several students to look out the window and report what they see. Talk about why different children may see different things.

What to Say:

Stand at a window and say, "Can anyone tell me what this is called? Yes, that's right. It's a window. We have windows in this building so we can look outside. Let's all look out the window and see what's outside. Who can tell me what they see? (At this point, hold an informal discussion, letting children share what they see.) We all have windows at home, don't we? What do we see out of our windows at home? (Lead discussion.)

Now we're going to draw a window at home and tell what we see outside. Then we can draw what we see. (Work with individual children, letting them have a chance to draw a shape, with assistance if needed, and tell about what they see outside their windows.)

Doing More:

Have students see pretend places out of their windows and describe them. Or to introduce the concept of sorting, have students look for things that are green, things that are little, things that are alive, etc., outside their windows.

Out of My Window *(cont.)*
NAEYC Appropriate Practices

Appropriate Practice:

Three-Year-Olds

"Adults listen to stories, tell or write down stories they dictate; and enjoy three-year-olds' sense of humor.

Concept Connection:

This activity enhances imagination and oral language skills, while at the same time asking children to be aware of shapes. By listening to a child's description of what he/she sees out of the window and then writing it down, the child is helped to feel affirmed, confident, and successful.

Appropriate Practice:

Four- and Five-Year-Olds

"Children are provided many opportunities to talk informally with other children and adults."

Concept Connection:

This activity allows teachers to work informally with individual children and provide them individual time. Children gain feelings of self-worth by having adults listen to their thoughts and stories.

Appropriate Practice:

Four- and Five-Year-Olds

"Children are provided many opportunities to experiment with writing by drawing and copying."

Concept Connection:

This activity gives children the opportunity to experiment with drawing and recognizing shapes which enhances math readiness and eye-hand coordination.

A Day at the Beach

Preparation Time:

One hour

Math Concept:

This activity introduces three-, four-, and five-year-olds to geometric, three-dimensional (solid) shapes and the names corresponding to these shapes.

Materials:

a sand table or outdoor sandbox, water, buckets, a variety of differently shaped beach toys (box shapes, cylinders, balls, pyramids, etc.), broom and dust-pan, an area for children to wash hands

What to Do:

In this activity children learn shapes and build sand castles, increasing their understanding of geometric concepts at a pretend day at the beach. To prepare for this activity, you will need a sand table with plenty of sand and in close proximity to water. You may prefer to do this activity outside as it does become very messy.

Begin this activity by preparing your beach area. Lay out your equipment in an attractive way. Let children familiarize themselves with the equipment and model how to use the different sand-castle forms. Ask which one is shaped like a box. Use words like square, box, rectangle, cone, cylinder, circle, etc. While children may not retain many of these words, any exposure to them will provide familiarity with the geometry concepts they will need later on.

You may want to have aides or parent helpers help you with this activity. Assist the children by giving them ideas of what they can do to make their day at the beach enjoyable. This activity can be as straightforward or as expanded as you wish. Some teachers will want to get totally into the beach party theme; others will simply provide the shape makers and let children take it from there. Either way will be fun and productive.

A Day at the Beach *(cont.)*

Self-Directed Teaching Focus:

Model activity and leave the space as part of your existing sand table or sandbox area. When conversing with children regarding their experiences at the sand table, reinforce shape words whenever possible.

Directed Teaching Focus:

Have everyone try to make a square shape and a round shape. Encourage them to make unusual shapes. Show children how to make a sand-castle village. See who can build a sand castle the fastest. Then have fun at the end knocking them all down.

What to Say:

We are going to have fun pretending we are at the beach today! How many of you have ever been to the beach? How many of you have built a sand castle before? (Model and discuss activity.) Let's look at the things I have to make castles with. You can use these box shapes or square shapes to make your castle. Or you can use these, which will make round shapes. This is called a cylinder. We can make lots of interesting shapes when we make our sand castles. Are you ready? Let's give it a try.

Doing More:

If you are near an ocean or lake, children love to do the real thing. If you take your children to a body of water, be sure to have plenty of volunteers to assist you and also that children are water safe. Prepare for the "real" day at the beach by discussing what children can expect and what rules they should follow.

Evaluation and Processing Through Storytelling:

Let children tell "day at the beach" stories or act out a day at the beach in dramatic play.

A Day at the Beach *(cont.)*
NAEYC Appropriate Practices

Appropriate Practice:

Three-Year-Olds

"Adults provide…sand and water with tools."

Concept Connection:

The beach activity gives children a variety of opportunities to pour, measure, and play with sand and water.

Appropriate Practice:

Four- and Five-Year-Olds

"Children choose among activities the teacher has set up."

Concept Connection:

This activity is perfect for self-directed fun, and some children will go to the "beach" daily while others will go just once in awhile. Provided as one of many choices, children have a chance to gain confidence in their choices and decisions.

Appropriate Practice:

Four- and Five-Year-Olds

"Teachers facilitate the development of positive social skills."

Concept Connection:

Using a "beach" area requires that children interact in a casual fashion and practice their skills of compromise.

Shapes Blindfold Game

Preparation Time:

One hour

Math Concept:

This activity introduces three-, four-, and five-year-olds to shapes and their names.

Materials:

cut-out shapes on pages 197–199, paper or
material bag in which to store shapes, scarves or bandannas for blindfolds

What to Do:

In this activity children learn the names of shapes and play a guessing game to see whether they can guess a shape blindfolded. To prepare this activity, use the shape patterns on pages 197–199 to create your own shapes. Use a variety of materials and textures to make different-feeling shapes. For example, cut a number of squares from heavy construction paper and then affix a variety of different kinds of surfaces to the shapes to make them tactile experiences for children feeling them in the blindfold game. Some surface ideas that work well are:

- ❖ sandpaper
- ❖ materials like velvet, felt, satin
- ❖ a variety of different kinds of paper (e.g., tracing paper, cardboard, watercolor paper, etc.)

To begin this activity, have children learn "The Shape Song" on page 196.

Have children work in pairs, alone, or with aides. Model the shape words and the shapes to the children. Let children repeat the names of the shapes. Then have children take turns picking one with a blindfold on and saying what they think it is. (For younger children who do not know these words yet, let them tell how it feels. Use words such as smooth, hard, soft, etc.)

Shapes Blindfold Game *(cont.)*

Self-Directed Teaching Focus:

Leave the shapes in the art center or tactile center for children to use whenever they wish. Exposure to the different shapes is more important than actually learning the names at this time.

Directed Teaching Focus:

Teach the shape song as a directed activity and then have children repeat the names of the shapes, or use the shape guessing game as part of an organized circle-game activity.

What to Say:

Today we are going to learn a simple song about shapes! Can anyone tell me what this shape is? (Hold up circle.) Right, this is a circle. Let's all make a circle motion with our hands like this. (Model circular motion which will later be used with the song.) Now let's see if we know the names for these other shapes.

Now we're going to learn the song. I will sing it for you, and you can join in when you wish. After we are done, we will all play a guessing game with shapes. We can play this game anytime we want to, and we will all learn the names of our shapes that way.

Doing More:

During circle time every day, have children find something in the room that is shaped like a circle or a square.

Evaluation and Processing Through Storytelling:

Have children tell stories about things that are square or things that are round, or have them dictate stories about their impression of the activity.

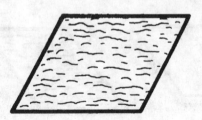

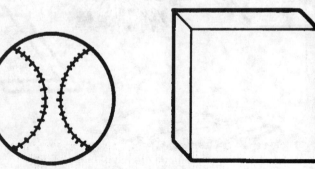

Shapes Blindfold Game *(cont.)*

NAEYC Appropriate Practices

Appropriate Practice:

Three-Year-Olds

"Adults encourage children to use language to solve problems and learn concepts."

Concept Connection:

As children talk about and touch shapes, they are encouraged to learn mathematical concepts and see the differences and similarities among objects.

Appropriate Practice:

Four- and Five-Year-Olds

"Children work individually or in small groups most of the time."

Concept Connection:

This activity lends itself to individual or small group play, and a child can explore shapes alone as easily as with a small, informal group.

Appropriate Practice:

Four- and Five-Year-Olds

"Children develop language and literacy through meaningful experience."

Concept Connection:

When children handle actual objects that have names, they can see immediate meaning behind the identifying words.

Shapes Blindfold Game *(cont.)*

Shape Song

(Sing to the tune of "Someone's in the Kitchen with Dinah.")

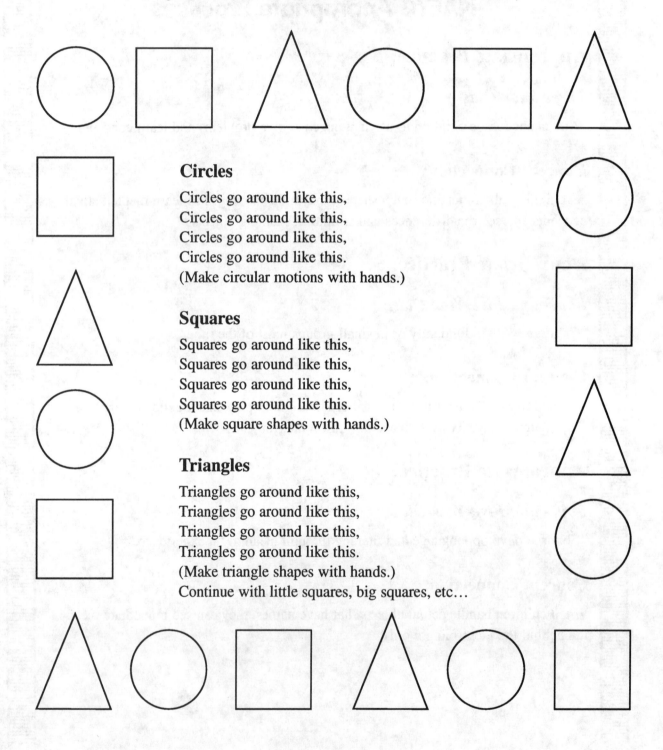

Circles

Circles go around like this,
Circles go around like this,
Circles go around like this,
Circles go around like this.
(Make circular motions with hands.)

Squares

Squares go around like this,
Squares go around like this,
Squares go around like this,
Squares go around like this.
(Make square shapes with hands.)

Triangles

Triangles go around like this,
Triangles go around like this,
Triangles go around like this,
Triangles go around like this.
(Make triangle shapes with hands.)
Continue with little squares, big squares, etc…

196

Shapes Blindfold Game *(cont.)*

Shape Patterns

Circle

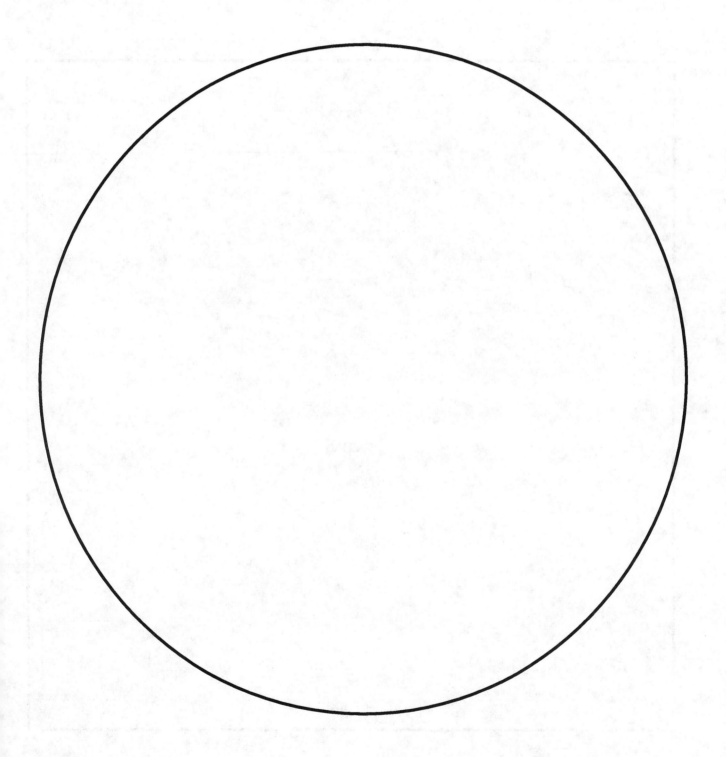

Shapes Blindfold Game *(cont.)*

Shape Patterns *(cont.)*

Square

Shapes Blindfold Game *(cont.)*

Shape Patterns *(cont.)*

Triangle

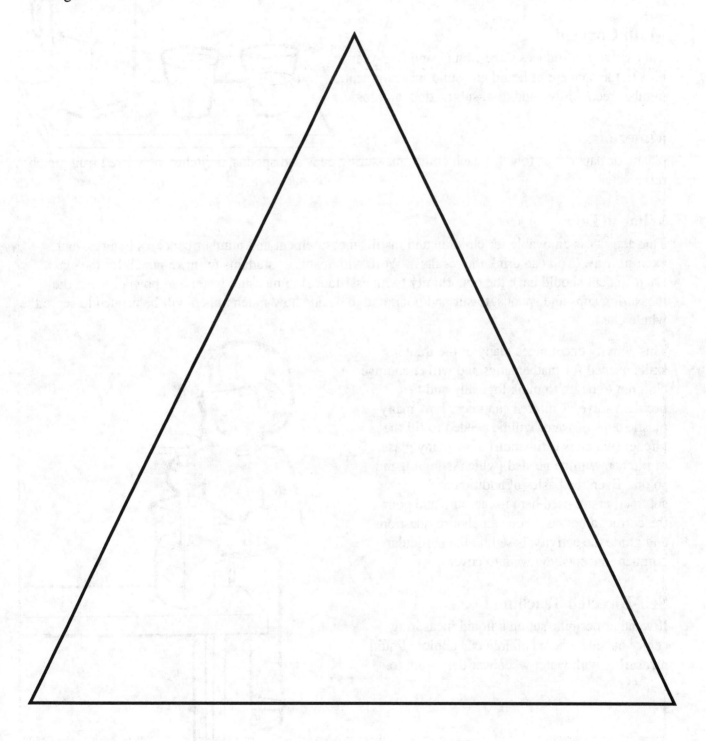

Tea Party!

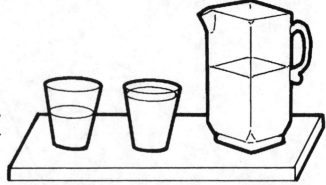

Preparation Time:

Thirty minutes

Math Concept:

This activity introduces three-, four-, and five-year-olds to the concept of liquid and solid measurement, number recognition, addition, subtraction, and logic.

Materials:

plastic or paper cups (one for each child), measuring cups and spoons, a pitcher, powdered fruit punch mix, water

What to Do:

This activity is enjoyable for children and instills measurement and number concepts in a relevant, exciting way. (You can drink the results!) Work with teams of students to make punch for the class. Each student should have the opportunity (with assistance) to measure water and powder using the measuring cups and spoons, to stir and pour, and to decide how much punch will be needed to serve the whole class.

This activity encourages many of the thinking skills needed for mathematics and will encourage children to begin to think logically and to problem solve. Children can guess how many plastic cups of water will be needed to fill the pitcher (which is estimation), how many glasses or pitchers will be needed (which is logic), and so on. Even the basics of addition and subtraction are used here to measure and pour the correct amounts. You can choose questions and guide the activity, based on the particular number concepts you wish to cover.

Self-Directed Teaching Focus:

If weather permits, set up a liquid measuring center outside where children can explore liquid measuring with water whenever they want to.

Tea Party! *(cont.)*

Directed Teaching Focus:

Measurement of food (or drink) is basically a directed activity.

What to Say:

Today we are all going to work together to make a special treat for the class. We are going to make fruit punch. First, we are going to measure the powder with these. These are called measuring spoons. They will tell us how much powder to put in our punch.

Then we will measure water with these. These are called measuring cups. After we are done, everyone will get to drink fruit punch. Now I'm going to read the directions. We need six cups of water and three spoonfuls of powder. Here are six cups…

(Model the activity, showing the children six cups and demonstrating how to fill them up and pour them into the pitcher, etc. Interact with small groups, allowing children to take charge of the activity whenever possible and providing assistance when needed. Words like "less," "more," "enough," "a little," "a lot," etc., should be used to begin to give children a working mathematical vocabulary. For example, you can say, "If we pour a glass for Jess, will there be less punch in the pitcher or more?" and "What will happen if we keeping pouring punch for everyone in the class?")

Doing More:

Make measuring cups and spoons available for play in the sandbox. Use measuring equipment to measure solids, sand, rice, popcorn, etc.

Evaluation and Processing Through Storytelling:

Encourage students to explain how they measured the water for the punch. Write down their dictated explanations for parents to enjoy.

Tea Party! *(cont.)*
NAEYC Appropriate Practices

Appropriate Practice:

Three-Year-Olds

"Adults provide opportunities for three-year-olds to demonstrate and practice their newly developed self-help skills and their desire to help adults…with feeding themselves. Adults are patient with occasional spilled food and unfinished jobs."

Concept Connection:

This activity, while introducing measurement and number concepts, allows children to help the teacher with a "grown-up" task. By interacting and supporting children in the process, the teacher helps children to become acquainted successfully with real-life skills.

Appropriate Practice:

Four- and Five-Year-Olds

"Children's natural curiosity and desire to make sense of their world are used to motivate them to become involved in learning activities."

Concept Connection:

This activity gives children hands-on experience with a real-life situation by actually experiencing and taking part in making punch. Having the opportunity to do something that a grown-up might normally do for them is very motivating.

Appropriate Practice:

Four- and Five-Year-Olds

"Children develop understanding of concepts about themselves, others, and the world around them through content areas (that) are all integrated through meaningful activities such as measuring water or ingredients for cooking."

Concept Connection:

This activity integrates math concepts into a concrete experience. Children measure, pour, and mix ingredients for fruit punch, experiencing a real-life situation that enhances their understanding of their own world.

How Tall Am I?

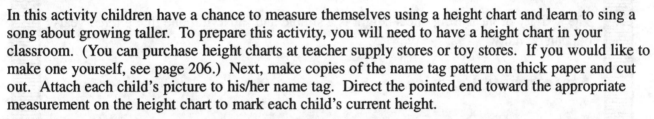

Preparation Time:

One hour

Math Concept:

This activity introduces three-, four- and five-year-olds to the concept of measurement in feet and inches, addition, logic, and one-to-one correspondence. This may be adapted fo metric measurement.

Materials:

measuring strip (page 206), "How Tall Am I?" name tags (page 207), "We Grow Taller Every Day" song (page 205)

What to Do:

In this activity children have a chance to measure themselves using a height chart and learn to sing a song about growing taller. To prepare this activity, you will need to have a height chart in your classroom. (You can purchase height charts at teacher supply stores or toy stores. If you would like to make one yourself, see page 206.) Next, make copies of the name tag pattern on thick paper and cut out. Attach each child's picture to his/her name tag. Direct the pointed end toward the appropriate measurement on the height chart to mark each child's current height.

Begin this activity by showing children the height chart and mentioning that the numbers on the chart relate to feet and inches. Model the heights of several children and use the words "feet" and "inches" to describe their heights. Point out the numbers on the height chart and let children name them. Then ask several children to measure themselves and have children compare who is taller and who is shorter.

Next, teach children the "We Grow Taller Every Day" song. Sing this song when children are measuring themselves. You will want to leave the chart up and periodically allow children to measure themselves and adjust their name tags to their new heights.

Self-Directed Teaching Focus:

To self-direct this activity, let children re-measure themselves anytime they want to. Some children will choose to do this daily.

Directed Teaching Focus:

Direct this activity by having children sing "We Grow Taller Every Day." The children will want to sing this song again and again and will enjoy singing the name of the person being measured.

What to Say:

Today we are going to see how tall we all are! Look over here at our new measuring chart. We can see how tall we are by using it. These little spaces are called inches and twelve inches added together equal a foot. When we measure ourselves, we talk about feet and inches. Who wants to try? (Model activity with a number of students.) Now I am going to teach a song we can sing while we are being measured. Let's all sing this together, and we will sing the name of the person we are measuring. Let's try it!

Evaluation and Processing Through Storytelling:

Have children dictate "When I Was Small" stories.

How Tall Am I? *(cont.)*

NAEYC Appropriate Practices

Appropriate Practices:

Three-Year-Olds

"Adults provide opportunities for three-year-olds to demonstrate newly developed self-help skills."

Concept Connection:

The activity of measuring one's height is a simple and satisfying one that a three-year-old can do daily.

Appropriate Practice:

Four- and Five-Year-Olds

"Teachers recognize that children learn from self-directed experimentation."

Concept Connection:

This activity provides children with a daily opportunity for experimentation.

Appropriate Practice:

Four- and Five-Year-Olds

"Children are provided many opportunities to see how reading and writing are useful."

Concept Connection:

Children can tell by taking part in measuring themselves that it is useful to be able to read names, to recognize numbers, etc.

How Tall Am I? *(cont.)*

"We Grow Taller Every Day" Song

(Sing to the tune of "Mary Had a Little Lamb.")

We grow taller every day,

Every day,

Every day,

We grow taller every day,

Look how tall _____ is!

(Insert a child's name into song and sing
as he/she measures him/herself.)

How Tall Am I? *(cont.)*

Height Chart

Copy the measuring strips on this page onto tagboard or heavy construction paper and tape together to make your own height chart. Each strip is 6" long (15.5 cm).

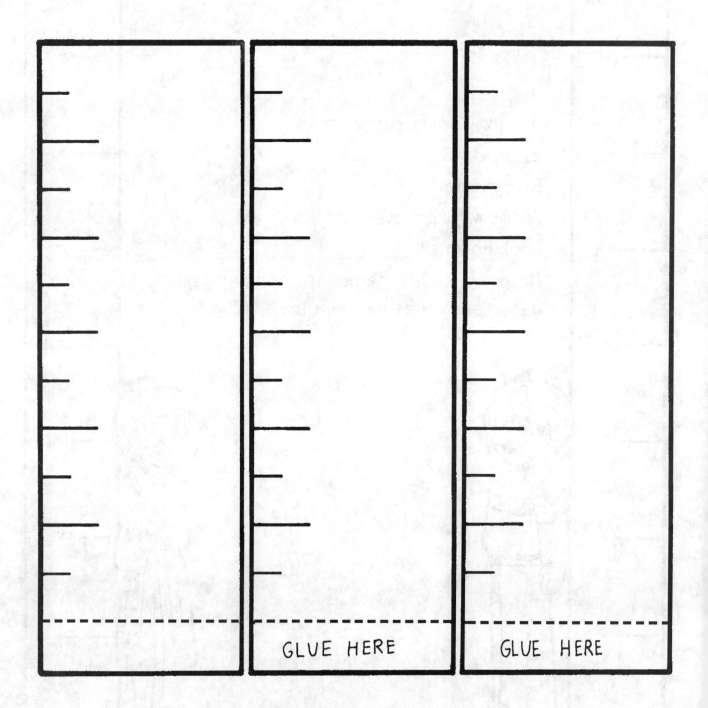

How Tall Am I? *(cont.)*
Name Tags

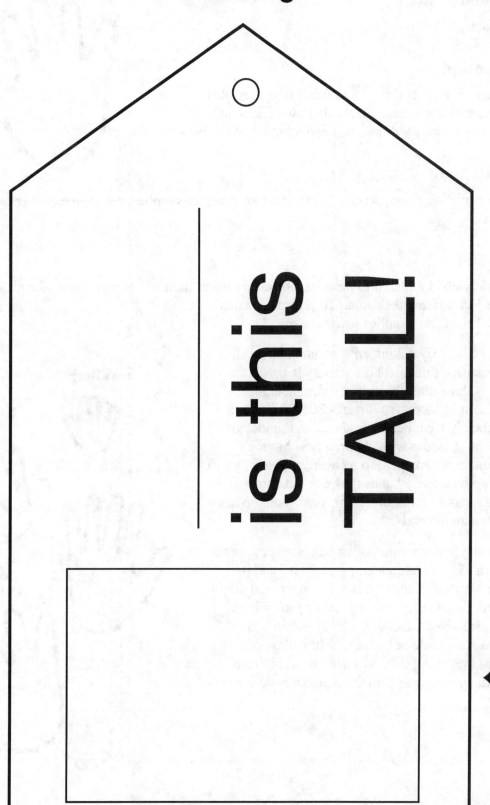

is this TALL!

Attach picture here.

Hand Measuring

Preparation Time:

Little or none

Math Concept:

This activity introduces three-, four-, and five-year-olds to the concept of measurement, number awareness and recognition, counting, addition, and estimation.

Materials:

colored construction paper, scissors, tape, paste or glue, art supplies, rulers, measuring tape, yardstick (meterstick)

What to Do:

In this activity children learn to measure objects by using their hands and then make hand patterns to measure objects around the room. To prepare for this activity, gather the art supplies listed above.

Begin this activity by talking with children about the idea of measuring things. (This activity is particularly useful if it is done after the children complete the "How Tall Am I?" activity on pages 203–207. Then they will already have been introduced to the idea of measurement. Discuss with children how big their hands are and then ask them to measure a table in your room, seeing how many hands they can put across it. Have them measure other objects in your room. Model the activity with the class.

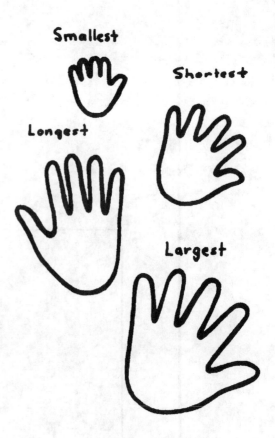

Next, help children trace their own hands and cut out a hand pattern. Have children compare their hand patterns. Use words like smaller, larger, longer, and shorter. This will enable them to start seeing things in the context of size. Next, use all the hand patterns to stretch across the table or the rug. Ask children how many hands they think they will need to reach from one place to another (this utilizes estimation skills).

Hand Measuring *(cont.)*

Self-Directed Teaching Focus:

Let children use their hand patterns, tape measures, rulers, and/or yardsticks (metersticks) to measure things around the classroom.

Directed Teaching Focus:

Guide children in the hand-measuring exercise. Play a "Who can measure fastest?" game or "Who can find the longest thing, the shortest thing, etc.?"

What to Say:

Today we are going to learn more about measuring. Remember when we all measured how tall we were? That was fun, wasn't it? Today we are going to use our hands to measure things. Let me show you. I can find out how many hands long this pencil is, or this desk, or the door. Let's all try it. Now we are going to trace our hands to make a hand cut-out. We will put these all together and see how long they are. That will be fun. Let's try!

Doing More:

Introduce children to rulers and yardsticks. Talk with children about what kinds of people use things to measure in their jobs. Ask a handyman friend to bring in his/her equipment and show how things are measured. Talk about why we might measure things at home (e.g., measuring a floor for carpet, measuring the depth of a pool, etc.).

Evaluation and Processing Through Storytelling:

Have children talk about the longest walk they ever took, or the highest place they ever saw, or the deepest ocean. Encourage them to discuss anything that introduces measuring words.

Hand Measuring *(cont.)*

NAEYC Appropriate Practices

Appropriate Practices:

Three-Year-Olds

"Adults recognize that three-year-olds are not comfortable with much group participation."

Concept Connection:

This activity is perfect for solitary play. A child does not have to interact with others to have fun measuring.

Appropriate Practice:

Four- and Five-Year-Olds

"Teachers prepare the environment for children to learn through active exploration."

Concept Connection:

The concept of measuring can be explored again and again; and, as a child does so, he/she learns about the environment.

Appropriate Practice:

Four- and Five-Year-Olds

"Teachers recognize that children learn from self-directed problem solving and experimentation."

Concept Connection:

Children are involved in a variety of experiments and problem-solving situations by making hand measurements.

Can You Set the Table?

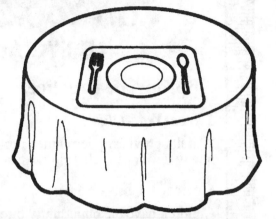

Preparation Time:

Fifteen minutes

Math Concept:

This activity introduces three-, four-, and five-year-olds to one-to-one correspondence and sets.

Materials:

plastic spoons and forks, colored construction paper

What to Do:

Most preschool facilities have playhouse and play kitchen setups. If this is the case in your facility, setup will be very easy. If you do not have playhouse setups, standard tables or desks may be used as tables. You can use plastic spoons and forks for eating utensils and sheets of colored construction paper for place mats. Make table settings available to children on a regular basis or use this activity during snack time.

Each child should have the opportunity to set the table, placing a place mat, a fork, and a spoon. Three-year-olds will be able to recognize the meaning of the activity and set a place for themselves. Four- and five-year-olds may be inspired to take the activity further, creating a playhouse situation and having a meal, etc.

Self-Directed Teaching Focus:

Leave table-setting supplies available in your house or kitchen center so children can set the table and role-play whenever they want to.

Directed Teaching Focus:

Review the table-setting process on a regular basis at circle time. Have individual students volunteer to show how they would set the table.

What to Say:

Today, we will have a chance to do something helpful just like grown-ups do. We are going to set the table. Does anyone know what this is? (Hold up a fork.) Yes, that's right. It's a fork. What do we use it for? (Encourage children to discuss their knowledge of forks and what they are used for. Repeat the same question and discussion with both the spoon and the place mat. Reinforce responses and offer information instead of correcting.) I am going to set a place for me. First, I put the place mat down, and then I put the fork here, and then I put the spoon here. Now, I'm going to close my eyes and think of my favorite thing to eat. My favorite thing is chocolate ice cream! If you would like, set the table and then tell me your favorite thing to eat. (You may wish to write the favorite food and name of each child on a place mat to use for a bulletin board display.)

Doing More:

Have children parallel-play in groups of two, setting the table and playing house. This is a cooperative-learning readiness activity.

Evaluation and Processing Through Storytelling:

Have children dictate stories about setting the table at home. Write their stories on paper place mats for display.

Can You Set the Table? *(cont.)*
NAEYC Appropriate Practices

Appropriate Practice:

Three-Year-Olds

"Adults provide opportunities for three-year-olds to demonstrate and practice their newly developed self-help skills and desire to help adults with setting the table."

Concept Connection:

Children have the opportunity through the activity to reinforce a newly-learned self-help skill and be encouraged and supported in their attempts.

Appropriate Practice:

Three-Year-Olds

"Adults provide many opportunities for three-year-olds to play by themselves or parallel play. Adults recognize that three-year-olds are not comfortable with much group participation."

Concept Connection:

The activity is set up so children may play individually while having an opportunity to share their results and look for support from an interested teacher. The activity also lends itself to parallel play.

Appropriate Practice:

Four- and Five-Year-Olds

"If learning is relevant for children, they are more likely to persist with a task and be motivated to learn more."

Concept Connection:

Setting the table is a relevant and exciting task for four- and five-year-olds because it gives them the opportunity to model adult behavior and reenact something that happens in their everyday lives.

Appropriate Practice:

Four- and Five-Year-Olds

"Children develop understanding of the world around them through observations, interacting with people and real objects, and seeking solutions to real problems."

Concept Connection:

This activity gives children the opportunity to handle real objects used daily and to understand their purpose and usefulness in an authentic setting.

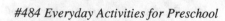

Play-Money Banks

Preparation Time:

Few to several hours

Math Concept:

This activity introduces three-, four-, and five-year-olds to money concepts, as well as counting, addition and subtraction, logic and estimation.

Materials:

money banks and play money (See pages 216–219.)

What to Do:

In this activity children enjoy playing with their own play banks. In addition, they learn about pennies, nickels, dimes, and quarters while reinforcing the math concepts of counting, addition, subtraction, and estimation. To prepare for this activity, make one bank and one set of play money for each child. You can have children help you by decorating their own banks.

Begin this activity by talking with children about money. (You may have already made some kind of cash register setup in the restaurant activity on page 89.)

Children love to play with money. The idea of having their own banks to play with pleases most children. You may wish to let children take their banks home after this activity to use as a real bank at home. Discuss pennies, nickels, dimes, and quarters with children. Talk about what kinds of things you can buy with each. (Most children of four or five will have some kind of understanding about what candy costs, etc.)

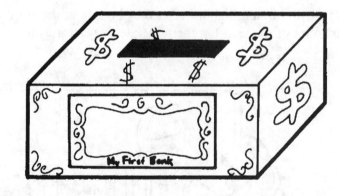

Then give each child a play bank. See if children can pick out the penny, the nickel, the dime, and the quarter. You may wish to have children use these banks as part of an already existing center or have them play bank, store, or any other kind of game where money is involved,

Self-Directed Teaching Focus:

Place the play money and the banks in each of your centers where money will be part of the role-playing fun. Encourage children to use it. A simple cash register can be made out of any cardboard box, even a shoe box.

Play–Money Banks *(cont.)*

Directed Teaching Focus:

Have children all sit with their money in front of them. Have children hold up a penny, a nickel, a dime, and a quarter. Try to guess how many pennies it takes to make a nickel and then show the children. Use words like "let's guess, let's estimate, let's count," etc.

What to Say:

We have something new and exciting for our classroom. I have made us some play–money banks. How many people here have a real piggy bank or a bank where they keep money at home? (Hold a class discussion.)

Can anyone tell me what this is? (Hold up each coin and explain.) How many pennies do we have here? Let's count them—one, two, three, four, five—we have five pennies. We can put these in our banks. Let's try that. We can use these banks in our store center and use the play money for our cash register, or we can use the money in our restaurant. That will be fun. Now let's look at the nickels (repeat for the dimes and quarters).

Show children bills in various amounts: one-, five-, and ten-dollar bills. Talk about what you can buy for these amounts. Use relevant things that children are interested in owning. For example, a stuffed animal costs about ten dollars. You would either need ten ones, or two fives, or a ten.

Add play dollars to your centers so children can be around pretend currency and use it in their imaginative play. Again, it is the exposure to these concepts, not the mastery, that you are interested in.

Evaluation and Processing Through Storytelling:

Have children tell about what they bought at the store or what they would do if they had a certain amount of money. Let them dictate these stories to you.

Play-Money Banks *(cont.)*
NAEYC Appropriate Practices

Appropriate Practice:

Three-Year-Olds

"Adults provide large amounts of uninterrupted time for children to persist at self-chosen tasks."

Concept Connection:

This activity lends itself to the kind of concentrated, self-directed, solitary play that appeals to three-year-olds.

Appropriate Practice:

Four- and Five-Year-Olds

"If learning is relevant for children, they are more likely to persist with a task and to be motivated to learn more."

Concept Connection:

This activity is relevant to the lives of four- and five-year-olds because they are becoming interested in how much things cost and how much money they will need to buy something.

Appropriate Practice:

Four- and Five-Year-Olds

"Children are provided concrete learning activities with materials and people relevant to their own life experiences."

Concept Connection:

This activity allows children the opportunity to practice handling money in a secure and stress-free environment."

Play-Money Banks *(cont.)*

Coin Patterns

Copy onto tagboard or heavy paper and cut out.

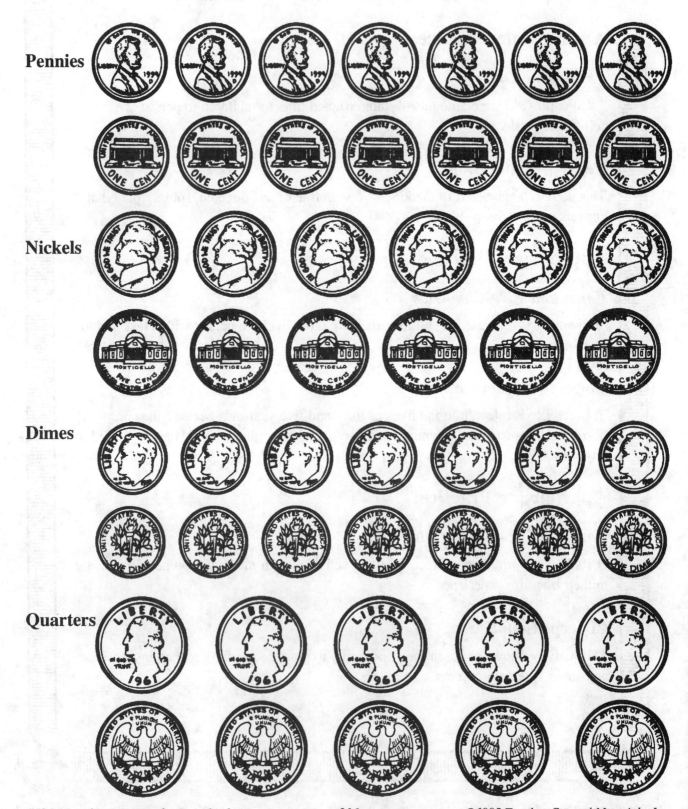

Play–Money Banks *(cont.)*

Currency Patterns

Copy onto paper (preferably green, if you want to be more realistic) and cut out.

$1.00

$5.00

$10.00

Play-Money Banks *(cont.)*

Make a Bank

Each child in your classroom should have his or her own play bank in which to store play money. You can make these banks yourself or have the children help with the decorations.

Materials:

small gift boxes or square boxes purchased from a crafts store, art supplies, scissors, craft knife, wrapping or colored paper, tape, glue

What to Do:

1. Place lid on box and seal with tape.

2. Cover box with wrapping or colored paper.

3. Color or paint bank labels (see page 219), cut out, and glue to the box.

4. Cut a 1" x 3" (2.5cm x 7.5cm) money slot in the lid, using a craft knife or scissors.

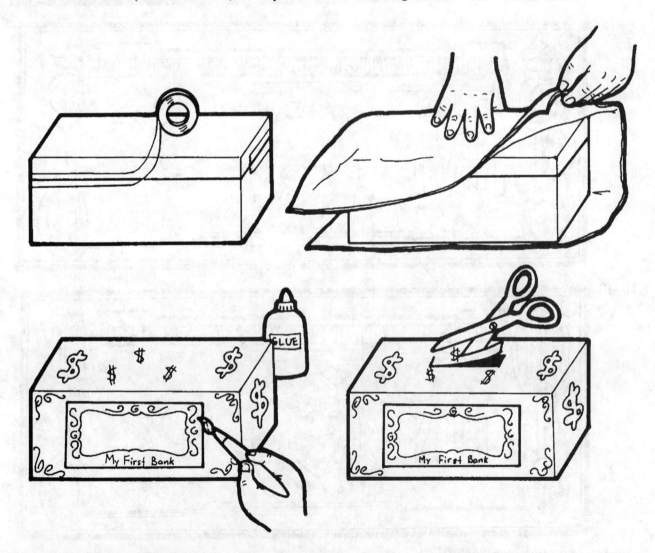

Play–Money Banks (cont.)
Bank Labels

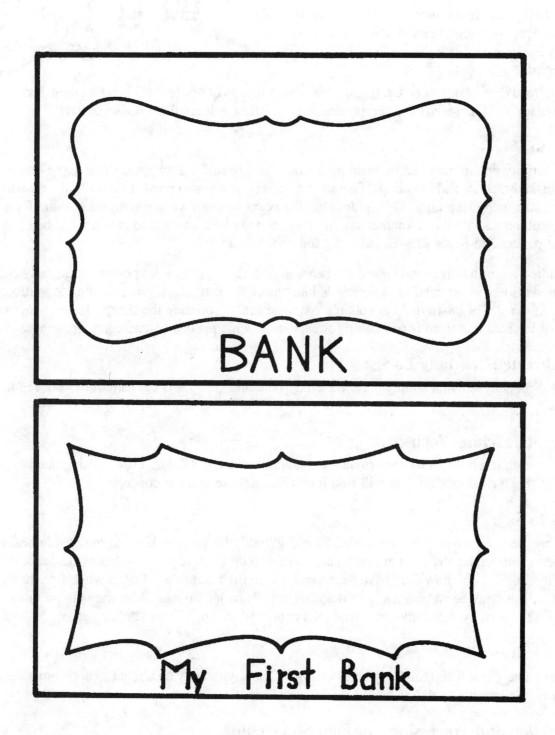

Teddy-Bear Addition and Subtraction

Preparation Time:

One to two hours

Math Concept:

This activity introduces three-, four-, and five-year-olds to the concept of addition, subtraction, and counting.

Materials:

sleeping teddy bears in sets of ten (page 223), sheep in sets of ten (page 224), Sleeping Teddy Bear rhyme (page 222), large box for bed (or cradle or existing doll cradle in house center)

What to Do:

In this activity children will enjoy learning a teddy-bear rhyme that exposes them to the concepts of addition, subtraction, and counting. There are a variety of ways to present this activity. A simple way is to set up a teddy bear crib. Let children put the bears to sleep when the rhyme is said. Even very young children can do this. Another way to use the teddy bear game is to create a felt-board activity. Use the patterns on pages 223–224 to make felt board characters.

As children learn the rhyme and place the bears in bed, they will have exposure to the early concepts behind addition and subtraction. Use words like "more," "less," "all," "none," etc., to reinforce these ideas. At the end of the rhyme, let children have the fun of counting the sheep. Help children become aware of the idea that there is one sheep for each bear, which is one-to-one correspondence.

Self-Directed Teaching Focus:

To self-direct this activity, simply leave the teddy bear and sheep sets out as part of your regular center activities.

Directed Teaching Focus:

Teach your children the teddy bear rhyme and practice it daily. Children love to sing and say rhymes together. Each time they do, you will find it reinforces these number concepts.

What to Say:

Today we are going to play a game called Sleeping Teddy Bears. Look at our new teddy bears and their bed. (Model activity.) Aren't they cute! Let's count them to see how many there are. There are ten teddy bears. Look how they have their numbers on their tummies. Listen while I recite the rhyme and show you how the game goes. (Model activity). Now let's try it. Who wants to put a teddy bear to bed? (Try activity with children.) And let's count the sheep. (Complete the activity.)

Doing More:

Play the same game with real teddy bears or toys. The rhyme may be altered to accommodate any of the children's favorite "pals."

Evaluation and Processing Through Storytelling:

Let children tell stories about going to bed.

Teddy Bear Addition and Subtraction *(cont.)*

NAEYC Appropriate Practices

Appropriate Practice:

Three-Year-Olds

"Adults provide many opportunities for three-year-olds to play by themselves."

Concept Connection:

This activity lends itself to self-directed play that is perfect for three-year-olds.

Appropriate Practice:

Four- and Five-Year-Olds

"An abundance of these types of activities is provided (participating in dramatic play and other experiences requiring communication)."

Concept Connection:

This activity provides children with an opportunity to participate in dramatic play using the figures of sleeping teddy bears and sheep to demonstrate a counting rhyme.

Appropriate Practice:

Four- and Five-Year-Olds

"Teachers prepare the environment for children to learn through active exploration and interaction with adults, other children, and materials."

Concept Connection:

Children have the opportunity to manipulate a variety of materials in this activity.

Teddy–Bear Addition and Subtraction

(cont.)

Sleeping Teddy Bears

Teddy bear, teddy bear,
Go to bed!
Rest your little sleepy head,
Teddy bear, teddy bear,
Go to bed,
Now there is one!
  (Replace with "Now there are two,
  three, four," etc., up to ten.)
Now the teddy bears are all asleep.
Let's help them stay asleep by counting sheep.
1..2..3..4..5..6..7..8..9..10!

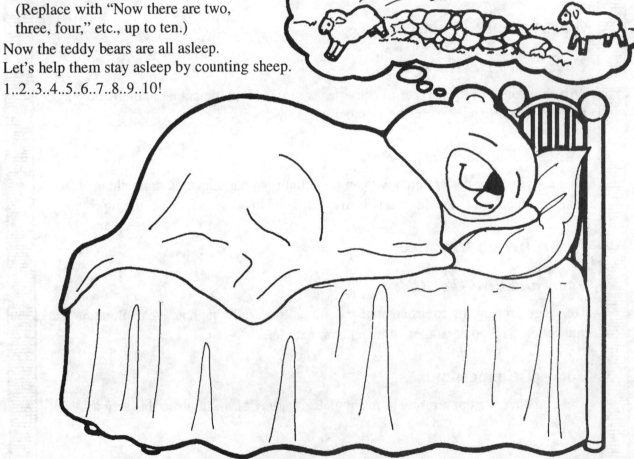

222

Teddy-Bear Addition and Subtraction *(cont.)*
Sleeping Teddy Pattern

Copy onto heavy paper, tagboard, or felt. In the circle on the teddy bear, write the numerals 1-10.

Teddy–Bear Addition and Subtraction *(cont.)*
Sheep Pattern

Copy onto heavy paper, tagboard, or felt. In the circle on the sheep, write the numerals 1-10.

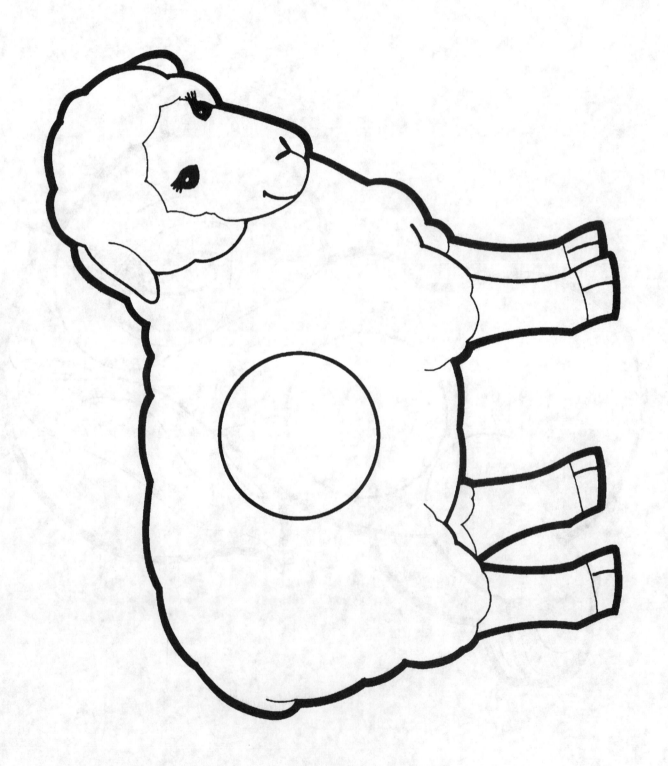

Table of Contents for Science and Curiosity

Mud-Pie Bakery

Preparation Time:

Several hours

Science and Curiosity Concept:

In this activity children gain creativity and competency in a hands-on activity. Children also experience the environment by experimenting with a variety of natural materials.

Materials:

mud, dirt, sand, rocks, twigs, leaves, etc. (This activity works best in an outdoor setting; however, it can be done indoors if you use sensory, sand, or water tables.)

What to Do:

To prepare this activity you will need a variety of kitchen tools and pie tins that will never see the inside of a house again. Use the parent volunteer letter on page 394 to request supplies you may not have at your preschool.

You may wish to prepare "pie ingredients" and place them in an inviting bakery setup with work stations, or you may prefer more of a pie free-for-all. Some teachers may wish to set up several stations (e.g., a mixing station, a baking station, a decorating station). This is a way to let children decide jobs and delegate and also make space for each other.

The following is a list of absolute necessities. You may wish to add more to this list.

- ❖ aprons or old, large shirts
- ❖ pie tins
- ❖ baskets or laundry hampers to hold baking equipment
- ❖ old, large spoons; spatulas; and other kitchen gadgets (Check for safety.)
- ❖ shovels and trowels (Make sure these are sturdy; real ones are better than play tools.)
- ❖ old cookie sheets
- ❖ plastic or metal mixing bowls and buckets for water, sand, and mud
- ❖ natural decorations: old leaves, twigs, acorns, seed pods, rocks, sand, flowers (To prevent any problems, check to be sure the plants you use are nontoxic.)

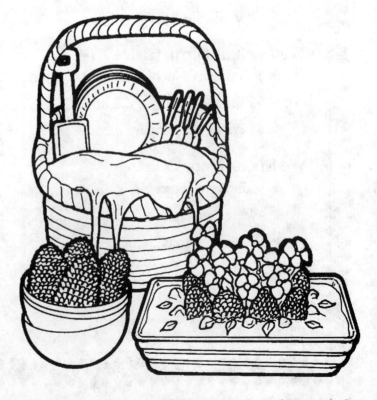

Mud-Pie Bakery *(cont.)*

What to Do *(cont.)*:

Another idea that works well is a pie bake-off. Let children enter their best pies in a pie contest. Serve real pie as a group prize. (Serve this outside before cleanup so you only have to clean up once.)

Self-Directed Teaching Focus:

After setting up the mud-pie center, leave it as part of your outdoor play center.

Directed Teaching Focus:

Any directed portion of this activity, like a pie-judging contest, will serve as a directed format for this activity.

What to Say:

Today we are going to work in our very own mud-pie bakery. I have set it up for us outside. Let's all come and take a look at it. How many children here have made mud pies before? They are lots of fun to make! (Model activity and center for children.) Okay, let's all have fun!

Doing More:

Vary the tools and supplies at your mud-pie bakery. Children can make bread, cake, cookies, or whatever they think would be a tasty addition to their bakery's inventory.

Evaluation and Processing Through Storytelling:

Have children dictate stories about their favorite pies or have them describe what they like best about playing in the mud.

Mud-Pie Bakery *(cont.)*

NAEYC Appropriate Practices

Appropriate Practice:

Three-Year-Olds

"Adults provide plenty of materials and time for children to explore and learn about the environment, to exercise their natural curiosity, and to experiment with cause and effect relationships."

Concept Connection:

This activity gives children an opportunity to enjoy experimenting with and combining dirt, sand, water, and other natural materials.

Appropriate Practice:

Four- and Five-Year-Olds

"Children develop understanding about themselves, others, and the world around them through observation, interacting with people and real objects."

Concept Connection:

This activity allows children to observe and interact with real objects in the environment.

Appropriate Practice:

Four- and Five-Year-Olds

"Outdoor activity is planned daily so children can learn about outdoor environments and express themselves."

Concept Connection:

This activity is best performed outdoors. It brings children into contact with natural objects and allows them to express themselves freely.

Nature Sort

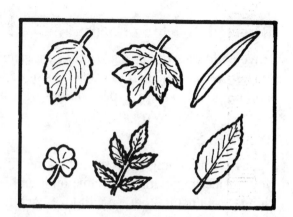

Preparation Time:

One hour or less

Science and Curiosity Concept:

This activity introduces three-, four-, and five-year-olds to the idea of observation, a foundation of science. (Additionally, this activity crosses over to math concepts of sorting, matching, addition, subtraction, and counting.)

Materials:

a small paper bag for each child (lunch bags work fine), large pieces of construction paper in a variety of colors

What to Do:

In this activity children collect nature samples and then work together to sort them. To prepare for this activity, all you need is your preschool yard or an available park and a paper bag for each child.

Begin this activity by explaining to children that they will all be collecting interesting items from nature. You may wish to let them know that they may collect only things that are lying on the ground. (This will prevent industrious children from uprooting plants!)

After children have collected a variety of samples, ask each child to pour his or her nature sample onto a large piece of construction paper that will serve as a sorting mat. (To do this activity again and again and save paper, laminate your sorting mats.) Be sure to look over each child's collection for things that should be returned outside, like bugs, worms, or anything you feel uncomfortable sorting.

Next, ask children to separate their leaves into a pile. Then ask children to put their leaves on a separate piece of paper. This will be the "leaf mat." You can have separate mats for rocks, pine cones, twigs, acorns, or whatever else children find. Another way to sort the items is by color and shape. For example, have children first sort all the green leaves and then all the green leaves that are little. Use words like same, different, big, little, a lot, a few, etc. This will give children a basic science/math vocabulary and begin to set a base for later skills.

You may wish to complete the activity by making mounted displays. Simply glue or paste the samples to the construction paper for a bulletin board or take-home display. Heavy samples may need a little tape.

Self-Directed Teaching Focus:

After the initial direction of the activity, children have a self-directed experience collecting their samples. Be sure to be available to assist them in decision making regarding their samples, etc. Also, if the sorting mats are laminated, this activity can be done again and again and can be placed in your preschool for self-directed play.

Nature Sort *(cont.)*

Directed Teaching Focus:

Have children work as a group to sort specific samples from their piles. Or ask children to collect only leaves one day and sort in categories of big, little, large, small, colors, textures, appearance, shiny, smooth, rough, etc. The possibilities for sorting are almost endless.

What to Say:

Today we are going to do something outside. We are going to have a nature sort! I will give each of you a paper bag with your name on it and in a few minutes, we will all go outside and find interesting things from nature that we will take back in the classroom to look at. Now first, let's talk about the things that we may choose.

It's very important not to choose anything alive. Do we all know what that means? That means we should not pull up a plant or pick a flower or take a bug or a little animal. We are looking for things like fallen leaves, little rocks, acorns, and twigs. You may take things that have fallen to the ground. (Model the activity and have children go outside and select their nature items.)

Now let's show all the pretty natural things we have found and take a look at them. I see that Sarah has collected many different and pretty leaves. Sarah, you've chosen leaves of many different colors. Let's all put our leaves on a separate mat. Can everyone bring up one leaf and put it here? Great. Look at all the leaves. Does anyone see a green leaf? Let's put our green leaves here. Great. Now we have sorted out the green leaves. We have a lot of green leaves. We have more green leaves than brown leaves, don't we? (Continue with different nature items.)

Doing More:

There are a variety of different items to sort in your classroom. Do the same activity with small toys or game pieces (and get your games organized at the same time).

Evaluation and Processing Through Storytelling:

After making nature pictures with the collections children have found, let children tell you about their pictures. Write their descriptions on the pictures.

Nature Sort *(cont.)*

NAEYC Appropriate Practices

Appropriate Practice:

Three-Year-Olds

"Adults provide plenty of materials and time for children to explore and learn about the environment, to exercise their natural curiosity, and to experiment with cause and effect relationships."

Concept Connection:

This activity provides three-year-olds a chance to have hands-on experience with their immediate environment, and to satisfy their natural curiosity about nature and the world around them.

Appropriate Practice:

Four- and Five-Year-Olds

"Experiences are provided that meet children's needs and stimulate learning in all developmental areas."

Concept Connection:

Children have a need to understand their environment. This activity lets four and five-year-olds gather information and ask questions about what they see.

Appropriate Practice:

Four- and Five-Year-Olds

"Children develop understanding of concepts about themselves, others, and the world around them through observation, interacting with people and real objects, and seeking solutions to concrete problems."

Concept Connection:

In this activity four and five-year-olds gain actual experience observing real obejects in a context that increases their knowledge.

Garden Explorers

Preparation Time:
Little or none

Science and Curiosity Concept:
This activity introduces three-, four-, and five-year-olds to the concepts of observation, comparison, investigation, and logical thinking.

Materials:
grassy area large enough for children to lie down, a long piece of string for each child (at least 40"/100cm long), towels or mats for children to lie on (optional)

What to Do:
In this activity children lie on the grass and look at their own "bug towns," investigating the tiny bugs and insects that pass through their very own circles. To prepare for this activity, all that is needed is a grassy area large enough for children to lie on. Each child should have a piece of string to make a circle on the grass to focus his/her attention.

Begin this activity by reading the story called "I Live in the Garden" on page 293. Let them know that they are going to have a chance to watch their own bugs. Have children lie on the grass and focus their attention within their string circles to see how many living creatures they can see. Interact with children, encouraging their discovery and assisting when necessary. Encourage children to talk about what they see.

Self-Directed Teaching Focus:
Encourage children to make string circles on the grass whenever they want to look at insects during outdoor time. Listen to their observations.

Directed Teaching Focus:
Set aside a definite time each week to repeat this activity with the whole class.

What to Say:
Today we are going to have fun looking at how bugs live. Let's all go outside and lie on the grass and see how many different bugs we can see. Then we will talk about them.

We will look for all the bugs we heard about in the story I just read. Who can remember what kinds of bugs we heard about? (Class discussion.)

Doing More:
Have children paint or draw pictures of the bugs and insects they saw.

Evaluation and Processing Through Storytelling:
Have children dictate stories about what they saw in their garden explorations.

Garden Explorers *(cont.)*

NAEYC Appropriate Practices

Appropriate Practice:

Three-Year-Olds

"Adults recognize that three-year-olds are not comfortable with much group participation."

Concept Connection:

This activity allows three-year-olds to spend time playing in a solitary or parallel manner.

Appropriate Practice:

Four- and Five-Year-Olds

"Teachers accept that there is often more than one right answer."

Concept Connection:

This activity allows children to have personal experiences. There is no incorrect way to do it and no incorrect outcome.

Appropriate Practice:

Four- and Five-Year-Olds

"Children are expected to be mentally active."

Concept Connection:

In this activity children must use a variety of thinking skills to observe, to process information, and to form conclusions.

My Voice Recording

Preparation Time:
One hour

Science and Curiosity Concept:
In this activity three-, four-, and five-year-olds gain increased self-expression and creativity through voice awareness (body awareness).

Materials:
two tape recorders, two tape cassettes, teacher voice script on page 235

What to Do:
In this activity children will have the opportunity to experiment with the sounds of their own voices and hear their own voices recorded on a tape recorder. To set up this activity, simply place two operational tape recorders in your music/dance center, one with a blank tape and one with a prerecorded teacher voice tape (page 235).

The prerecorded teacher voice tape will provide children with ideas about voice sounds; the use of this tape will help make this activity self-directed. (Make sure that after recording your voice tape that you punch out the two square plastic pieces in the top of your cassette tape, thus preventing little fingers from accidentally recording over it.)

To begin this activity, let children hear the teacher voice tape at circle time. Inform them that this new activity will be available for them to try in their music center. Model the use of the tape recorders and make sure that each child has an understanding of how to use them before you place them in the center.

Self-Directed Teaching Focus:
After initial explanation of activity, make the voice recording center available to children. This works well as part of the dance/music center.

Directed Teaching Focus:
Read the teacher voice script as a group exercise and forgo the recording step.

What to Say:
Today we'll be experimenting with taping your voices. Can anyone tell me what this is? (Display tape recorders and model their use.) How many of you have used a tape recorder like this before? I was sure some of you had! Now let's all listen to a tape I made. After you hear it, I will put it in our music center and you may all use it whenever you want to make recordings of your own voices. Won't that be fun? (Play voice tape and set up center activity.)

Doing More:
Keep individual children's voice recordings separate by giving each child a tape to use and keep in his/her cubby. These tapes can later be saved as a permanent voice record or family keepsake.

Evaluation and Processing Through Storytelling:
Use tape recorder for children to record oral stories and share by playing their own tapes during circle time.

My Voice Recording *(cont.)*

Teacher Voice Script

Remember that there are many ways to create a voice tape. You may enhance these ideas with themes and ideas familiar to your children, or use this voice tape to lead your children in the direction you think is most beneficial.

Record your tape after your children go home and your facility is quiet. Take your phone off the hook so a perfect rendition of the ABC song won't be ruined by a phone call! Play it back, and record it again until you are happy with it. (You do not have to be a singer to have fun recording a song, and being comfortable with your own voice is one of the gifts you can give your children, and maybe even yourself.)

Script

Isn't it fun to use a tape recorder? I am recording my voice. I will say my name!

My name is _____

My last name is_____

I know how to laugh (laugh into the tape recorder). I can whisper like this (whisper into the recorder). I can even make a funny voice like this (make a funny sound). I know a song. I will sing it for you. (Sing a common song like the ABC song.) That's all for now! Bye, bye! You can make a tape too! Say anything you want, sing a song, or count. It's all up to you!

My Voice Recording *(cont.)*
NAEYC Appropriate Practices

Appropriate Practice:

Three-Year-Olds

"Adults encourage children's developing language...responding to children's verbal initiatives."

Concept Connection:

In this activity three-year-olds have the opportunity to explore language by taping and listening to their own voices. Children become aware of their own verbalizations and the sounds of their own voices.

Appropriate Practice:

Four- and Five-Year-Olds

"An abundance of activities is provided to develop language and literacy through meaningful experience."

Concept Connection:

In this activity four- and five-year-olds enhance their speaking vocabularies and develop language skills. Additionally, they become familiar and comfortable with their own speaking voices.

Appropriate Practice:

Four- and Five-Year-Olds

"Activities are designed to develop children's self-esteem and positive feelings toward learning."

Concept Connection:

By mastering the use of a tape recorder and having the experience of creating their own language and voice tapes, children have an increased sense of mastery and self-esteem.

Sound-Effect Fun

Preparation Time:

Several hours

Science and Curiosity Concept:

In this activity three-, four-, and five-year-olds will gain creativity and competency through awareness of sounds and the ability to mimic sounds. (This activity also builds oral language skills.)

Materials:

two tape recorders, blank cassette tapes, prerecorded sound-effect tape (see page 239), a variety of sound-effect equipment (use musical and rhythm instruments)

What to Do:

In this activity children hear a variety of prerecorded sound effects and have the opportunity to make their own sound effects and record them. To begin this activity, see page 239 for making your own sound-effect tape. (There is also a variety of sound-effect recordings available commercially, like sea and ocean sounds, etc. Be sure to listen to these tapes carefully before adding them to your center and be careful not to use any subliminal message tapes that are sometimes sold with nature sounds.)

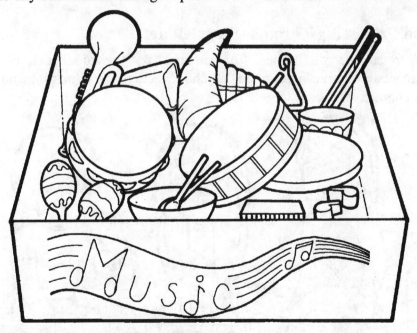

Begin by letting children hear the sound-effect tapes and showing them their new activity center and the box of sound-effect equipment. Be sure to allow plenty of time for discovery and experimentation with these new sound toys. Set up the sound-effect center so children may use it whenever they wish to make their own sound-effect tapes. Talk about the different sound effects people hear on TV and in the movies, etc. Show children some simple sound effects they can record, and model recording a door knock, a sneeze, etc. Set up your center and let the sound-effect fun begin!

Sound-Effect Fun *(cont.)*

Self-Directed Teaching Focus:

Leave the sound-effect activity as a regular part of the children's music and dance center so children may have self-directed play whenever they wish. Give children separate tapes for their cubbies or ask them to use their voice tapes for sound effects (see previous activity).

Directed Teaching Focus:

Play a "Who can make this noise?" game. Start and stop prerecorded sound-effect tapes to let children imitate the noises in a group activity.

What to Say:

Today we are going to have fun with noises. Let's all make noise. Ready! Go! (Model a variety of noises such as laughing, clapping, singing, etc., and let children think of as many others as possible.) Now we are going to talk about the many different noises we hear every day. I am going to play a tape that has many different noises on it, and then we are going to get to make our own tapes of noises we like. (Model activity.) Let's set up these tapes in our center. Then, whenever you want to, you can make a tape of noises you like.

Doing More:

Encourage children to use noises and sound effects in their oral and taped storytelling.

Evaluation and Processing Through Storytelling:

Add sound effects to tape-recorded stories. For example, say, "I heard a knock on the door" (record a knock), or "I heard a baby sneeze" (record an "ah-choo"). Anything is possible, and children will enjoy thinking of alternatives.

Sound-Effect Fun *(cont.)*

Sound-Effect Tapes

Making a sound-effect tape gives you a chance to use your own imagination and make your children happy too. Anything that makes a great sound will do. The sky is the limit! Here are some successful suggestions:

- ❖ knock on table or door
- ❖ laugh
- ❖ pretend to cry
- ❖ sneeze
- ❖ walk in place for footsteps
- ❖ bang pot lids together
- ❖ ring bells
- ❖ beat a drum
- ❖ use a musical instrument of any kind
- ❖ zip a zipper
- ❖ turn on a water tap
- ❖ pour water
- ❖ make splashing sounds
- ❖ open a squeaky door
- ❖ whistle
- ❖ clap your hands
- ❖ snap your fingers
- ❖ rattle paper or cellophane for fire noises
- ❖ turn on any electric appliance that makes a noise, such as an electric fan or a blender
- ❖ flush a toilet (Children love this.)
- ❖ make animal noises
- ❖ record a real cat or dog
- ❖ record crickets
- ❖ birds chirping
- ❖ phone ringing
- ❖ doorbell
- ❖ siren
- ❖ playground whistle

These are just a few suggestions. Get in the habit of listening, and you will discover that great sound effects are everywhere. Make sure you have some private time to work on recording this tape. It does not have to be perfect quality; just aim for recognizable sounds.

Sound-Effect Fun *(cont.)*

NAEYC Appropriate Practices

Appropriate Practice:

Three-Year-Olds

"Adults know that children are rapidly acquiring language, experimenting with verbal sounds, and beginning to use language to solve problems and to learn concepts."

Concept Connection:

This activity allows three-year-olds to form a relationship between sounds and how they are made; in addition, they learn the names of objects, which enhances their language.

Appropriate Practice:

Four- and Five-Year-Olds

"Different levels of ability, development, and learning styles are expected, accepted, and used to design appropriate activities."

Concept Connection:

The very nature of this activity allows all children, no matter what their ability and development, to experiment and create their own sound effects. There is no correct way to experience this activity, and all children achieve enhanced development no matter what their level of ability is.

Appropriate Practice:

Four- and Five-Year-Olds

"Children work individually or in small informal groups most of the time."

Concept Connection:

In this activity children have the opportunity to work by themselves and at their own pace in self-directed play.

Guess This Sound!

Preparation Time:

None (after completing preparation for Sound-Effect Fun)

Science and Curiosity Concept:

In this activity three-, four-, and five-year-olds foster competency and self-confidence through sound identification.

Materials:

prepared sound-effect tapes, one tape recorder

What to Do:

In this activity children listen to prerecorded sound-effect tapes, or sound-effect tapes they have made themselves in the previous activity, and take turns guessing the sounds they hear. Use the existing sound-effect tapes from the previous activity and set up the center so children may listen to the tapes and then draw pictures about the sounds they hear.

Self-Directed Teaching Focus:

To self-direct this activity, make paper and drawing materials available by the tape recorder and sound-effect tapes. Encourage children to draw pictures showing the things they hear on the tape.

Directed Teaching Focus:

To direct this activity, have children sit in a circle while you play the tape. Ask children to call out the things they think they hear. You may also do this activity with small informal groups or individuals. It is not necessary to make it a whole-group activity. Respond with affirmation and acknowledgment about what they hear and use the time for explanation about confusing sounds and the feelings that certain sounds might bring. For example, the sound of thunder might scare some children. The sound of a sneeze might remind some children of an illness they have had. This format provides an opportunity for discussions and may be done in small groups or with the use of parent volunteers.

What to Say:

We are going to have more fun with sounds today. I have set up a new guessing game for us. Listen to these sounds and try to guess what they are. (Model activity with tape.) Now I am going to put this tape recorder and drawing supplies over here, and we can listen to sounds and draw pictures about sounds whenever we want to.

Doing More:

Encourage children to take tape recorders outside and record birds, playground noises, etc. Give children a chance to share the noises they recorded.

Evaluation and Processing Through Storytelling:

Have children dictate stories about pictures they have already drawn while listening to sound-effect noises.

Guess This Sound! *(cont.)*
NAEYC Appropriate Practices

Appropriate Practice:

Three-Year-Olds

"Adults encourage children's developing language by speaking clearly and frequently to individual children and listening to their responses."

Concept Connection:

This activity creates an opportunity for adult-child communication. Children have the opportunity to interact in a positive and productive manner with adults and get encouragement, information, and increased language mastery.

Appropriate Practice:

Four- and Five-Year-Olds

"Children are expected to be mentally active."

Concept Connection:

This activity encourages children to think and develop both cognitive and deductive thinking skills. Children process information and base a guess on a number of complex variables.

Appropriate Practice:

Four- and Five-Year-Olds

"Children's natural curiosity and desire to make sense of their world are used to motivate them to become involved in learning activities."

Concept Connection:

This activity inspires children to think about the sounds in the world around them and to become aware of their surroundings, both natural and man-made.

Pet Masks

Preparation Time:

One hour

Science and Curiosity Concept:

In this activity three-, four-, and five-year-olds gain self-esteem through creativity and mastery and learn more about the animals in their environment.

Materials:

brown paper bags (large enough to fit over children's heads), art supplies

What to Do:

In this activity children will make and wear paper-bag kitty and doggy masks. To prepare this activity, you will need one paper bag for each child. Use the cat and dog faces for children to make quick-and-easy masks, or use your own design if you prefer (see pages 245-246 for patterns.) Begin by discussing cats and dogs with your class. Ask them to make the noise a cat makes and the noise that a dog makes. Let them know they will get a chance to dress up like their favorite pets.

Precut the cat and dog faces for children and give them the opportunity to paste these on a paper bag. They can paste the cat face on one side and the dog face on the other. Allow children to color the faces. Next, help children make eyeholes in their masks that will allow them to see. Let children put on their masks and present a dog-and-cat parade, or let them use their masks for dramatic play or as part of their storytelling.

Self-Directed Teaching Focus:

To self-direct this activity, after masks are created, add them to the pretend center as additional costume choices.

Directed Teaching Focus:

Let children play the animal noises game. You say an animal name, and they make the sound that animal makes. Children also love to sing "Old MacDonald Had a Farm" and make the animal noises that go with the song.

What to Say:

How many of you have a pet at home? What kind of pets do you have? (Let children talk about their pets and share their pets' names.) Now let's all make the noises that cats make. Meow!!! And cats also make a purring noises. Let's all purr. Isn't this fun! Now let's make the noises that dogs make. That's right—dogs go "woof, woof." We are all going to make our very own pet masks, and then we will get to wear them and pretend we are cats and dogs. (Model activity.)

Doing More:

Make a farmyard of animal faces. Let children make masks of their favorite farm animals. Have children tell their own farm stories.

Evaluation and Processing Through Storytelling:

Let children tell stories about their pets at home. Or record stories and let children do animal sound effects.

Pet Masks *(cont.)*

NAEYC Appropriate Practices

Appropriate Practice:

Three-Year-Olds

"Adults provide plenty of material and time for children to explore and learn about the environment, and to exercise their natural curiosity."

Concept Connection:

Children are very interested in animals, and this activity encourages them to become familiar with pets and the words and sounds related to them.

Appropriate Practice:

Four- and Five-Year-Olds

"Children are provided concrete learning activities relevant to their own life experiences."

Concept Connection:

As children play pretend in cat and dog masks, they are exploring relevant real-life experiences and things they are familiar with.

Appropriate Practice:

Four- and Five-Year-Olds

"Children's natural curiosity and desire to make sense of their world are used to motivate them to become involved in learning activities."

Concept Connection:

Playing "cats and dogs" allows children to form a concept relevant to their lives and find out more about animals that interest them.

Pet Masks *(cont.)*

Cat Face Pattern

Make enough copies for the children in your class. Let children paint, color, and/or decorate; then have them glue the faces onto their paper bags. Cut out eyeholes so the children can see.

Pet Masks *(cont.)*
Dog Face Pattern

Make enough copies for all the children in your class. Allow children to decorate the faces and then glue them to their paper bags. Cut out eyeholes so the children can see.

Classroom Pets

Preparation Time:

Two hours

Science and Curiosity Concept:

In this activity three-, four-, and five-year-olds gain a variety of concepts and skills such as socialization and self-esteem through the act of caring for a pet.

Materials:

a class pet of some kind (a variety of different choices are available and inexpensive; however, it's a good idea to opt for a sturdy pet), pet food, water, a cage, any special equipment needed for your pet (check with the pet store), pet-care chart (page 250), helper name tags (or use the picture helper chart if you do not want to stress letter and word awareness)

What to Do:

In this activity children have the experience of taking care of a classroom pet by taking turns being pet helpers. To prepare for this activity, you will first have to select a pet. Some excellent and sturdy choices are:

- ❖ mice, rats, guinea pigs, hamsters
- ❖ harmless snakes
- ❖ fish (even goldfish will do)
- ❖ turtles or tortoises (Sometimes turtles and tortoises hide or just sit there indefinitely which tends to be frustrating for the pet owners, and some varieties are on the endangered list and should not be kept in the classroom.)

First, prepare the pet's living area and get everything needed for the pet's new habitat. Some teachers will want to make children aware of this process and discuss the pet selection beforehand by looking at pictures and discussing how they will take care of their pet once it arrives. Next, prepare the pet-care chart and the name tags for the chart. (There are two choices for charts, depending on what you prefer in your classroom. One can be used with name tags; the other has slots for Polaroid picture name tags for nonreaders.

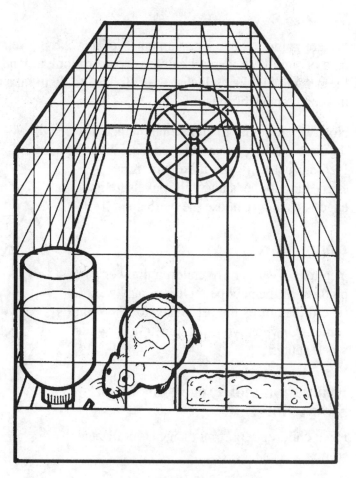

Classroom Pets *(cont.)*

What To Do *(cont.)*:

Discuss with children the responsibilities of pet care. Model the care of the pet a number of times on different days with your children. Let them all look on as a group until everyone is really comfortable with taking care of the pet. You will want to oversee this activity carefully until you are sure your children have mastered it. (However, many children have some responsibilities at home regarding their pets.)

You may wish to have a team be the pet monitors weekly, or choose one student at a time.

Self-Directed Teaching Focus:

This activity lends itself to being self-directed after children are comfortable and sure of how to do it. You will want to oversee it and ensure that the pet is doing well, etc. It is also important to check in with the pet monitors daily to see how they are doing and to set a definite time of day that the pet is fed and cared for.

Directed Teaching Focus:

Each week when the pet monitors are chosen, you may wish to have a group discussion about how the pet is doing and what interesting things the children have noticed about the pet's behavior that week.

What to Say:

We are going to have a new member of our class! We are getting a pet for all of us to have and take care of right here. Now I want everyone to look at where our pet will live, and we will talk about what the pet will be like and what we will have to do to take care of it. (Show pet's living area and model upkeep responsibilities.)

Now we are going to choose pet helpers for the first week. The people I choose will feed our pet daily and make sure it has everything it needs and will make sure its cage is clean. (Choose the pet helpers.)

Doing More:

You may wish to have children draw or paint pictures of the new pet. Or you may want to record the noises the pet makes for the sound center. Or video your pet in action for your video center.

Evaluation and Processing Through Storytelling:

Have children report on their pet in dictated stories.

Classroom Pets (*cont.*)

NAEYC Appropriate Practices

Appropriate Practice:

Three-Year-Olds

"Adults provide a safe, hazard-free environment and careful supervision."

Concept Connection:

Children have the thrill of caring for a living thing and fostering a sense of caring and responsibility in a hazard-free and controlled environment.

Appropriate Practice:

Four- and Five-Year-Olds

"Teachers prepare the environment for children to learn through active exploration and interaction."

Concept Connection:

This activity is an ongoing opportunity for children to learn about themselves and living things; it fosters many important socialization skills such as compassion, understanding, and empathy.

Appropriate Practice:

Four- and Five-Year-Olds

"Learning about math, science, social studies, health, and other content areas are all integrated through meaningful activities such as those when children explore animals..."

Concept Connection:

Children have a realistic opportunity to integrate the subject areas when they have the hands-on experience of caring for a pet.

Classroom Pets *(cont.)*

We take care of our

	M	T	W	Th	F

Classroom Pets (cont.)

Pet-Care Labels

Attach the appropriate labels to your pet care chart.

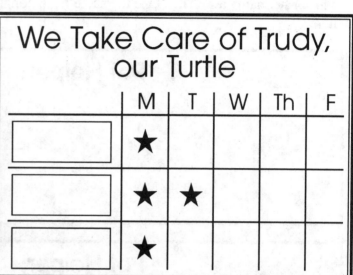

We Take Care of Trudy, our Turtle	M	T	W	Th	F
	★				
	★	★			
	★				

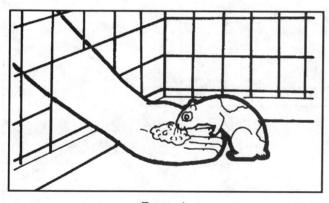

Feed

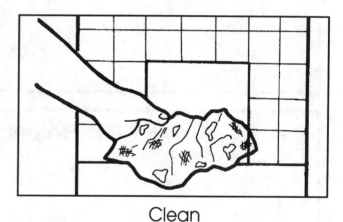

Clean

Observe

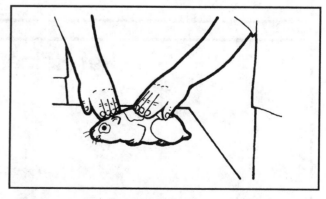

Give Attention (pet, play with, etc.)

　　　　251　　　　*#484 Everyday Activities for Preschool*

Classroom Pets *(cont.)*

Pet-Care Name Tags

Make enough copies of name tags so each child in your classroom has one. Affix each child's picture to his or her name tag. Then tape the name tag belonging to your chosen pet monitor next to his or her chore.

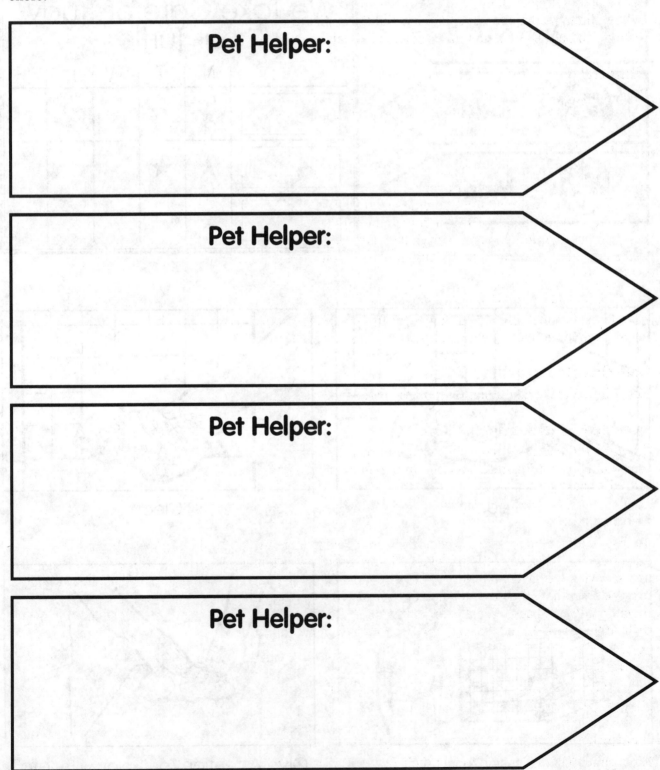

Pet Helper:

Pet Helper:

Pet Helper:

Pet Helper:

Alfred, the Lollipop Dragon

Preparation Time:
Several hours

Science and Curiosity Concept:
In this activity three-, four-, and five-year-olds gain self-esteem through competence, creativity, and the ability to distinguish between real and make-believe animals.

Materials:
dragon (see page 257), lollipops in assorted colors, paper lollipop (page 256—one copy for each child), crayons, tape, "Alfred, the Lollipop Dragon" (page 254)

What to Do:
In this activity children will listen to the story "Alfred, the Lollipop Dragon," and then make paper lollipops to put on a lollipop dragon. To prepare this activity, reproduce page 257 on heavy paper or oaktag to make your own lollipop dragon. Use the pattern on page 256 for lollipops and have children color their own. Create your own dragon bulletin board but make sure it's low enough so when children put their lollipops on Alfred, they are able to easily reach the bulletin board. (As an alternative make this a felt-board activity by cutting the dragon and lollipops out of felt.)

To begin this activity, read "Alfred, the Lollipop Dragon." Then let children know they will all have a chance to make a colored lollipop to stick on the back of a dragon. After children are finished, let them have their own real lollipops as a present from their dragon friend, Alfred. (If you prefer not to serve sugar to children, there are a variety of sugarless lollipops available.)

Self-Directed Teaching Focus:
Let children make additional lollipops as part of their art center.

Directed Teaching Focus:
After reading the story, have children color their lollipops. Then let children go up one by one to tape their lollipops onto Alfred. Ask children to guess the color of each lollipop before it is placed on Alfred's back.

What to Say:
Today we are going to read a wonderful story about a dragon who loved lollipops. Let's all listen. (Read story.) Now, we will all make lollipops out of paper to put on our own Alfred. Look over here and see what we have—our very own Alfred, the Lollipop Dragon! Now after we make our lollipops, everyone will have a chance to stick one on Alfred's back. Let's all say the colors aloud as we put them on Alfred's back. What color is this one? Red? Great! (Continue until all the children have put their lollipops on Alfred's back.) Now we all have a present from Alfred—our own lollipops to eat!

Doing More:
Let children dress as princesses and princes and act out dragon stories or act out "Alfred, the Lollipop Dragon" as you read it.

Evaluation and Processing Through Storytelling:
Have children dictate stories about their favorite kinds of candy.

Alfred, the Lollipop Dragon (cont.)
"Alfred, the Lollipop Dragon"
by Grace Jasmine

Alfred was a little dragon.

A little dragon who loved candy.

He dreamed of candy when he slept. He thought about candy when he was awake—oh, how he loved candy!

Alfred loved all kinds of candy.

He loved, candy bars, candy kisses, candy canes, gumdrops, and jelly beans.

But most of all, Alfred loved lollipops!

He loved the grape ones because they were purple and tasted just like grapes.

He loved the lemon ones because they were yellow and tasted just like the sour lemons off the tree!

He loved the cherry ones because they were red, his favorite color.

He loved the lime ones because they were green like him!

He loved the orange ones because they were named the same as their color—orange.

And he loved the pineapple ones because they were white and yummy!

Oh, how he loved them. Everyone in the kingdom knew how Alfred loved lollipops. His family knew. His little dragon friends knew. Even the king and queen and all their little children knew.

One day for a big surprise, everyone who knew how much Alfred loved lollipops brought him one! He was so happy he tap-danced around the royal garden. One by one, his friends stuck their lollipops for Alfred on his back.

And that is how Alfred became the lollipop dragon.

254

Alfred, the Lollipop Dragon *(cont.)*

NAEYC Appropriate Practices

Appropriate Practice:

Three-Year-Olds:

"Adults provide many experiences and opportunities to extend children's language."

Concept Connection:

Children enhance their language ability by listening to Alfred's story.

Appropriate Practice:

Four- and Five-Year-Olds

"Experiences are provided that meet children's needs and stimulate learning in all developmental areas."

Concept Connection:

Children find the idea of lollipops enjoyable and exciting and are interested in hearing about them and taking part in an activity that builds language skills.

Appropriate Practice:

Four- and Five-Year-Olds

"An abundance of these types of activities is provided to develop language and literacy through meaningful experiences—listening to and reading stories and poems, dictating stories, etc."

Concept Connection:

Children listen to a story in this activity and have the opportunity to further integrate what they hear and understand by acting it out.

Alfred, the Lollipop Dragon *(cont.)*
Lollipop Pattern

Make enough copies so that each child in your classroom has a lollipop. Cut out and allow children to color them. Make extra copies to place in your art center for use as a self-directed activity.

Planting an Outdoor Garden *(cont.)*

Self-Directed Teaching Focus:

Encourage children to look at their garden daily; leave weeding materials available for children to spend self-directed time weeding their garden. Be sure to show children the difference between weeds and their plants so they will not accidentally uproot their plants.

Directed Teaching Focus:

Spend a morning or two showing children different plants in books and talking about what kinds of plants there are. Or bring a variety of vegetables and/or flowers to school and show children what their plants will look like when grown. Have children name each of the vegetables and/or flowers.

What to Say:

Today we are going to become farmers and plant our own vegetable/flower garden. How many of you have ever helped in a garden? (Discuss gardens and plants with children and give them an opportunity to share what experiences they have had, according to their age level and understanding.) Now let's all look at our garden. (Model the activity.) Now we are all going to plant vegetable and/or flower seeds, and they will begin to grow. After we take care of them for a long, long time, we will have some vegetables/flowers that we can eat/admire.

Doing More:

Visit a farm or local grower, or visit the house of one of your children who has a parent who gardens. Use the parent expert letter on page 395 to get parent volunteers for not only this but many other activities.

Evaluation and Processing Through Storytelling:

Have children tell about why they like farming or about their experiences planting their own garden.

Planting an Outdoor Garden (cont.)

NAEYC Appropriate Practices

Appropriate Practice:

Three-Year-Olds

"Adults provide plenty of space and time outdoors."

Concept Connection:

Planting an outdoor garden gives children motivation to explore their outdoor world.

Appropriate Practice:

Four- and Five-Year-Olds

"Children are provided many opportunities to develop social skills such as cooperating, helping, etc."

Concept Connection:

Taking part in creating and caring for a garden gives children many opportunities to practice working-together skills.

Appropriate Practice:

Four- and Five-Year-Olds

"Children are provided many opportunities to see how reading and writing are useful."

Concept Connection:

Children use plant labels and pictures to see another interesting reason for reading.

Planting an Outdoor Garden *(cont.)*

Plant Labels

Make copies of these labels (or design your own); then cut out and glue to a craft stick. Insert in the soil to label rows of seeds.

Corn

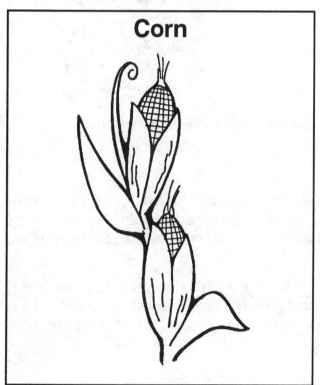

Beans

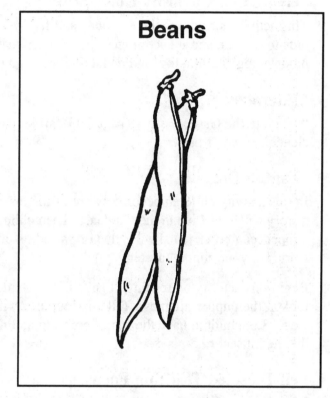

Carrots

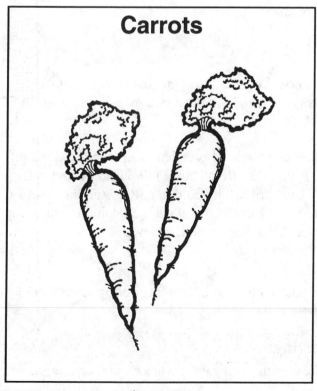

Radishes

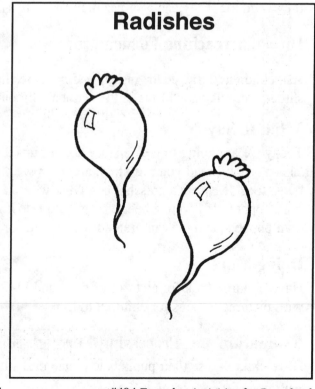

I Live in the Garden

Preparation Time:
One hour

Science and Curiosity Concept:
This activity introduces three-, four-, and five-year-olds to insects, and it encourages observation, making models, logical thinking, and deductive reasoning.

Materials:
"I Live in the Garden" story (page 293), art supplies, puppets (pages 295–303), craft sticks or pipe cleaners, glue or paste

What to Do:
In this activity children become aware of the insects and other creatures that live in a garden by hearing a story called "I Live in the Garden." Then children make insect puppets (pages 295–303). These puppets can be mounted with glue or pasted on craft sticks or pipe cleaners and used to dramatize stories in your puppet theater.

Begin this activity by reading "I Live in the Garden." Discuss the various insects and creatures and look at the puppet-pictures. Tell children they will get to play their favorite insects or creatures in the story. Let children have the fun of coloring and mounting their own puppets and using them for self-directed insect role-plays.

Self-Directed Teaching Focus:
Leave puppets out as part of your pretend center so children can play "I Live in the Garden" anytime they want to. They can also use their puppets as part of storytelling.

Directed Teaching Focus:

Ask children to imitate the insects and creatures in the story. Let bees buzz, grasshoppers hop, snakes slither, etc. Play an "I Live in the Garden" Simon-Says game (i.e., "Simon says to wiggle like a worm.").

What to Say:
Today we are going to hear a story about bugs and other creatures. It is called "I Live in the Garden." Listen while I read you this story, and then we will talk about it. (Read story.) We can pretend to be bugs, too. If I were a grasshopper, what would I do? That's right. I would hop. Let's all hop like a grasshopper. If I were a bee, what would I do? I'd go buzz! buzz! Now we are all going to make our own puppets, and we can pretend we are bees or flies or butterflies anytime we want to.

Doing More:
Have children look for pictures of bugs and insects in your collection of books, or bring several books with pictures of bugs for children to look at.

Evaluation and Processing Through Storytelling:
Have children use their puppets to create oral stories regarding their favorite insects and creatures.

I Live in the Garden *(cont.)*

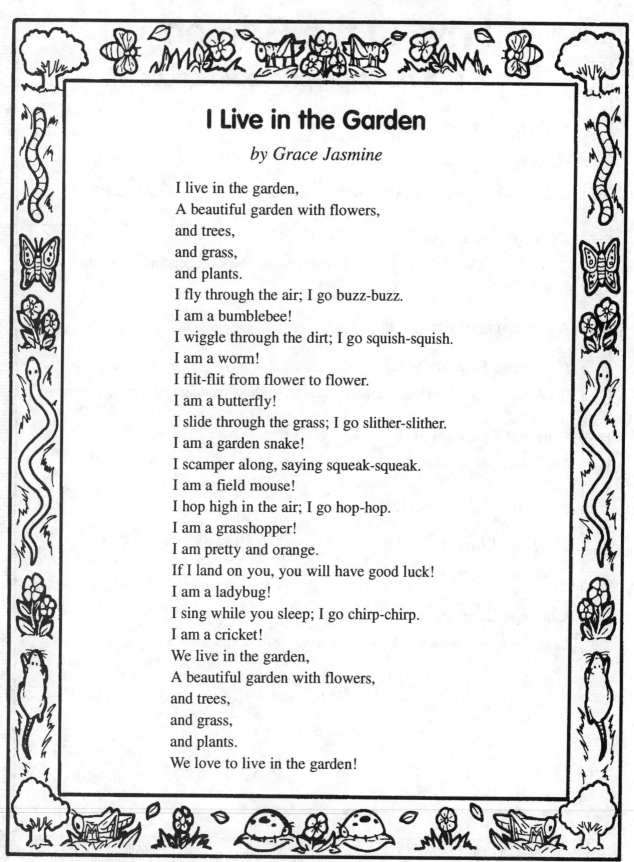

I Live in the Garden

by Grace Jasmine

I live in the garden,
A beautiful garden with flowers,
and trees,
and grass,
and plants.
I fly through the air; I go buzz-buzz.
I am a bumblebee!
I wiggle through the dirt; I go squish-squish.
I am a worm!
I flit-flit from flower to flower.
I am a butterfly!
I slide through the grass; I go slither-slither.
I am a garden snake!
I scamper along, saying squeak-squeak.
I am a field mouse!
I hop high in the air; I go hop-hop.
I am a grasshopper!
I am pretty and orange.
If I land on you, you will have good luck!
I am a ladybug!
I sing while you sleep; I go chirp-chirp.
I am a cricket!
We live in the garden,
A beautiful garden with flowers,
and trees,
and grass,
and plants.
We love to live in the garden!

I Live in the Garden (cont.)

NAEYC Appropriate Practices

Appropriate Practice:

Three-Year-Olds

"Adults provide many opportunities to extend children's language abilities."

Concept Connection:

"I Live in the Garden" exposes children to common words, ideas, and meanings about a garden.

Appropriate Practice:

Four- and Five-Year-Olds

"Children are provided many opportunities to see how reading and writing are useful."

Concept Connection:

Exposure to stories encourages children's interest in reading and writing.

Appropriate Practice:

Four- and Five-Year-Olds

"Children are expected to be mentally active."

Concept Connection:

Children develop thinking skills when listening to stories.

I Live in the Garden *(cont.)*
Puppets

Butterfly

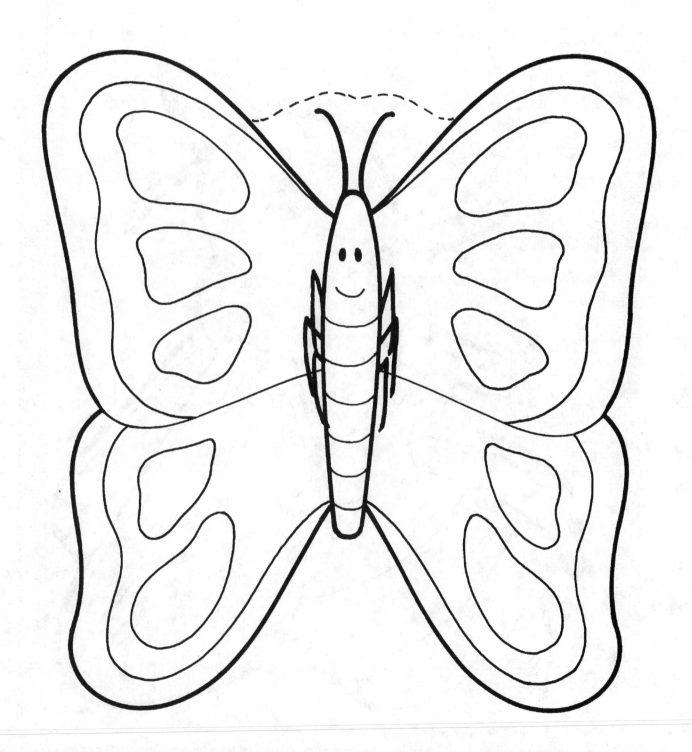

I Live in the Garden (cont.)

Puppets (cont.)

Bumblebee

I Live in the Garden (cont.)

Puppets (cont.)

Worm

I Live in the Garden (cont.)
Puppets (cont.)

Fly

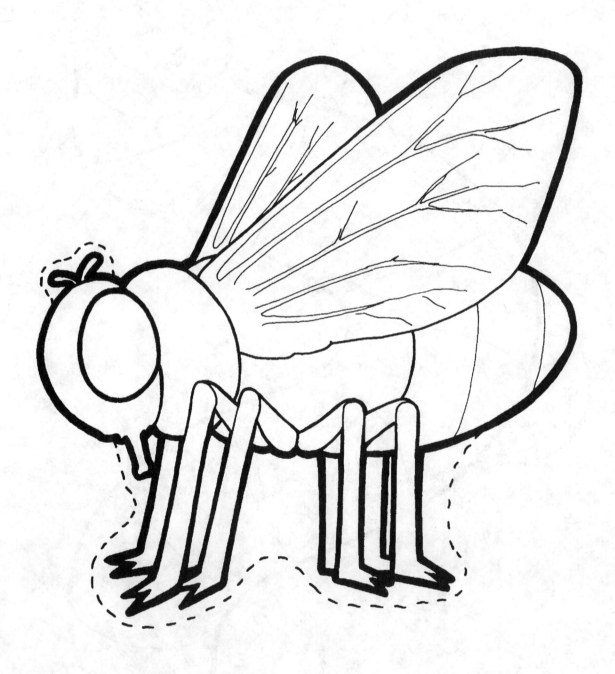

298

I Live in the Garden (cont.)
Puppets (cont.)

Ladybug

I Live in the Garden (cont.)
Puppets (cont.)

Grasshopper

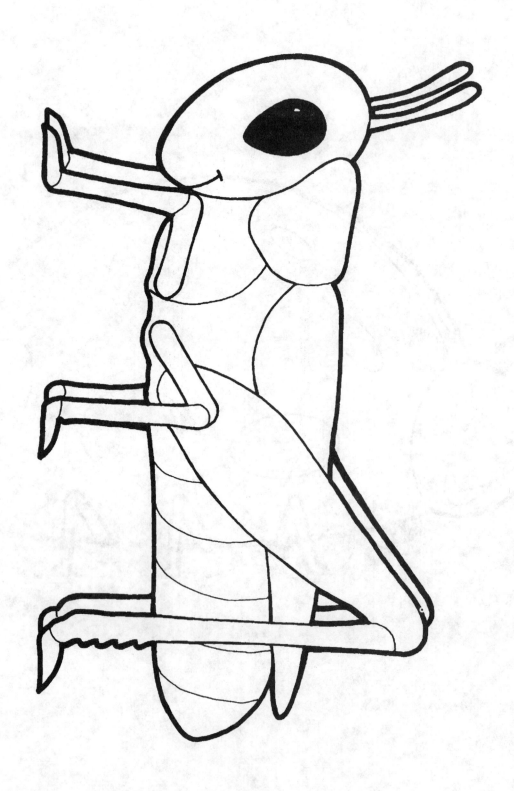

I Live in the Garden (cont.)

Puppets (cont.)

Moth

I Live in the Garden (cont.)
Puppets (cont.)

Garden Snake

I Live in the Garden (cont.)
Puppets (cont.)

Mouse

Rainbow Watercolors

Preparation Time:

One hour

Science and Curiosity Concept:

This activity introduces three-, four-, and five-year-olds to a variety of curiosity and scientific concepts including: cause and effect, investigation, experimentation, and forming conclusions.

Materials:

twenty plastic cups (clear, not colored), a box of food coloring in assorted colors (red, yellow, blue, green), plastic spoons, butcher paper, tape, paper towels

What to Do:

In this activity children have the opportunity to observe and experiment with different colors. (Please note that this is a messy experiment and the Messy Letter, page 396, should be sent home ahead of time.) To begin this activity, create a temporary color station. You should have a low, easy-to-reach table, chairs, and a throw-away covering like butcher paper taped to the table top. Next, have a variety of clear plastic cups, plastic spoons, and paper towels. Model the way that colors combine to form other colors. (As a quick review, we have listed easy color combinations for you here:

Typical assortments of food coloring contain blue, red, yellow, and green food coloring. To create additional colors:

> blue + red = purple
>
> red + yellow = orange
>
> yellow + blue = green
>
> yellow + green = lime green

You can also make lighter versions of each of the colors by mixing a lot of water with a small amount of food coloring. For example, you can make pink by adding water to a small amount of red food coloring.

Give children an opportunity to mix colors and see what different combinations they can come up with. Use words that help them to build a science vocabulary— "look," "watch," "let's see what happens," "observe," "changes," "stays the same," etc.

Rainbow Watercolors *(cont.)*

Self-Directed Teaching Focus:

Have nontoxic colors available in paint center for children to mix and experiment with. This activity is a very good one for children to guide themselves, for they can do much of it alone.

Directed Teaching Focus:

Conduct an organized experiment. Ask children to show you certain colors or try to mix colors to come up with a requested color. Have children line up their plastic glasses to make a rainbow.

What to Say:

Today we are going to have fun experimenting with different colors. Let's all look at the watercolor table I have set up. But before we start and I show you what to do, we have to put on our messy shirts.

Now let's see how these colors can mix together. If I mix red and yellow, what do you think will happen? Shall we try it? Oh, look! It's orange. Shall we try another one?

Doing More:

Have snack-time milk fun by adding a drop of food coloring to it. Or call a day "Red Day" and have children find as many red objects as they can.

Evaluation and Processing Through Storytelling:

Have children dictate stories about their favorite color, or what they liked about mixing colors together.

Rainbow Watercolors *(cont.)*

NAEYC Appropriate Practices

Appropriate Practice:

Three-Year-Olds

"Adults provide plenty of time and materials for children to learn about their environment."

Concept Connection:

In this activity three-year-olds have an opportunity to explore color and learn about the colors in their environment while satisfing their natural curiosity.

Appropriate Practice:

Four- and Five-Year-Olds

"Teachers prepare the environment for children to learn through active exploration with materials."

Concept Connection:

Children have the opportunity to actively explore colors in this activity.

Appropriate Practice:

Four- and Five-Year-Olds

"Teachers move among groups and individuals to facilitate children's involvement with materials and activities by asking questions, offering suggestions, or adding more complex ideas to a situation."

Concept Connection:

These color experiments create the perfect environment for teacher facilitation and give teachers many opportunities to explore cause and effect with their children.

306

Water Painters

Preparation Time:
One hour

Science and Curiosity Concept:
In this activity three-, four-, and five-year-olds are introduced to a variety of curiosity concepts, including experimenting with water and gases, observation, and cause and effect.

Materials:
a variety of clean paintbrushes; buckets, coffee cans, or plastic bowls; an outside paved play area

What to Do:
In this activity children have fun painting with water while at the same time being exposed to a variety of science concepts, most importantly the evaporation of water. To prepare this activity, all that is needed is a number of clean paintbrushes in different sizes and something in which to hold water. Children can paint with water almost anywhere outside. Have children paint objects like fences, the blacktop, sidewalks, paved playground areas, and outside walls. Mention the science words related to what they are doing to help them build a science vocabulary. Use words and phrases such as "watch," "see what happens," "evaporates," "gas," "liquid," "dry," and "wet." Even though children will not master the meanings of all of these words, their use will help expose the children to a basic science vocabulary. Children can do this again and again. Preschoolers enjoy it!

Self-Directed Teaching Focus:
Leave painting materials available for outside play. Make sure that the weather is somewhat warm so children will not get wet and cold.

Directed Teaching Focus:
Interact with individual children, talking with them about what is happening as it happens.

What to Say:
Today we are going to paint with water. Painting with water is really fun, because you can paint things that you usually cannot paint. Water won't hurt fences, the playground, play equipment, or the outside walls. Let's walk around and I'll show you all the things you can paint. Then we will try it once to see. When I paint this swing with the water, it gets wet. What do you think will happen to it when the sun shines on it for awhile? Will it dry up? Yes, that's right. It was water, and then it disappeared into the air; it's what we call "evaporation." It has become water vapor. Clouds are made of water vapor. Let's try painting whenever we want to!

Doing More:
Have children paint with small brushes. Encourage them to paint "magic" pictures, letters, numbers, or their names.

Evaluation and Processing Through Storytelling:
Have children tell a story about the activity. Have a parent who is a house painter or an artist come in and show the children his/her paints.

Water Painters *(cont.)*
NAEYC Appropriate Practices

Appropriate Practice:

Three-Year-Olds

"Adults provide plenty of material and time for children to explore and learn about the environment, to exercise their natural curiosity, and to experiment with cause and effect relationships."

Concept Connection:

This activity gives three-year-olds a perfect opportunity to find out for themselves what water will do.

Appropriate Practice:

Four- and Five-Year-Olds

"Experiences are provided that meet children's needs and stimulate learning."

Concept Connection:

This activity meets the four- and five-year-old's need to actively explore the world in which he/she lives.

Appropriate Practice:

Four- and Five-Year-Olds

"Children work individually or in small informal groups most of the time."

Concept Connection:

This activity provides an opportunity for relaxed parallel play; children can work alone or share their discoveries, as they wish.

Pretend Seasons

Preparation Time:
Several hours

Science and Curiosity Concept:
In this activity three-, four-, and five-year-olds use their imaginations to foster thinking skills that will later be related to probability and forming hypotheses.

Materials:
three bedsheets (one white, one tan, and one blue); snow equipment (optional); beach equipment (optional)

What to Do:
In this activity children have the fun of pretending to play at the beach or in the snow, or possibly both. In it, children become aware of indicators of the season and develop thinking skills that will later be used for scientific experimentation.

Begin this activity by designating a beach and snow play area. Use the tan sheet for the beach sand area and the blue sheet for the ocean. Or use the white sheet for snow and the blue sheet for ice. This activity can be as simple or as in-depth as you wish. You may use props like snow clothes and toy and beach equipment to make play more fun, or you can let children gather things from the pretend center and water-table areas to complete the activity in the way they see fit.

Begin the activity by telling children they are going to use their imaginations to play at the beach or in the snow. Set up the areas in an inviting fashion and let children move in and out of these imaginary seasons as they will.

Self-Directed Teaching Focus:
Leave a seasons play area set up for children to play in during self-directed play. It's more fun if the seasonal play area is in contrast to the real weather. Children enjoy playing winter when it is warm and sunny outdoors.

Directed Teaching Focus:
Have children talk about things they would like to play with in the snow or at the beach. Talk with children about a day they spent either in the snow or at the beach during circle time.

What to Say:
Today we have a new and fascinating place to play! This is our new pretend beach. We can play this is the ocean and this is the sand. Even when it's freezing outside as it is today, we can have fun here at our very own beach. We can use our sand-table toys to play with or our toy boats. Let's try it!

Doing More:
Try a "Winter in July" party theme to extend this activity. Have children watch "Frosty the Snow Man" or any other appropriate video. "Frosty" is good because it deals with a variety of science concepts, including heat and the cold, temperatures, and water evaporation.

Evaluation and Processing Through Storytelling:
Have children tell "a day at the beach" or "a day in the snow" stories. Use the actual pretend play area for a stage to act out children's stories.

Pretend Seasons *(cont.)*

NAEYC Appropriate Practices

Appropriate Practice:

Three-Year-Olds

"Adults provide plenty of materials and time for children to explore and learn about the environment, to exercise their natural curiosity."

Concept Connection:

This activity provides the perfect opportunity for three-year-olds to experiment with make-believe and to understand their own abilities to change their environment through creative play.

Appropriate Practice:

Four- and Five-Year-Olds

"Teachers prepare the environment for children to learn through active exploration and interaction."

Concept Connection:

Children have the opportunity to elaborate on their understanding of the different seasons by using the toys and equipment that go with different seasons as part of creative play.

Appropriate Practice:

Four- and Five-Year-Olds

"Children work individually or in small, informal groups most of the time."

Concept Connection:

This activity lends itself really well to solitary or parallel play situations.

Table of Contents for Appendix

Teacher Note: Use the patterns and pictures in the appendix in whatever way you wish. You may decide to use them only as directed in the various activities, or you may use them to do some of the following activities:

- ❖ create book covers or mini-books

- ❖ cut out of felt and use as a felt-board activity

- ❖ color and decorate for artistic creations

- ❖ place around your classroom as reminders of various concepts

- ❖ send home to reinforce concepts learned

You are limited only by your creativity and available time.

Rhyming Words

Heart

Cart

Pot

Cot

312

Rhyming Words *(cont.)*

Cake

Snake

Hand

Sand

Rhyming Words *(cont.)*

Pants

Ants

Pear

Hair

314

Rhyming Words *(cont.)*

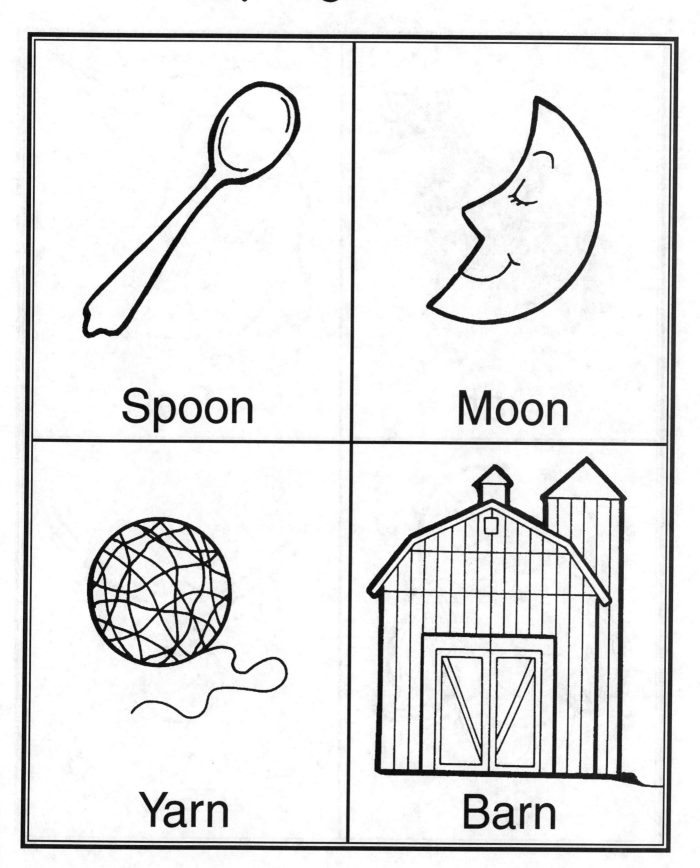

Spoon

Moon

Yarn

Barn

Rhyming Words *(cont.)*

Bat

Rat

Girl

Pearl

Rhyming Words *(cont.)*

Boy

Toy

Crown

Clown

Rhyming Words *(cont.)*

Bear

Chair

Mouse

House

Rhyming Words *(cont.)*

Star

Car

Boat

Coat

Rhyming Words (cont.)

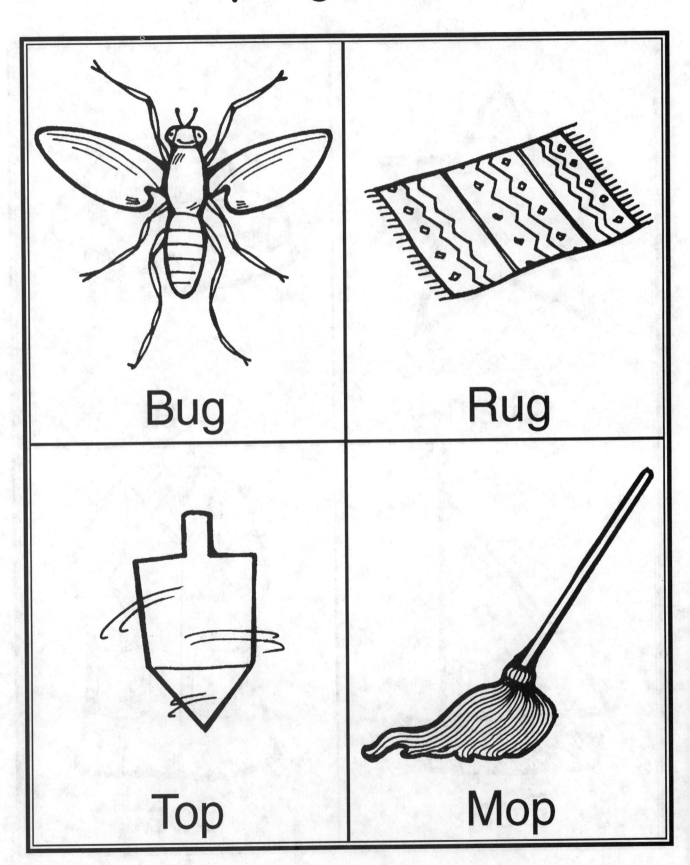

Bug

Rug

Top

Mop

320

Rhyming Words *(cont.)*

Whale

Snail

Cat

Hat

Uppercase Alphabet

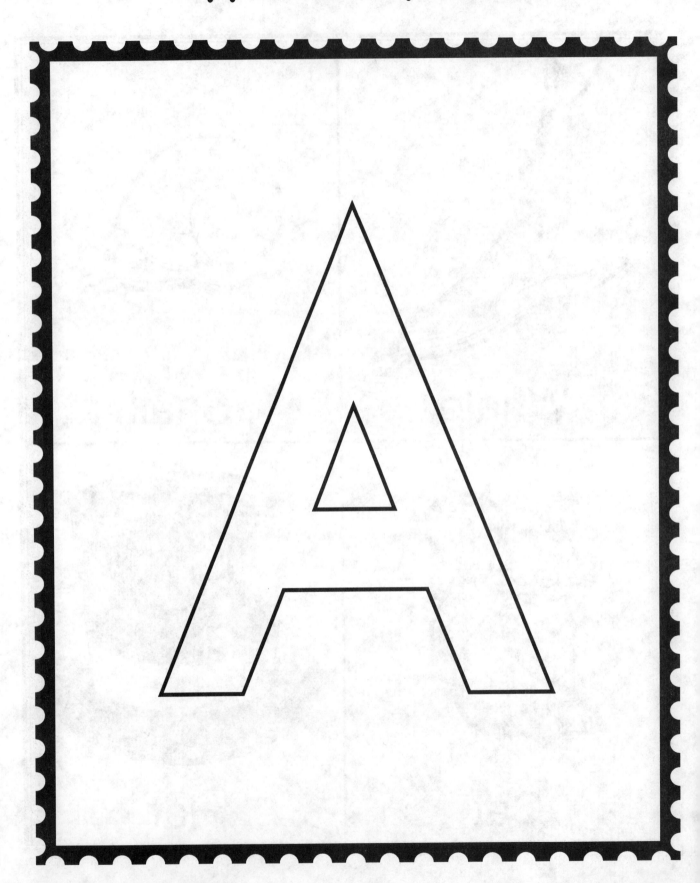

Uppercase Alphabet *(cont.)*

Uppercase Alphabet *(cont.)*

Uppercase Alphabet *(cont.)*

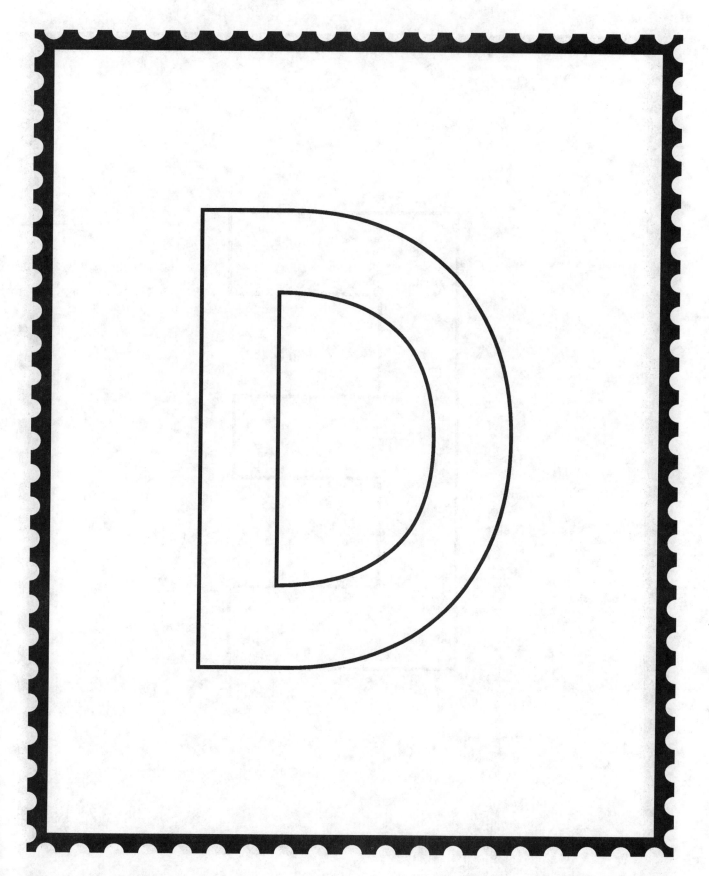

Uppercase Alphabet *(cont.)*

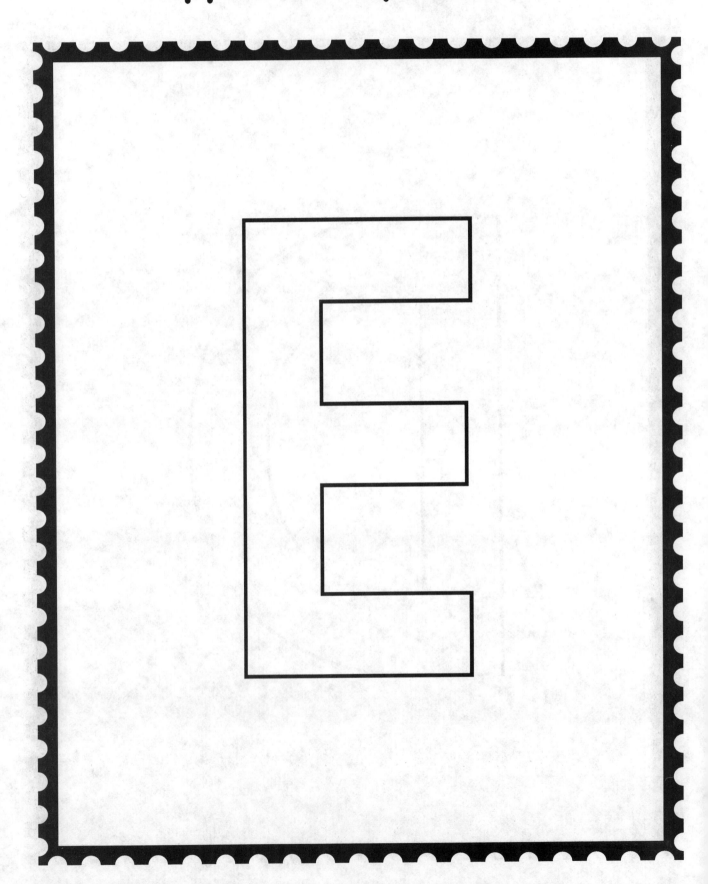

326

Uppercase Alphabet *(cont.)*

Uppercase Alphabet *(cont.)*

328

Uppercase Alphabet *(cont.)*

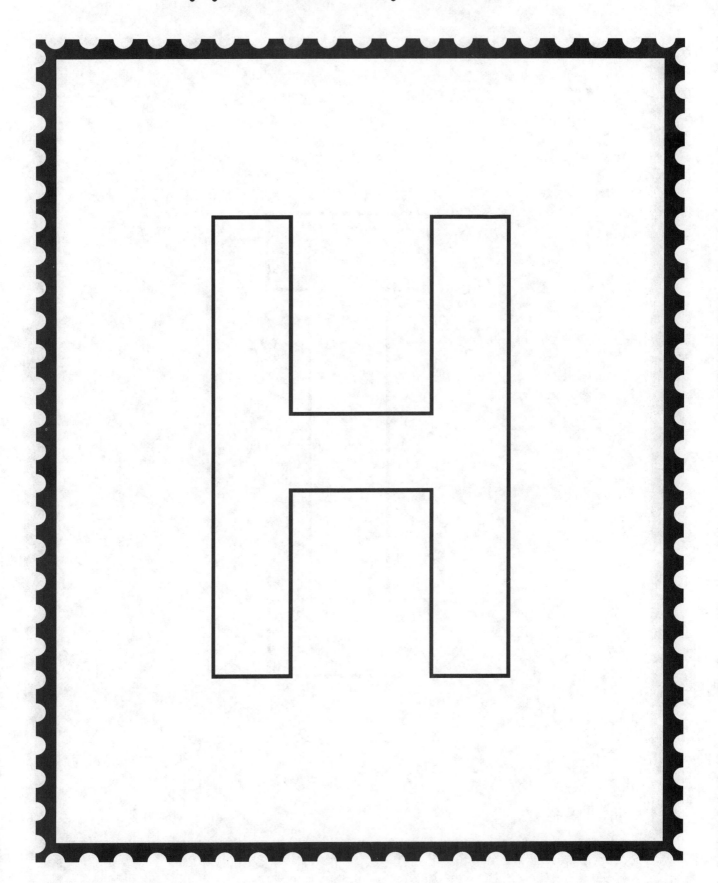

Uppercase Alphabet *(cont.)*

Uppercase Alphabet *(cont.)*

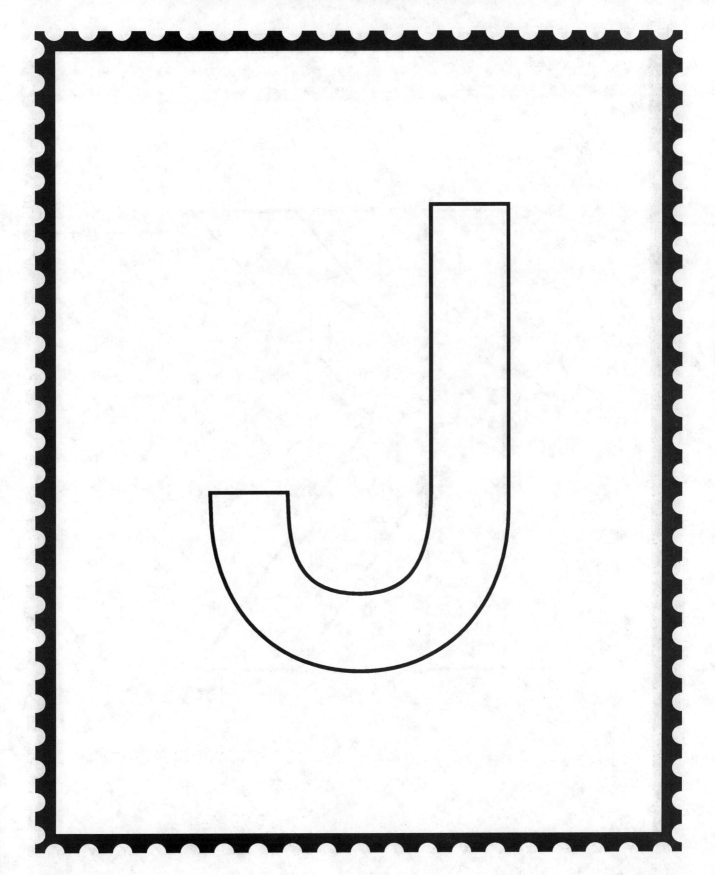

Uppercase Alphabet *(cont.)*

Uppercase Alphabet *(cont.)*

Uppercase Alphabet *(cont.)*

Uppercase Alphabet *(cont.)*

Uppercase Alphabet *(cont.)*

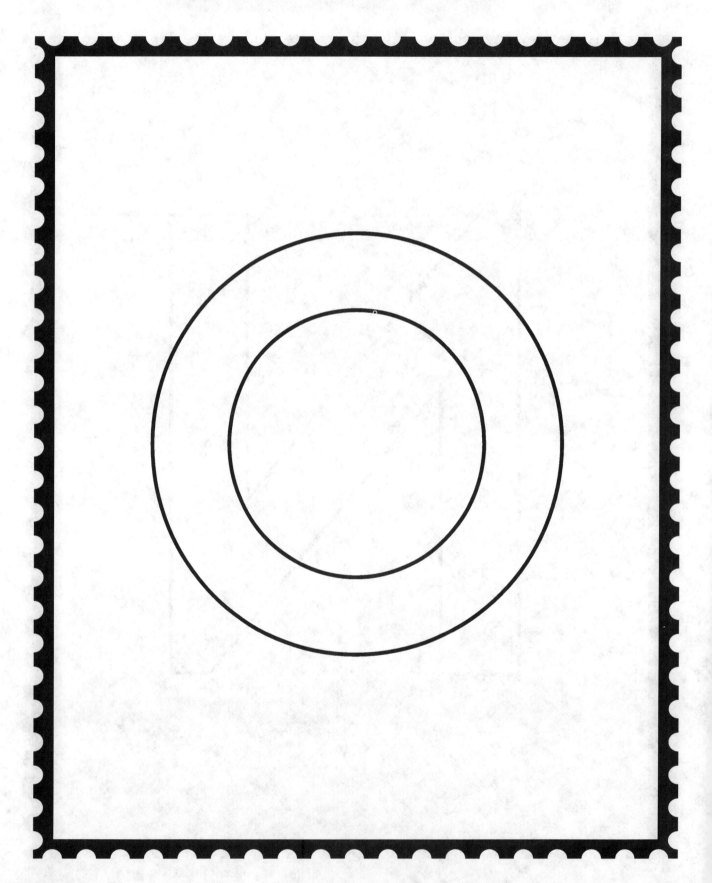

Uppercase Alphabet *(cont.)*

Uppercase Alphabet *(cont.)*

Uppercase Alphabet *(cont.)*

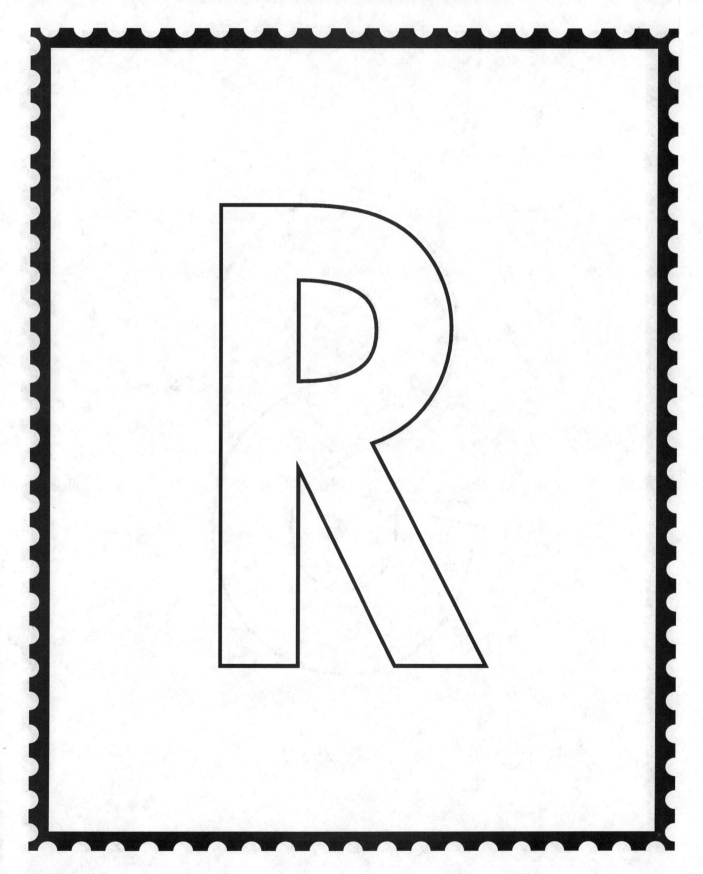

Uppercase Alphabet *(cont.)*

Uppercase Alphabet *(cont.)*

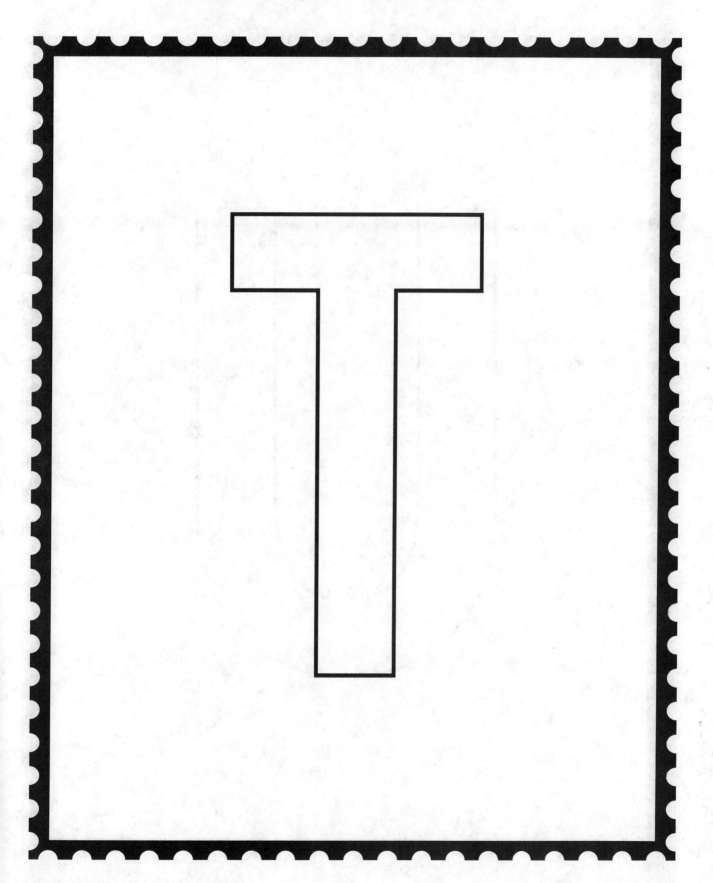

Uppercase Alphabet *(cont.)*

342

Uppercase Alphabet *(cont.)*

Uppercase Alphabet *(cont.)*

Uppercase Alphabet *(cont.)*

Uppercase Alphabet *(cont.)*

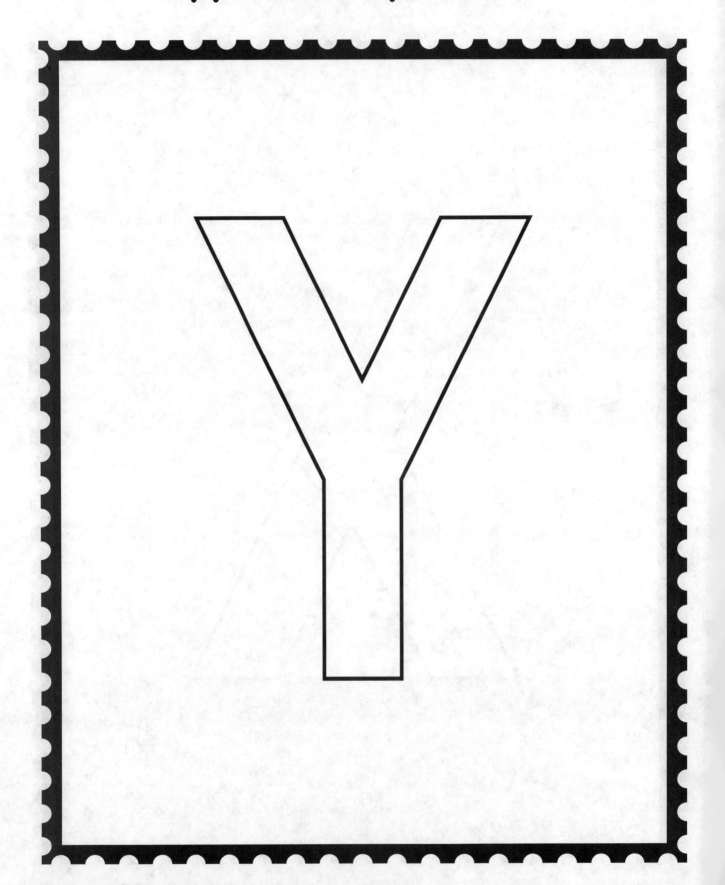

Uppercase Alphabet *(cont.)*

Lowercase Alphabet

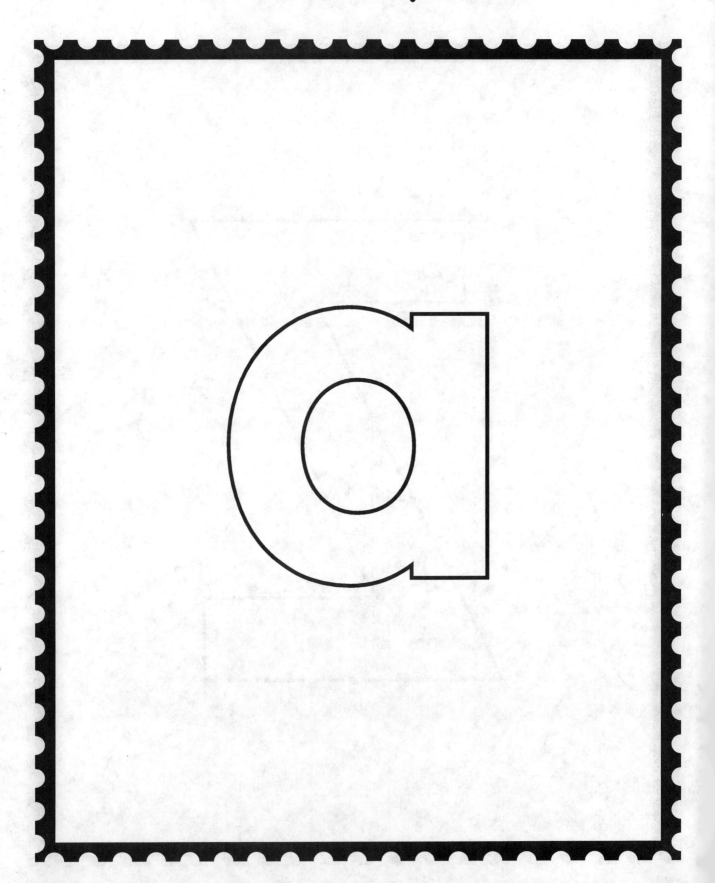

348

Lowercase Alphabet *(cont.)*

Lowercase Alphabet *(cont.)*

350

Lowercase Alphabet *(cont.)*

Lowercase Alphabet *(cont.)*

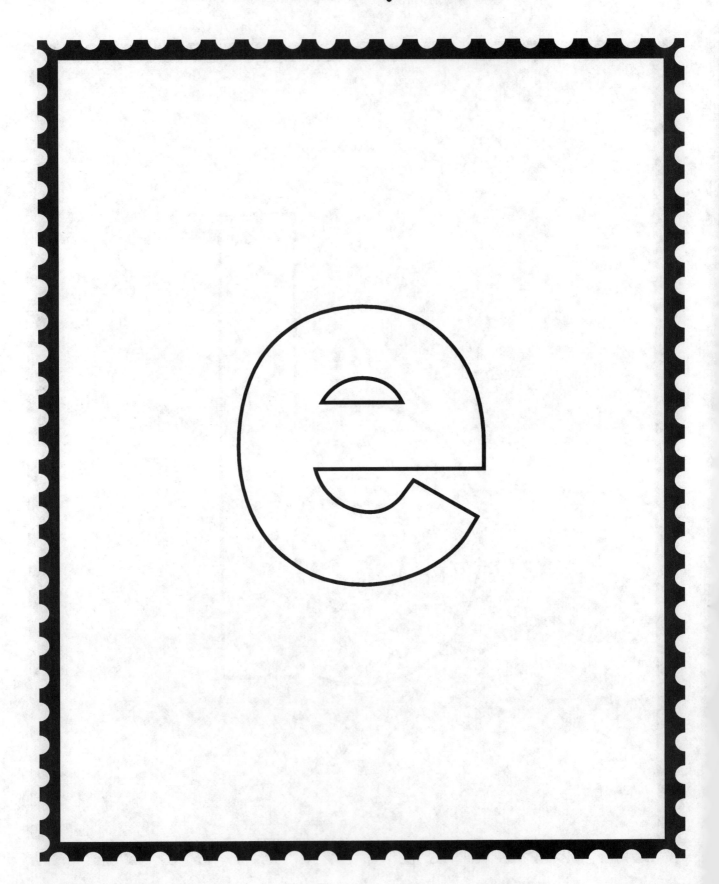

Lowercase Alphabet *(cont.)*

Lowercase Alphabet *(cont.)*

Lowercase Alphabet *(cont.)*

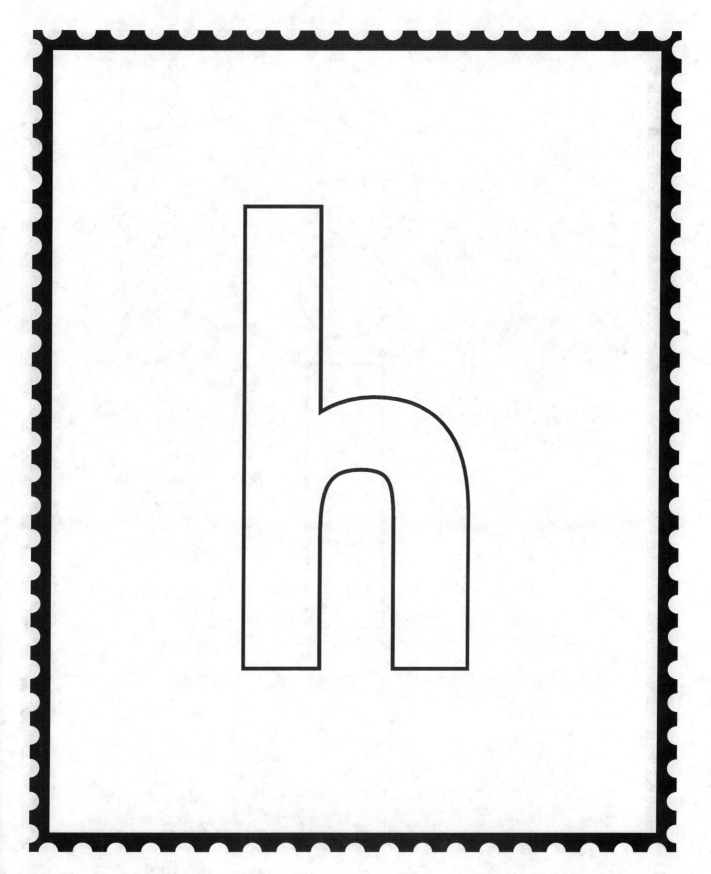

Lowercase Alphabet *(cont.)*

Lowercase Alphabet *(cont.)*

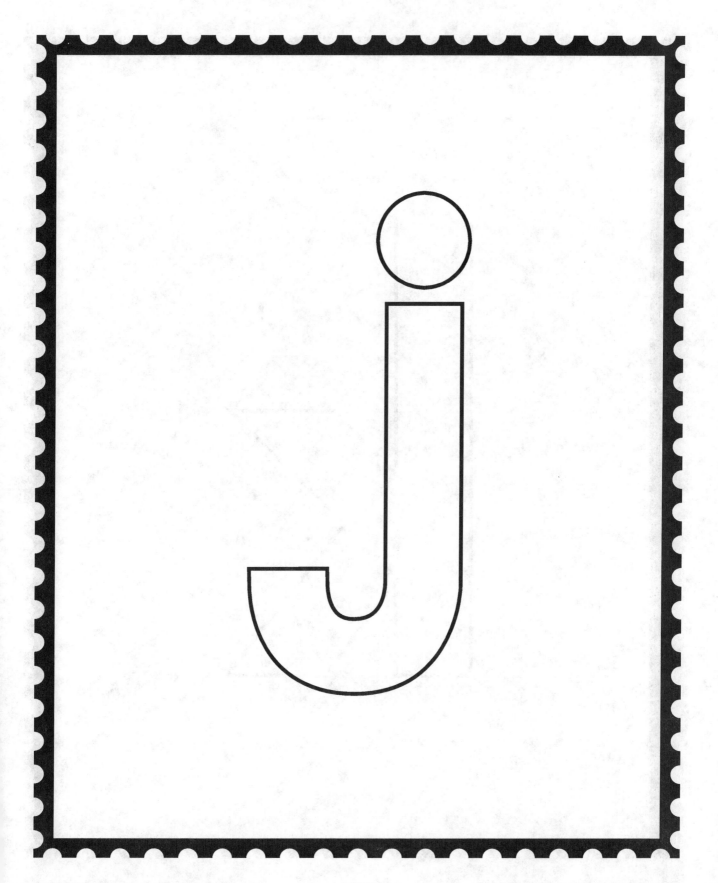

Lowercase Alphabet *(cont.)*

Lowercase Alphabet *(cont.)*

Lowercase Alphabet *(cont.)*

360

Lowercase Alphabet *(cont.)*

Lowercase Alphabet *(cont.)*

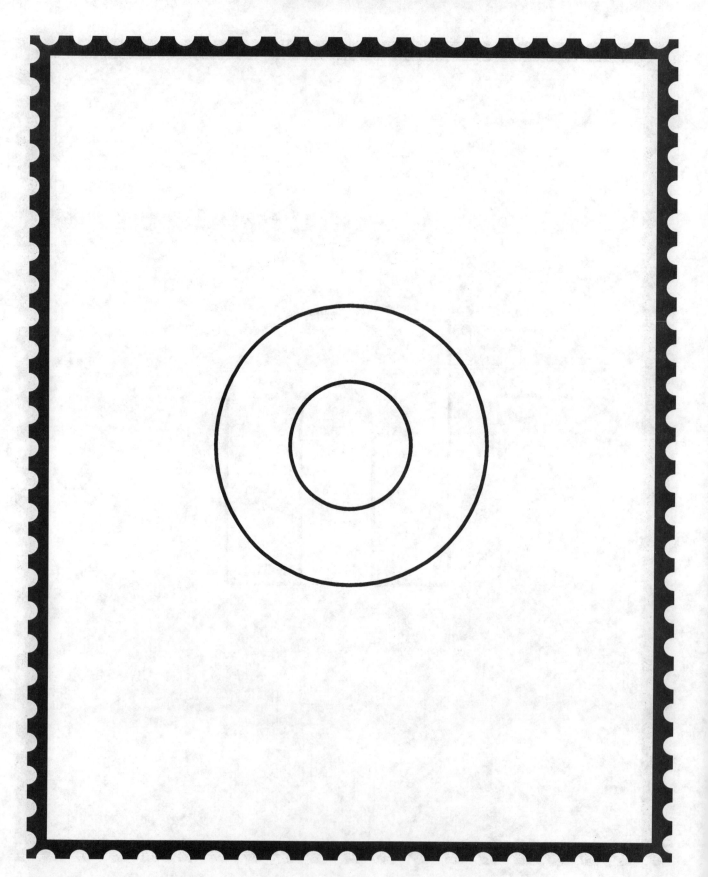

362

Lowercase Alphabet *(cont.)*

Lowercase Alphabet *(cont.)*

Lowercase Alphabet *(cont.)*

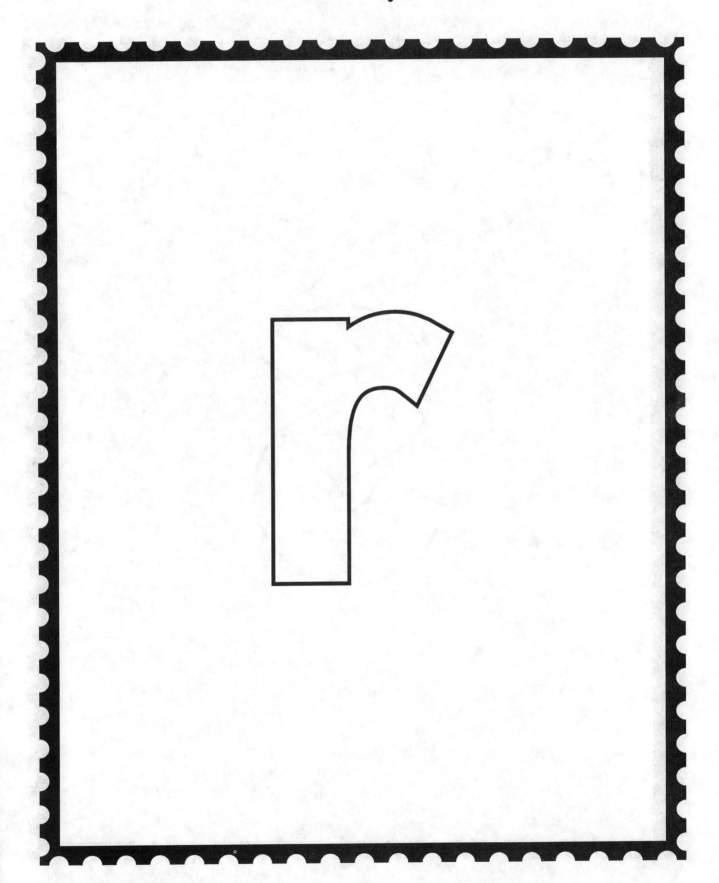

Lowercase Alphabet *(cont.)*

Lowercase Alphabet *(cont.)*

Lowercase Alphabet *(cont.)*

Lowercase Alphabet *(cont.)*

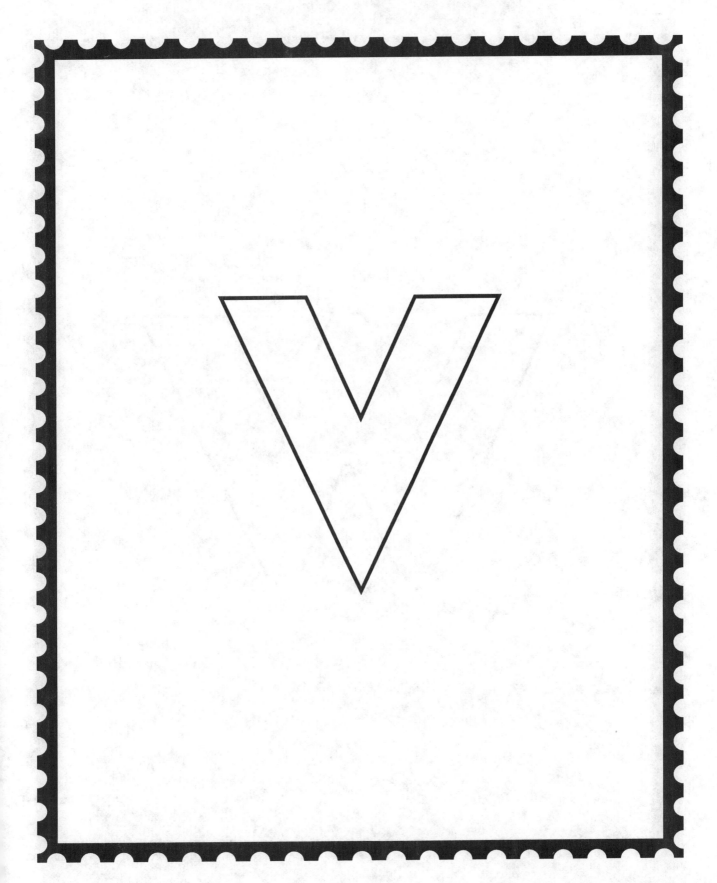

Lowercase Alphabet *(cont.)*

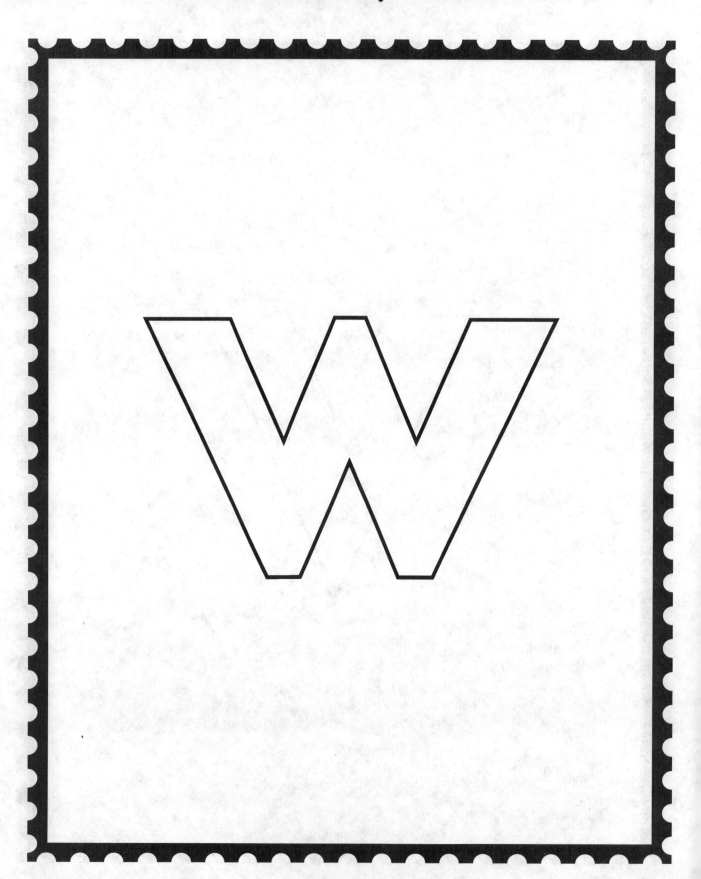

Lowercase Alphabet *(cont.)*

Lowercase Alphabet *(cont.)*

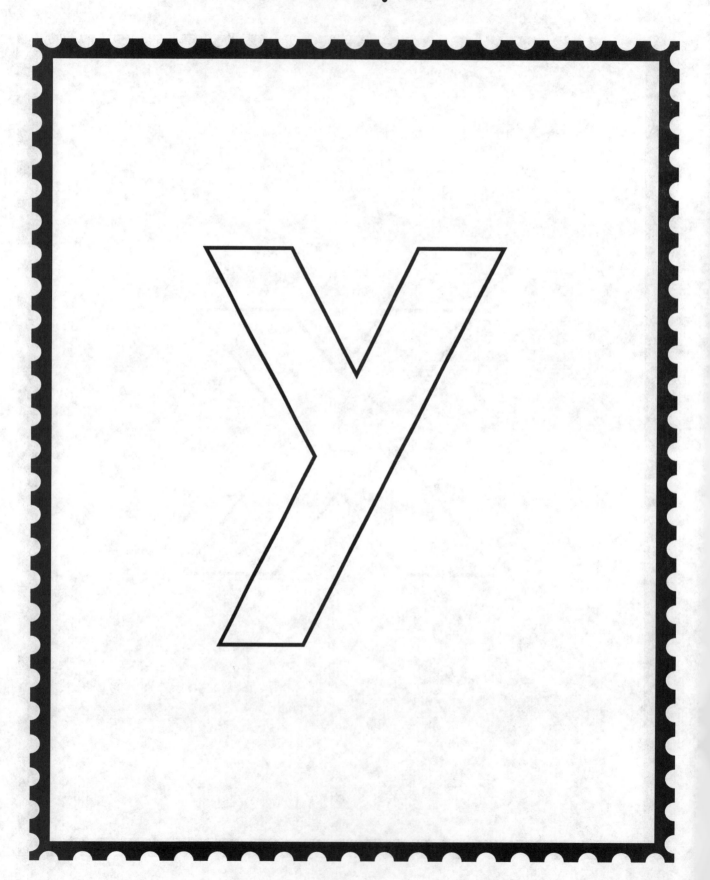

Lowercase Alphabet *(cont.)*

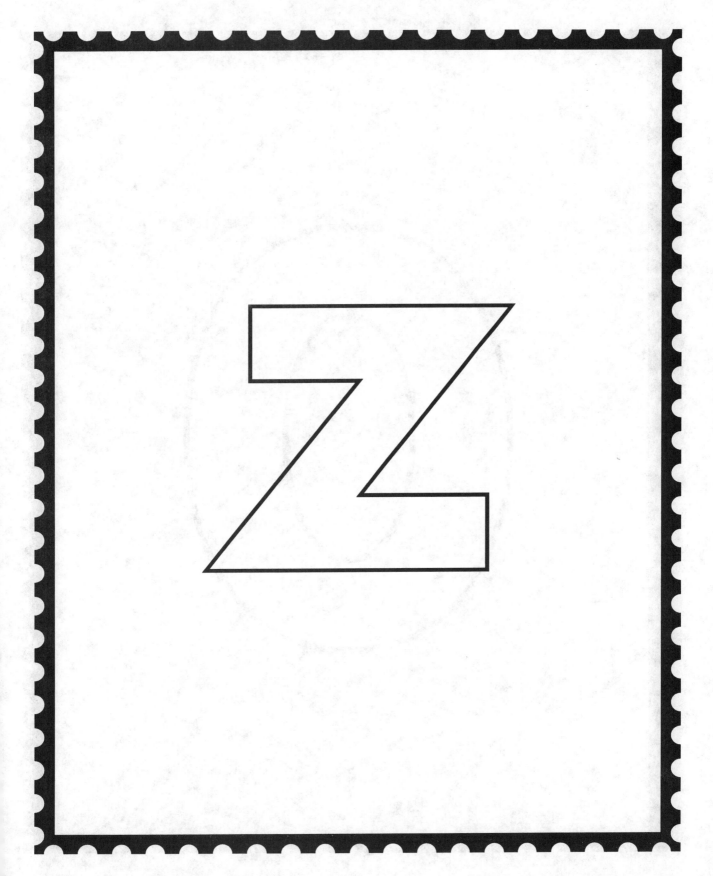

Numbers

Numbers *(cont.)*

375

Numbers *(cont.)*

Numbers *(cont.)*

Numbers *(cont.)*

Numbers *(cont.)*

Numbers *(cont.)*

Numbers *(cont.)*

Numbers *(cont.)*

382

Numbers *(cont.)*

Numbers *(cont.)*

Numbers Sets: One

Numbers Sets: Two

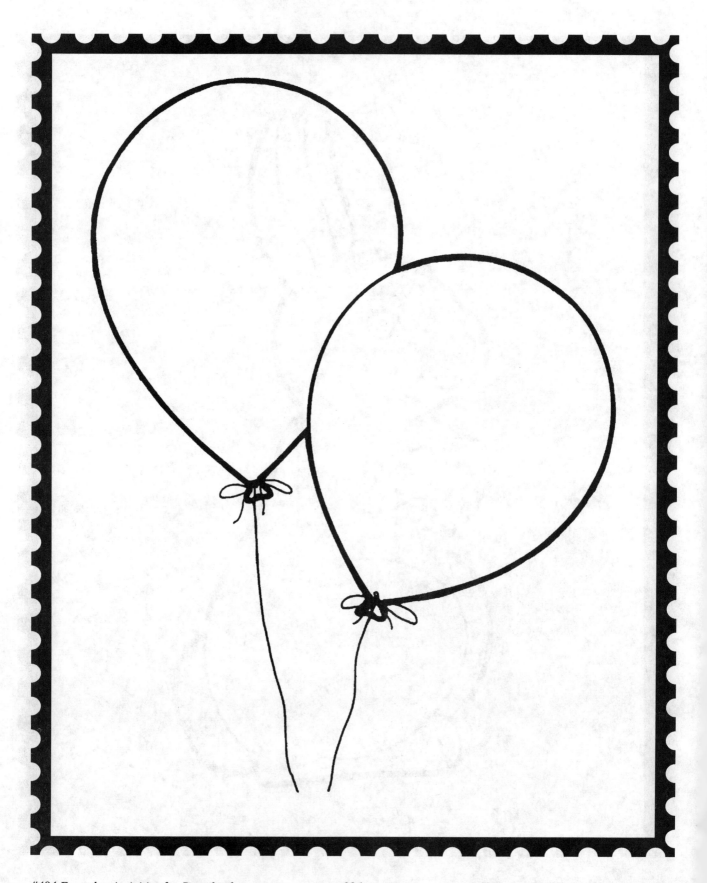

Numbers Sets: Three

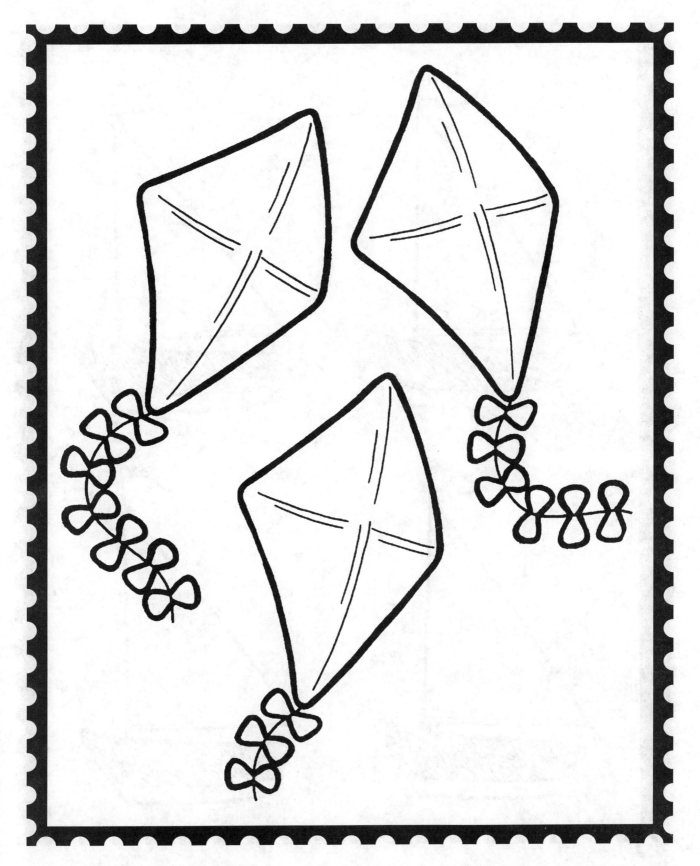

Numbers Sets: Four

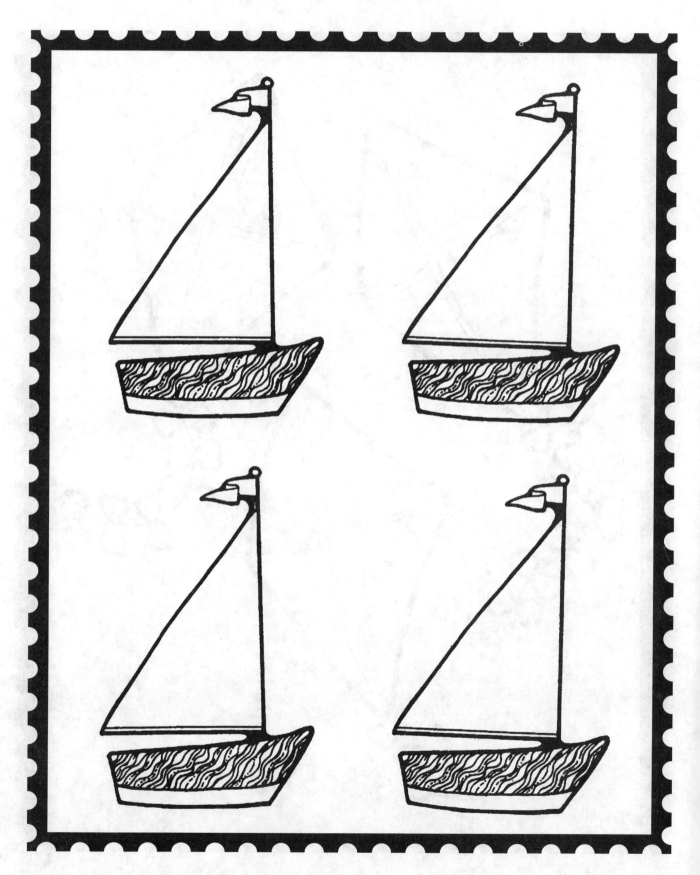

Numbers Sets: Five

Numbers Sets: Six

390

Numbers Sets: Seven

Numbers Sets: Eight

Numbers Sets: Nine

Numbers Sets: Ten

General Supplies Letter

Dear Parents,

We would like to add to our preschool supplies. We can use practically anything old and serviceable you want to donate. We especially need any of the following items that are checked.

_____ costumes

_____ clothes

_____ art supplies

_____ clean and safe food boxes

_____ egg cartons

_____ cardboard boxes

_____ empty oatmeal boxes

_____ empty coffee cans

_____ new or usable cassette tapes

_____ tape recorders

_____ party supplies—paper plates, napkins, forks, and spoons

_____ old, clean sheets

_____ old dolls or toys (that your child is not attached to)

_____ other _____

_____ other _____

_____ other _____

Thank you in advance for whatever you can donate.

Sincerely,

- -

Please call me regarding a donation.

Name _____

Child's name _____

Phone _____ Best time to call _____

Parent Expert Letter

Dear Parents,

In order to make your child's early childhood learning experience as meaningful as possible, we need your help. There are many opportunities for parent volunteers to share what they know with our children. This is enjoyable for the children, it broadens their learning experiences, and it is a very memorable way for you to be part of your child's learning.

We can use parent experts in any of the following areas:

❖ storytellers
❖ actors
❖ musicians
❖ dancers
❖ parent professions

We can use information about cultures in the following areas:

❖ customs
❖ languages
❖ foods
❖ holidays
❖ traditional dances and songs
❖ historical or interesting memories

If you can think of something other than what is listed here that you would like to suggest, please feel free to do so! We look forward to learning much from all of you. Thank you in advance for helping to make your child's learning experience extra special.

Sincerely,

- -

I would like to volunteer in this area:

Name _____

Child's name _____

Phone _____ Best time to call _____

Anticipate Messy Children Letter

Dear Parents,

As part of our emphasis on active learning experiences, we will be having a "messy" learning experience on _____ . In order to make sure your child does not ruin his/her clothing, please do one or both of the following:

1. Send an old shirt (adult size) to school with your child to serve as a smock. This smock can remain at school for other messy activities.

2. Make sure that your child wears old clothing on the day mentioned above.

As usual, there are many opportunities for you to be part of your child's learning experience. Please feel free to visit our classroom, or call me to schedule regular volunteer time. We always enjoy seeing you!

Sincerely,

- -

Please fill in and return if you would like to be called.

Name _____

Child's name _____

Phone _____ Best time to call _____

General Parent Request Letter

Dear Parents,

From time to time our facility has needs that we look to our parents to help us meet. We can utilize practically anything used that you might throw away or give away, as well as many disposable items like old cartons, boxes, and food containers. Here is a list of our ongoing needs.

- ❖ clothes
- ❖ dolls
- ❖ dress-up clothes
- ❖ big appliances boxes
- ❖ clean, empty food packages
- ❖ old, safe kitchen equipment
- ❖ paper plates, cups, napkins
- ❖ other

Thank you in advance for your help. Please feel free to contact us regarding anything you would like to donate.

Sincerely,

Parent Thank You Letter

Dear _____,

I want to take this opportunity to express my most sincere thanks for taking the time to

_____

_____

In this day of busy schedules, it is expecially gratifying to have you give freely of your time in assisting our school in meeting its educational goals for our students.

I want to especially mention _____

_____

_____

_____

Thank you for your help. You are truly special.

Appreciatively,

Bibliography and Acknowledgements

Bateman, C. Fred. *Empowering Your Child.* Hampton Roads Publishing Company, Inc., 1990.

Bayless, Kathleen M. and Marjorie E. Ramsey. *Music: A Way of Life for the Young Child.* Merrill Publishing Company, 1987.

Bos, Bev. *Before the Basics.* Turn the Page Press, 1983.

Bos, Bev. *Don't Move the Muffin Tins.* Turn the Page Press, 1993.

Brown, Naima, Editor. *Science and Technology in the Early Years.* Open University Press, 1991.

Christie, James F. *Play and Early Literacy Development.* State University of New York Press, 1991.

Derman-Sparks, Louise and the A.B.C. Task Force. *Anti-Bias Curriculum: Tools for Empowering Young Children.* National Association for the Education of Young Children, 1991.

Foyle, Harvey C., and Lawrence Lyman, and Sandra Alexander Thies. *Cooperative Learning in the Early Childhood Classroom.* National Education Association of the United States, 1991.

Hendrick, Joanne. *The Whole Child: New Trends in Early Education.* The C.V. Mosby Company, 1975.

Lewis, M.M. *How Children Learn To Speak.* Basic Books, Inc., 1959.

McDaniel, Sandy Spurgeon. *Recipes for Parenting.* Spurgeon House Publication, 1990.

Paciorer, Karen Menke and Joyce Huth Munko, Editors. *Early Childhood Education, 92–93, 93–94.* The Dushkin Publishing Group, Inc.

Paley, Vivian Gussin. *The Boy Who Would Be a Helicopter.* Harvard University Press, 1990.

Pave, Routledge and Kegan. *Reading and Loving.* London, Henley, and Boston, 1977.

Piaget, Jean. *The Language and Thought of the Child.* The Humanities Press, Inc., 1959.

Rowf, Deborah Wells. *Preschoolers as Authors.* Hampton Press, 1994.

Winsor, Charlotte B. *Dimensions of Language Experience.* Agamon Press, Inc., 1975.

Yawkey, Thomas D. and others. *Language Arts and the Young Child.* F.E. Peacock Publishers, 1981.

Acknowledgments

Grace Hoag Cottage, Newport-Harbor Assistance League Day Care Center, Newport Beach, California

Ronald J. Evans, Ph.D., Professor of Mathematics, University of California at San Diego, San Diego, California

Rita Jamieson, Director of Step By Step Early Learning Center, Early Childhood Instructor, University of California, Riverside; Irvine Valley and Orange Coast Colleges, California

Guillermo G. Romero, MD., and Ph.D., Assistant Professor of Pharmacology, University of Pittsburgh, Pennsylvania

Frank Wagoner, All Business Support Services, Irvine, California

Yvonne Woods, Professor of Child Development, Cerritos College, Norwalk, California